Lecture Notes in Artificial Intelligence   1537

Subseries of Lecture Notes in Computer Science
Edited by J. G. Carbonell and J. Siekmann

Lecture Notes in Computer Science

Edited by G. Goos, J. Hartmanis and J. van Leeuwen

Springer

Berlin
Heidelberg
New York
Barcelona
Hong Kong
London
Milan
Paris
Singapore
Tokyo

Nadia Magnenat-Thalmann
Daniel Thalmann (Eds.)

Modelling and Motion Capture Techniques for Virtual Environments

International Workshop, CAPTECH'98
Geneva, Switzerland, November 26-27, 1998
Proceedings

 Springer

Series Editors

Jaime G. Carbonell, Carnegie Mellon University, Pittsburgh, PA, USA
Jörg Siekmann, University of Saarland, Saarbrücken, Germany

Volume Editors

Nadia Magnenat-Thalmann
University of Geneva, Department of Information Systems
24 Rue du Général Dufour, CH-1211 Geneva 4, Switzerland
E-mail: Nadia.Thalmann@cui.unige.ch

Daniel Thalmann
Swiss Federal Institute of Technology (EPFL)
CH-1015 Lausanne, Switzerland
E-mail: thalmann@lig.di.epfl.ch

Cataloging-in-Publication Data applied for

Die Deutsche Bibliothek - CIP-Einheitsaufnahme

**Modelling and motion capture techniques for virtual
environments** : international workshop ; proceedings / CAPTECH
'98, Geneva, Switzerland, November 26 - 27, 1998. Nadia Magnenat-
Thalmann ; Daniel Thalmann (ed.). - Berlin ; Heidelberg ; New York
; Barcelona ; Hong Kong ; London ; Milan ; Paris ; Singapore ;
Tokyo : Springer, 1998
  (Lecture notes in computer science ; Vol. 1537 : Lecture notes in
  artificial intelligence)
  ISBN 3-540-65353-8

CR Subject Classification (1998): I.2.10, I.4, I.3, I.6

ISBN 3-540-65353-8 Springer-Verlag Berlin Heidelberg New York

© Springer-Verlag Berlin Heidelberg 1998
Printed in Germany

Typesetting: Camera ready by author
SPIN 10692980   06/3142 – 5 4 3 2 1 0   Printed on acid-free paper

Preface

The CAPTECH'98 workshop took place at the University of Geneva on November 26–27, 1998, sponsored by FIP Working Group 5.10 (Computer Graphics and Virtual Worlds) and the Suisse Romande regional doctoral seminar in computer science. The subject of the conference was ongoing research in data capture and interpretation. The goals of capturing real-world data in order to perceive, understand, and interpret them and then reacting to them in a suitable way are currently important research problems. These data can be very diverse: sounds, emotions, shapes, motions, forces, muscles, actions, etc. Once captured, they have to be treated either to make the invisible visible, or to understand a particular phenomenon so as to formulate an appropriate reaction, or to integrate various information in a new multimedia format.

The conference included six sessions of presented papers and three panel discussions. Invited speakers treating various aspects of the topic were: Professor R. Earnshaw from Bradford University, Professor T. L. Kunii from Hosei University, and Professor P. Robert from EPFL. Professor K. Bauknecht, of the University of Zürich, President of IFIP, offered the welcoming address. Mr. E. Badique, project officer for the EU in Brussels, discussed recent results of the EU ACTS research program. Finally, the Geneva Computer Animation '98 Film Festival highlighted the evening of November 26.

October 1998

Nadia Magnenat-Thalmann
Daniel Thalmann
Conference and
Program Co-Chairs

Program Committee

Conference and Program Co-Chairs

Nadia Magnenat-Thalmann (University of Geneva, Switzerland)
Daniel Thalmann (Swiss Federal Institute of Technology, Lausanne, Switzerland)

Local Committee Co-Chairs

Christian Zanardi (University of Geneva)
Laurent Moccozet (University of Geneva)

International Program Committee:

Gustavo Alonso (ETH Zurich, Switzerland)
Norman Badler (University of Pennsylvania, USA)
Steve Carson (GSC, USA)
Tat-Seng Chua (National University of Singapore, Singapore)
Rae Earnshaw (University of Bradford, UK)
Jose Encarnacao (Institut für Graphische Datenverarbeitung, Germany)
Dieter Fellner (University of Braunschweig, Germany)
Eddy Flerackers (Limburg University Center, Belgium)
Pascal Fua (EPF Lausanne, Switzerland)
Simon Gibbs (Sony, USA)
Armin Gruen (ETH Zurich, Switzerland)
Prem Kalra (Indian Institute of Technology, India)
Arie Kaufman (State University of New York at Stony Brook, USA)
Eric Keller (University of Lausanne, Switzerland)
Stanislav Klimenko (Institute for High Energy Physics, Russia)
Tosiyasu L. Kunii (Computational Science Research Center, Japan)
Dimitris Metaxas (University of Pennsylvania, USA)
Tim Niblett (Turing Institute, UK)
Alex Pentland (MIT, USA)
Juris Reinfelds (New Mexico State University, USA)
Larry Rosenblum (Naval Research Lab, USA)
Sung Yong Shin (KAIST, Korea)
Vaclav Skala (University of West Bohemia, Czech Republic)
Yasuhito Suenaga (Nagoya University, Japan)
Jose Carlos Teixeira (Centro de Computacao Grafica, Portugal)
Paul ten Hagen (CWI, Netherlands)
Demetri Terzopoulos (University of Toronto, Canada)
Luc Van Gool (KU Leuwen, Belgium)
Philip J. Willis (Bath University, UK)
Franz E. Wolter (University of Hannover, Germany)

Table of Contents

Human Motion Analysis

Human Motion Capture and Manipulation

Image and Video Manipulation

Motion Control

Human Body and Objects 3D Reconstruction

Image/Video Based Facial Animation

Author Index

Motion Analysis in Clinical Practice Using Ambulatory Accelerometry

Kamiar Aminian[1], Eduardo De Andres[2], Karen Rezakhanlou[1], Carlo Fritsch[2], Y. Schutz[3], Michèle Depairon[4], Pierre-François Leyvraz[2], and Philippe Robert[1]

[1] Swiss Federal Institute of Technology – Lausanne (EPFL), Metrology Laboratory, CH-1015 Lausanne, Switzerland
[2] Hôpital Orthopédique de la Suisse Romande, Av. Pierre-Decker 4, CH-1005 Lausanne, Switzerland
[3] University of Lausanne, Institute of Physiology, CH-1011 Lausanne, Switzerland
[4] CHUV, Division of Hypertension and Vascular Medicine, CH-1005 Lausanne, Switzerland

Abstract. A new system, *Physilog*, for ambulatory monitoring of movement is proposed and its applications in orthopaedic, physiology, angiology and quality of life are presented. Body accelerations were recorded by a portable measuring device. Significant parameters of body motion, namely, movement coordination, temporal parameters, speed, incline, distance covered, kind of physical activity and its duration, are extracted from the subject accelerations in its daily environment. The accuracy of these parameters guarantees the reliability of accelerometry in clinical application.

1 Introduction

Accelerometry consists of measuring the body segmental kinematics using accelerometers. In these recent years, technical progress made it possible to realise miniature acceleration sensors with integrated conditioning and calibration module. In addition due to very low consumption, these accelerometers can be supplied by battery and lends themselves a promising tool for long term ambulatory monitoring [1]. In contrast to classical motion analysis such as image-based system [2], ambulatory accelerometry allows to detect body movement outside the laboratory and in the daily environment of the subject.

Theoretically, to describe the three-dimensional motion of each body segment, six accelerometers should be used [3], [4]. However due to the non linear relation between the linear and angular kinematics variables, and the influence of the gravitational acceleration component, multiple accelerometers (up to 12) attached to a single segment have been used to resolve its complete kinematics [5], [6]. This leads to a high number of sensors for whole body motion analysis. In addition, angular and linear displacement estimation using double integration of accelerations is often perturbed by the drift and movement artefact belonging to the acceleration signals and requires knowledge of the initial conditions [7].

In clinical practice, using a high number of sensors attachment sites, which increase also the number of connecting tools (such as cable and connector), is a disturbing factor which can modify patient's natural movements. However, in many clinical studies, the physician do not need a complete kinematics of motion, but rather some particular features of the movement. In these situations, the number of sensors and their sites of attachment can be optimised in order to resolve a defined problem. For

Nadia Magnenat-Thalmann, Daniel Thalmann (Eds.): CAPTECH'98, LNAI 1537, pp. 1-11, 1998.

example, in physical activity monitoring, where we are interested to know the type and duration of each posture, two accelerometers and a relatively simple identification algorithm are sufficient, while in orthopaedic, up to 7 accelerometers with an artificial neural network model are used to assess the coordination of movement.

In this paper a new ambulatory movement monitoring system, *Physilog* (BioAGM, CH), is proposed and its application in orthopaedic, physiology, angiology and quality of life are presented. All these applications have in common that body motion were recorded using a set of accelerometers. Whatever the sensors configuration (number, site of attachment, single or multi axis), the data processing and analysing can differ from one application to the other.

2   Measuring Device

Human movements were detected by miniature body fixed sensors. Piezoresistive accelerometers which have the advantage of being accurate, miniature, solid-state, inexpensive and relatively wide frequency range (0-350Hz) were used [8], [9]. Movements were measured in one or three dimensions using one or three accelerometers mounted in orthogonal direction supported on a miniature cube. Single and three axis accelerometers were fixed on the body through a belt around the trunk or directly attached on the skin using medical tape and supports. A digital portable recorder, the size of a Walkman, digitised, filtered, amplified and saved the acceleration signals on solid state memory cards. At the end of the recordings the data were transferred to a Personal Computer and the acceleration data were calibrated, analysed and the motion parameters estimated.

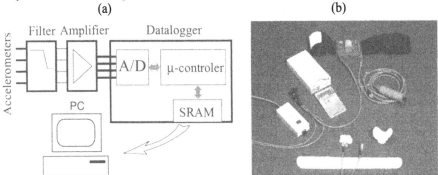

Fig. 1. Block diagram (a) and different components(b) of the measuring system.

Fig.1 show the block diagram of the measuring device. Up to 8 input channels with 12 bits resolution (0-5V) can be recorded on memory card which can reach up to 16Mbytes. The sampling rate can be fixed for each application from 0.001 Hz to 1500Hz. The batteries are rechargeable and allow from few hours to several days of operation depending on application.

3   Clinical Applications

3.1   Orthopaedic: Gait Coordination

Osteoarthritis is the most frequent joint pathology throughout the world. Thanks to the continuing development of joint arthroplasties, physical therapy and psychosocial support, it is now possible to restore the patients' near normal quality of life. Obtaining objective, dynamic and quantified data allowing the evaluation of the outcome of patients before and after hip arthroplasty is crucial. The most common means used for this evaluation are based on scores derived from questionnaires. Although the questions on such a scale are standardized, the answers are often subjective and the discrepancy between patient and physician's evaluation is significant [10], [11] , [12].

Walking is a *multisegmental* movement, which involve *coordinated* motor commands [13]. A new method for gait coordination analysis is proposed [14], [15]. Trunk and lower limbs accelerations during walking were recorded. The cross correlation functions of these accelerations were used to assess multisegmental coordination during walking. A set of significant parameters of cross correlation function was extracted. These parameters constitute the input of a neural network classifier [16] which provides a score for each walking.

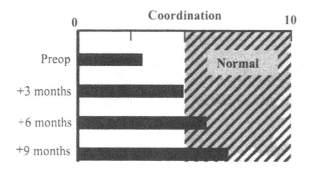

Fig. 2. Coordination score obtained for a patient with left coxarthrosis.

The coordination score of patients after hip arthroplasty was determined using this technique. The scores were then normalized from 0 (bad) to 10 (excellent). Fig. 2 shows the coordination improvement profile of a patient obtained before and after operation, compared to the scores of normal population. Coordination scores were then compared to two standard questionnaire scores completed by each patient [17]. In comparison with the questionnaire scores the coordination score is more severe with higher variability over patients and has a better accordance with the physician appreciation. In order to improve the functional score, the coordination score can be combined with temporal gait parameters presented in the next paragraph.

3.2   Orthopaedic: Temporal Gait Analysis

Walking is a cyclic movement. There are two main phases in the gait cycle [18]: during *stance* phase, the foot is on the ground, whereas in *swing* phase the same foot is no longer in contact with the ground. The stance phase is subdivided into three separate periods: *first double support* (both feet are in contact with the ground), *single limb stance* (one foot is swinging through while the other's is on the ground) and *second double support* (both feet are again on the ground). The time span of each phase of gait cycle are known as temporal parameters. Evaluation of temporal parameters during walking is a helpful means not only to assess some aspects of pathological walk among osteoarthritic patients but also to quantify their subsequent improvement after hip or knee arthroplasty [19], [20].

Signals from two accelerometers, fastened to lower limbs, were recorded during walking. Using an original method, the temporal parameters were computed [21]. Comparison between these results and those obtained by help of pressure sensors put under the sole for six healthy and four arthritic subjects has validated the proposed method. A good agreement of order of 4% was found.

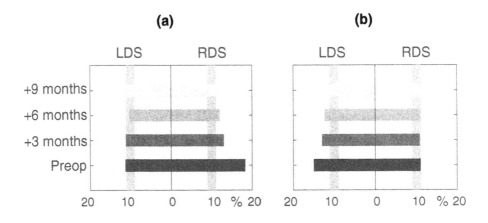

Fig. 3. Left and right double support (LDS and RDS) averaged over 7 patients with left coxarthrosis(a) and 5 patients with right coxarthrosis(b), compared to the corresponding normal values (grey lines around 10%).

The method was applied to data obtained from 12 hip osteoarthritic patients measured before and after operation – at three, six and nine months. A significant discrepancy between duration of left and right double limb support, depending on affected hip, was observed (fig.3). The contrast with their almost equal values for a population of normal subjects is paramount.

This result underlines that the weight transfer phase is the most demanding task during a gait cycle and certainly a painful one for patients. Furthermore a tendency toward normality was also observed after arthroplasty (fig.4).

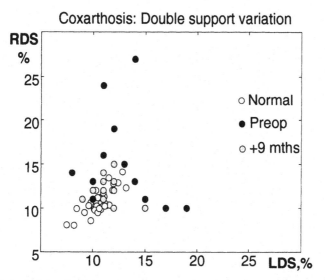

Fig. 4. Left and right double support (LDS and RDS) for 12 patients with coxarthrosis compared to their values for normal population.

3.3   Sport Performances

Walking and running are the most common physical activity of daily life. An accurate estimation of these two activities is fundamental in different fields such as sport performances, physical activity improvement, jogging and energy expenditure estimation.

Trunk and right ankle accelerations during walking and running were recorded [22], [23], [24], [25], [26]. The acceleration measured at the right ankle allowed the identification of heel strike in each cycle. The gait cycle (2 steps) was computed as the time between two heel strikes. For each cycle, a set of parameters exhibiting an appreciable correlation with speed and incline had been chosen to form the pattern of walking and running. Two Artificial neural Networks (ANN) were designed to recognise each pattern and to estimate the speed and incline of walking and running. Each subject performed a treadmill walking (resp. running) of 15 minutes ("calibration") before his self paced walking (resp. running) outdoor. The ANNs were first trained by known patterns of treadmill walking. Then, the inclines, the speeds and the distance covered during walking and running in free-living conditions were estimated (fig.5). The results show a good estimation of these variables, since the incline and the speed error are respectively less than 2.8% and 6% (fig.6.a and 6.b).

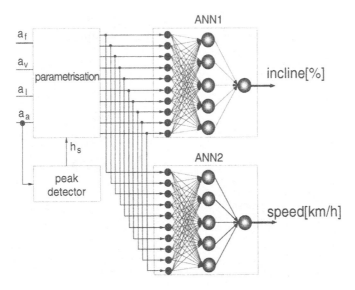

Fig. 5. Block diagram of the incline and the speed estimation. a_f, a_v, a_l are resp. the forward, vertical and lateral acceleration of the trunk, a_a is the forward acceleration of the right ankle. h_s correspond to the heel strike.

3.4   Physiology

Quantifying the energy expenditure of physical activity in daily life is a complex task in physiology. Different methods such as self-report questionnaire, heart rate monitoring and oxygen uptake measurement, are used in this purpose [27], [28]. These methods are often not accurate or/and not adapted for ambulatory monitoring. The energy expenditure of walking (EE) depends principally on the subject's weight, the speed and the incline of ground [29]. In this study, speed and incline were found using the above method (fig.5). The values of EE were assessed using indirect calorimetry [30]. Each subject underwent 22 measurement periods, each lasting 5 minutes, which was sufficient to obtain steady state calorimetric values. The first period corresponded to metabolism in the upright stationary position. Subsequently, the subject walked on treadmill in level and at three inclines in uphill (resp. downhill). Each subject walked at three different speeds for each incline. During the measurements, the subjects breathed only through their mouth via a tube and the air circulating in the tube was constantly analysed. Oxygen consumption and CO_2 production were determined every 15 seconds by an acquisition system. The EE was calculated from these results and over the two last minutes of each measurement period when oxygen consumption had reached a steady state. Polynomial multiple regression analysis was used to determine the relationship between EE versus speed and incline, and its validity was tested on 12 subjects.

   The calibrated data obtained from accelerometry and calorimetry on the treadmill were used, respectively to train the ANN – in order to compute the speed and incline and to calibrate the energy expenditure model. During the prediction, the subject walked on an outdoor circuit for an unspecified distance. The speed, incline and the energy expenditure were then determined from the acceleration data on the one hand and from the information provided by the calibration on the other.

The energy expenditure estimated from the acceleration is compared to that obtained from calorimetry, correlation of 0.97 with a coefficient of variation of 5% are found. Fig.6.c shows a typical estimation of energy expenditure of a subject walking without constrains on an outdoor circuit.

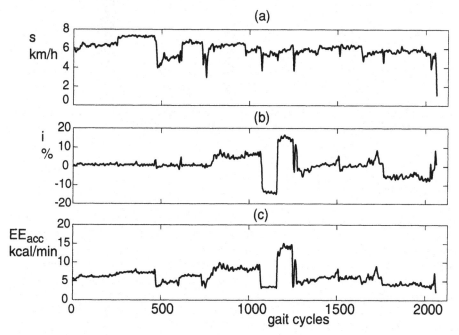

Fig. 6. Speed (s), incline (i) and energy expenditure EE_{acc} obtained by accelerometry, during 43 minutes of outdoor walking.

3.5 Quality of Life

Daily physical activity (or the restriction of it) is a determining factor in the quality of life. To date, this variable has only rarely been evaluated objectively and in most cases unsatisfactorily or imprecisely. However, a credible measurement of physical activity in everyday life would represent a decisive clinical element in the assessment of the utility of numerous symptomatic treatments [31], [32].

The chest and thigh accelerations, during daily physical activities, were recorded by *Physilog*. An algorithm was developed to classify the main activities: lying, sitting, standing, locomotion (dynamic). The results compared to video observation show an overall misclassification of 10.7%, which is mainly due to the confusion between dynamic and standing while the misclassification between postures is negligible. Fig.7 show typical physical activity estimation obtained from accelerometry and compared to video observation.

Using this feature, *accelerometry* is a promising tool for long term mobility monitoring in clinical application, particularly in chronic-pain, cardiac disease, spasticity, Parkinson's disease and their therapeutic evaluation.

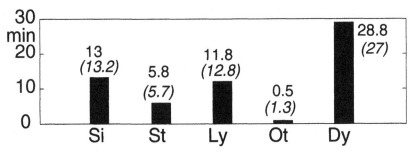

Fig. 7. Histogram of activities obtained by accelerometry and video (italic), during one hour: Dynamic (Dy), Sitting (Si), Standing (St), Lying (Ly) and others (Ot).

3.6   Angiology

The physiopathology of the intermittent claudication, based on post stress ischemia, is very complex and not completely understood. The clinical studies regarding arteriopathy of the lower limbs use, as an evaluation parameter of the severity of the illness, the painless and maximal walking distances determined on a treadmill. However, for these patients, walking on a treadmill is different to overground walking particularly because of the lack of training and the help provided by the handle bar of the treadmill. In addition the test has to be carried out inside the laboratory and it cannot be performed by all the patients [33], [34].

Walking distance in patients suffering from arterial insufficiency was measured with *Physilog*. Measurement was carried out on 10 patients who had intermittent claudication. Each patient performed 2 tests before and after a period of medication. Each test consisted of 2 walking trials. The first one was used to calibrate (trained) the ANN for speed estimation (fig.5). During the second phase, the patient walked at his desired speed on the metered walkway and the painless and maximum distance of walking were measured manually. The trunk and ankle accelerations were recorded simultaneously and the walking distance was computed from the values of speed estimated from ANN. Fig.8 shows a good agreement (r=0.99) between walking distance measured by *Physilog* (D_{ph}) and walking distance measured manually (D_{mn}), for all the tests. A mean error of 2.1% was found.

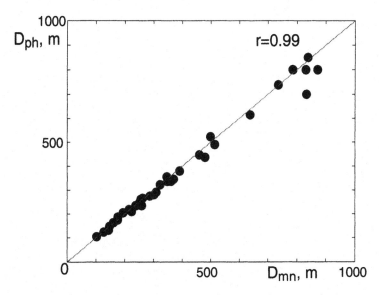

Fig. 8. Walking distance measured by *Physilog* (D_{ph}), compared to walking distance measured manually (D_{mn}).

4   Conclusion

The purpose of these studies was to show the possibility offered by accelerometry to measure and analyse body movements. The accelerometry appears to be the ambulatory means which is best accepted by the patients for long-term motion monitoring. Through different clinical applications, the possibilities to obtain significant parameters of motion are outlined. Significant parameters of body motion, namely, movement coordination, temporal parameters, speed, incline, covered distance, kind of physical activity and its duration, are extracted from the subject accelerations in its daily environment. The accuracy which is obtained for these parameters guarantees a reliability of accelerometry in clinical application. Completed by other motion and physiological sensors, this technique can be extended to other medical fields where the body motion is affected by the pathology suffered by patients. The monitoring of abnormal movements in neurological diseases (such as Parkinson), the improvement of the quality of life either after a surgery or by a specified medication or else by rehabilitation programs, are such examples. This extension, carried out in a large scale in clinical investigations, will allow improvement in accelerometry performances and validate the results on large population. However, it is very important to seek new techniques of the acceleration signal processing in order to extract significant parameters related to each specified pathology.

References

1 Rudolf F., Arbab B., Orhant O.: Low power accelerometer for portable and remote instrumentation, Proceeding of the Sensors Expo San Jose , Technical Conference.San Jose (1998) 417-423

2. Ferrigno G., Pedotti A: ELITE: A digital dedicated hardware system for movement analysis vis real-time TV signal processing. IEEE Trans. Biomed. Eng. 32 (1985) 943-950

3. Morris, J.R.W.: Accelerometry - a technique for the measurement of human body movements. J. Biomech. 6 (1973) 729-736

4. Willemsen, A.TH., Frigo C., Boom H.B.K.: Lower extremity angle measurement with accelerometers-error and sensitivity analysis. IEEE Trans. Biomed. Eng. 38 (1991) 1186-1193

5. Wu G., Ladin Z.: The study of kinematic transients in locomotion using the integrated kinematic sensor. IEEE trans. Rehabil. Eng. 4 (1996) 193-200

6. Kane T.R., Hayes W. C., Priest J.D.: Experimental determination of forces exerted in tennis play. In Biomech.IV, baltimore, MD (1974) 284-290

7. Wu G., Ladin Z.: The Kinematometer-An Integrated kinematic sensor for Kinesiological measurements. J. Biomech.Eng. 115 (1993) 53-62

8. Aminian K., Robert Ph., Jéquier E., Schutz Y.: Classification of level and grade walking using neural network. Proceeding of Iranian Conference on Electrical Engineering (ICEE-94) 6 (1994) 13-19

9. Aminian K., Robert Ph., Jéquier E., Schutz Y.: Level, downhill and uphill walking identification using neural network. Electron. Lett. 29 (1993) 1563-1565

10. Lieberman JR, Dorey F., Shekelle p., Schumaker L., Thomas BJ., Kilgus DJ., Finerman GA.: Differences between patients and physicians evaluations of outcome after total hip arthroplasty. Journal of Bone and Joint Surgery 78 A (1996) 835-838

11. Anderson G.: Hip assessment: a comparison of nine different methods. Journal of bone and joint surgery 54B (1972) 621-625

12. Liang MH., Fosset A., Larson M.. Comparisons of five health status instruments for orthopedic evaluation. Medical Care 28 (1990) 632-642

13. Bernstein N.: The coordination and Regulation of Movement. Pergamon Press London (1967)

14. Aminian K., Robert Ph., de Andrès E., Fritsch C.: Functional Performance Analysis of Hip and Knee Arthroplasty using Accelerometry. Proceeding of 8th Conference European Orthopeadic Research Society, EORS'98, Amsterdam, The Netherland. (1998) O 53.

15. de Andrès E., Aminian K., Fritsch C., Leyvraz P.-F., Robert Ph.: Interest of Gait Analysis in Hip and Knee. Proceeding of 2nd Mediterranean Congress of Physical Medicine and Rehabilitation, Valencia, Spain. (1998) 347

16. Kohonen,T.: Self-organisation and associative memory (3rd Edn.). Springer-Verlag, Berlin (1989)

17. de Andrès E., Aminian K., Fritsch C., Leyvraz P.-F., Robert Ph., Depairon M., Schutz Y.: Intérêts des analyses fonctionnelles lors d'arthroplastie (hanche-genou). Recueil des communications du 6ème Congrés de l'Union des Sociétés Chirurgicales Suisses, Lausanne, Suisse, supplement 1 (1998) 80

18. Vaughan C.L.: Dynamics of human gait. Human Kinetics Publishers, Champaign, 1992

19. Wall J.C., Ashburn A., Klenerman L.: Gait Analysis in The Assessment of Functional Perfoemance Before And After Total Hip Replacement. J. Biomed. Eng. 3 (1981) 121-127

20. Giannini S., Catani F., Bendetti M.G. and Leardini A., Gait Analysis: methodologies clinical applications, IOS Press Amsterdam (1994)

21. de Andrès E., Aminian K., Rezakhanlou K., Fritsch C., Robert Ph., Leyvraz P.-F.: Analysis of hip arthroplasty using accelerometry. Proceeding of 11th Annual symposium of the

International Society for Technology in Arthroplasty, Marseille, France (1998) *to be published.*

22. Aminian K., Robert Ph., Jéquier E., Schutz Y.: Incline, speed and distance assessment during during unconstrained walking. Med.Sci.Sports Exec. 27 (1995) 226-234
23. Aminian K.,. Robert Ph, Jéquier E., Schutz Y.: Estimation of speed and incline of walking using neural network. IEEE Trans.Inst.Meas. 44 (1995) 743-746
24. Schutz Y., Aminian K., Jequier E., Robert Ph.: Use of neural network for assessing the speed and incline of walking in man by means of 3-D accelerometry. Proceeding of the 27th annual Meeting of the USGEB/USSBE, Fribourg (1995)
25. Herren R., Sparti A., Aminian K., Schutz Y.: Assessment of speed and incline of outdoor running in humans by accelerometry, Med.Sci.Sports Exec. (1998) *to be published*
26. Schutz Y., Aminian K., Robert Ph.: A new device to predict under free-living conditions the speed and incline of walking. Proceeding of the7th ICO Satellite meeting, Quebec (1994)
27. Baranowski T.: Energy expenditure in level and grade walking. Res. Q. Exerc. Sport 59 (1988) 314-327
28. Eston RG., Rowlands AV., Ingledew DK.: Validity of heart rate, pedometry and accelerometry for predicting the energy cost of children's activities. J. Appl. Physiol. 84 (1998) 362-371
29. MARGARIA, R.: Biomechanics and energetics of muscular exercise, Oxford: Clarendon Press (1976) 67-139
30. Rose J., Ralston H.J., Gamble J.G.: Energetics of walking. In Rose J. and Gamble J.G. (Eds), Human Walking. Williams &Wilkins, Baltimore (1994) 45-72
31. NG A.V., Kent-Braun J.A.: Quantitation of lower physical activity in persons with multiple sclerosis. Med. Sci. Sports Exerc. 29 (1997) 517-523
32. Sieminski D.J, Cowell L.L., Montgomery P.S., Pillai S.B., Gardner A.W.: Physical activity monitoring in patients with peripheral arterial occlusive disease. J. Cardiopulmonary Rehabil. 17 (1997) 43-47
33. Cristol R., Graisel Y.B.: Evaluation de la claudication intermittente sur tapis roulant avec mesure de la pression systolique à la cheville après effort. J. Mal. Vasc., Paris 10 (1985) 101-107
34. Greig C., Bulter F., Skelton D., Mahmud S., Young A.: Treadmill walking in old age may not reproduce the real situation. J. Am. Geriatr. Soc. 41 (1993) 15-18

A Robust Human-Silhouette Extraction Technique for Interactive Virtual Environments

James W. Davis and Aaron F. Bobick

MIT Media Lab, Cambridge MA 02139, USA
{jdavis, bobick}@media.mit.edu

Abstract. In this paper, we present a method for robustly extracting the silhouette form of the participant within an interactive environment. The approach overcomes the inherent problems associated with traditional chroma-keying, background subtraction, and rear-light projection methods. We employ a specialized infrared system while not making the underlying technology apparent to those interacting within the environment. The design also enables multiple video projection screens to be placed around the user. As an example use of this technology, we present an interactive virtual aerobics system. Our current implementation is a portable system which can act as a re-usable infrastructure for many interactive projects.

1 Introduction

When designing interactive environments, it's imperative for the system to be engaging as well as be reliably "aware" of the person (or people) interacting within the space. Many installations are designed with a single large video display, which is the main focus of attention for the user [14,11,13,3]. As for sensing the person in the space, some installations use specialized light, lasers, electromagnetics, or electric field sensing to detect bodies, hands, or objects [14,11,13,8]. Other approaches use similar variants of chroma-keying (i.e. blue-screening) [3], background subtraction [15,7], or rear-light projection [9] to enable a video camera to extract a silhouette the person, where the person may or may not be required to wear special clothing. We are interested in the latter approaches where a full-body silhouette is visually extracted from the participant; properties of the silhouette such as position, shape, and motion are then used as input for driving the interaction.

The main problem with the current technology for extracting the silhouette is that it relies primarily on the color components of the video signal to perform the extraction. For example, chroma-keying methods require the person stand in front of a background consisting of a uniform-colored wall or screen. The system examines the incoming video signal for the background color of the wall. As long as the person doesn't have that background color on their clothing, the system can extract the person from the video by detecting and removing all the background color in the image. This type of system, commonly used by

Nadia Magnenat-Thalmann, Daniel Thalmann (Eds.): CAPTECH'98, LNAI 1537, pp. 12–25, 1998.
© Springer-Verlag Berlin Heidelberg 1998

meteorologists in TV studios, restricts the user not to have the color of the background anywhere on his/her clothing. If the space is to be used as an inter-active environment, the color-based methods as well as the rear-light approach are perceptually obtrusive distracting the user from the interactive experience. Immersion is a strong requirement when building interactive environments [10], and part of this illusion may be broken if such walls are incorporated.

One slight variant of the chroma-keying method is commonly referred to as background subtraction (as used in [3,7,15]). A snapshot of the environment containing no people is stored as a reference image. Frames of incoming video imagery are compared with the reference image. Anything that differs, at a pixel-wise level, is assumed to belong to an object (e.g. a person) in the environment. Using the snapshot allows a more natural scene, rather than just a colored or rear-light wall, to be the background. Now however, the colors on the person still need to be *different* everywhere than those of the wall and/or objects be-hind them. Furthermore, the lighting in the environment must remain relatively constant, even as the person moves about. When these constraints hold, the system works quite well. But if regions of the environment look similar to the person (e.g. a white patch of wall behind a person wearing a white shirt), or if inter-reflection from the person's clothing onto the background is significant, then the person extraction will have either holes or false appendages, respec-tively. To overcome these problems, a strong model of the body would seem to be required.

In this paper we present a method to overcome the inherent problems as-sociated with the above methods, while opening a new venue for multi-screen interaction. We begin by presenting our design specification for the proposed environment (Sect. 2). Next, we briefly present a virtual aerobics application which uses the proposed environment (Sect. 3), and lastly conclude with a brief summary of the framework (Sect. 4).

2   Design Specification

We divide the specification of the system into three main components. First, the environment itself is examined. We next present how specialized non-visible lighting can be used to enable robust sensing of the participant. Lastly, simple image processing techniques are shown for extracting the silhouette from the video stream.

2.1   The Environment

The prototype environment for showing the utility of the approach consists of two large video projection screens, with one behind and one in front of the user (see Fig. 1). The primary interaction screen is the frontal video display, though video or graphics can be displayed on both screens, enabling virtual objects or interactions on either of these displays. The use of back-projected video screens is necessary (at least for the back wall) for the method which extracts the silhouette of the user in the space (to be discussed). We employ collapsible "snap-on" screens that allow the system to be easily transported to different locations, unlike systems that use large projection TVs.

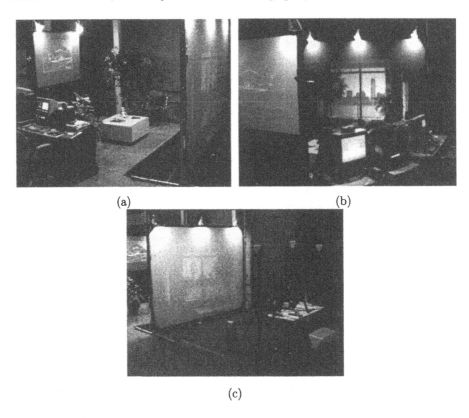

(a)   (b)

(c)

Fig. 1. Dual-screen environment. The environment consists of two video projection screens, with one in front of and one behind the user. (a) View from the outside the rear. (b) View from outside the front. (c) View from behind the environment showing the infrared emitters aimed at the rear screen.

Behind the user is a 10x8 foot back-projection screen used as the back wall. In front of the user is an 5x4 foot back-projection screen, which is elevated 3 feet off the floor (using two support legs), resembling a large-screen TV. (Later we explain why an elevated smaller screen is used as the front screen instead of a full-sized screen.) The distance between these two screens is 10 feet, large enough not to crowd the user in the space between the screens. Also, the resolution of the projected video on the front screen dictates this pleasing viewing distance.

2.2   Infrared Lighting

To allow the reliable extraction of the frontal silhouette of the user with a "live" video screen behind him/her, we direct invisible infrared light (using 6 consumer

840nm IR emitters) through the large back-projected screen behind the user (see Fig. 1(c)). These emitters are positioned such that the IR light is distributed across the back screen. By using an infrared-pass/visible-block filter tuned to this wavelength of infrared light, we can then restrict an inexpensive black-and-white video camera[1] placed well in front of the user to see only this infrared light. A person standing in front of the rear screen physically blocks the infrared light diffused through the screen, causing a video camera placed in front of the user to see a bright image with a black silhouette of the person. To get the most flat, frontal view of the person, the camera needs to reside approximately hip-level to the user[2]. Because the camera cannot sit behind the front screen (with the screen blocking the view, and the camera causing shadows on the screen from the projector light) or in front of the screen (such a visible sensor reduces the sense of immersion), we attached the camera to the bottom of an elevated front screen (3 feet off the ground). The elevated front screen resembles a large-screen TV at eye-level in the space and provides an adequate "virtual window" for interactive applications.

One advantage of using infrared light is that many video projectors emit very little infrared light or can be outfitted to do so with infrared-block filters. Therefore, we can project any video or graphics we wish onto the two projection screens without any concern of the effects on the silhouette extraction process. Also, standard fluorescent room lighting does not emit much infrared light and thus can be used to illuminate the environment without interfering with the infrared system. Our current system uses 5 inexpensive fluorescent spot lights, which are attached to the top of the screens.

This silhouetting process is illustrated in Fig. 2. Figure 2(a) shows a standard camera view of someone standing in front of the back-wall projection screen with graphics displayed. In Fig. 2(b), we see the same scene from the camera but now with infrared light being shown from behind the screen using the 6 infrared light emitters[3]. By placing an infrared-pass/visible-block filter over the video camera lens, a brightly lit screen (with no graphics visible) and a clean silhouette of the user is seen, as shown in Fig. 2(c). The IR light is not visible to the human visual system and thus one sees only video projected on the display screen (as shown in Fig. 2(a)).

This method overcomes the color dependencies associated with chroma-keying approaches because it is based on the blocking (or eclipsing) of specialized light (see Fig. 3) rather than the color differences between the person and background. In our system, the person is always able to wear arbitrarily colored clothing.

---

[1] Many video cameras have an infrared-block filter which limits the use of this process. One may need to remove this filter, or use a camera without this filter installed. We used a Sony SSC-M370 black and white camera which passes much of the IR light.

[2] If the camera were placed above a screen or on the floor, the silhouette would be a bit more distorted from perspective effects. Also, the rear screen through which the infrared light passes is only slightly diffusive, and thus an off-center video camera would not register fully the light coming from the multiple infrared emitters spaced behind the screen.

[3] The camera has no infrared-blocking filter and is thus sensitive to infrared light.

Furthermore, chroma-key and background subtraction systems require careful control of environment lighting, whereas the IR system is insensitive to arbitrary visible light. In comparison to systems that use bright rear-lighting, this system is similar but *hides* the technology from the participant by using the non-visible part of the light spectrum. The method also permits the display of video

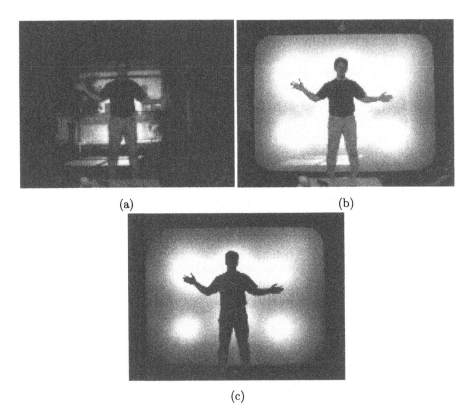

(a)   (b)

(c)

Fig. 2. Infrared light. (a) An image of the person in front of a video projection screen in the environment. (b) The same as shown in (a), but with infrared light directed through the screen. (c) The same image, but now filtered through an infrared-pass/visible-block filter. The image in (c) no longer shows the video projected on the screen, and the person now appears as a silhouette. To the naked eye, the version shown in (b) would appear as (a).

graphics behind the user, unlike the rear-lighting systems. Because the subject is rear-lit with the camera in front, any the reflection or absorption of the IR light occurs toward the rear screen, away from the camera. Therefore any hair, clothing, and material on the person that may cause reflective problems do not influence the imaging system.

We note that this system could be employed to the meteorologist scenario in the TV studios. Currently, a blue-screen (or green-screen) method is used to extract the meteorologist and place his/her image into a high-resolution weathermap. The meteorologist must look off-camera to a remote monitor to view the resultant composite and see if his/her hand is over the correct region. With our approach, it is possible to accomplish the same composite result, but now have the added benefit of projecting the actual weathermap onto the back wall to help the meteorologist.

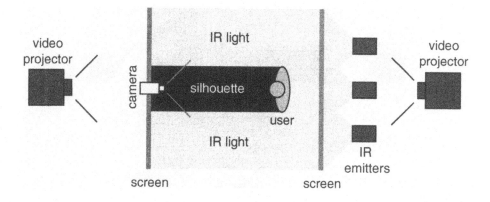

Fig. 3. Conceptual drawing of blocking (eclipsing) infrared light from the camera to generate a silhouette of the person.

It is also possible to have another camera and side-screen with its own infrared emitters to recover an additional silhouette of the user as viewed from the side (see Fig. 4). Additional information (e.g. three-dimensional information) of the person could be attained using the two silhouettes (one from the front and one from the side). The side-screen infrared camera/emitters would need to be tuned at a different wavelength, modulation, or synchronization than the back screen camera/emitters as not to interfere with each other.

2.3   Image Processing

The advantage of creating a robust silhouette image of the person using the above lighting approach is that we can use simple image processing methods to easily and quickly (in real-time) extract the silhouette from the digitized video. We could use a simple thresholding of the image to find the silhouette, but the emitters are not widely diffused by the projection screen and there are varying degrees of brightness (i.e. the IR light is not uniformly distributed across the screen as shown in Fig. 5(a)). Instead, we chose to follow the common background subtraction methodology [3,15,7], where first a reference picture is taken without a person in front of the screen (see Fig. 5(a)). Then for any new image containing the person (see Fig. 5(b)), all the pixels in the screen area are compared between the reference image and this new image, where a pixel

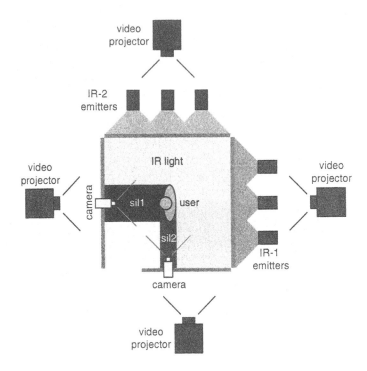

Fig. 4. Multiple screen environment using two independent IR emissions.

is marked as belonging to the person if the difference between the reference and current image at that pixel is above some threshold (see Fig. 5(c)). Due to imaging noise and digitizing resolution (in our case, 160x120), spurious pixels may be set and small thin body regions may end up disconnected from the rest of the body. We can apply simple image morphology (dilation) to the difference image to re-connect any small regions which may have become disjoint, and then perform simple region growing to find the largest region(s) in the image [6] (see Fig. 5(d)). This retains only the person while removing the noise. The result is a slightly fuller silhouette of the person, which can be further examined using computer vision algorithms for measuring the location, posture, and motion of the person to drive the interaction.

3   Virtual Aerobics

In this section we discuss the design and implementation of a *virtual Personal Aerobics Trainer (PAT)* employing the above IR silhouetting environment[4]. The aerobics application demonstrates the usefulness and capability of the IR silhouetting approach.

---

[4] An extended description of the virtual aerobics system can be found in [5].

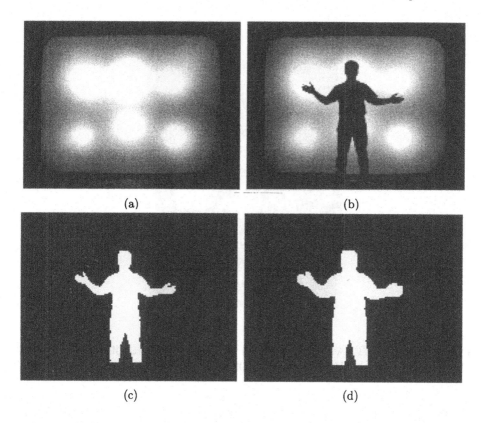

Fig. 5. Image processing. (a) Reference image. (b) Input image. (c) Binarized difference image. (d) Image morphology and region growing result.

The PAT system creates a personalized aerobics session for the user and displays the resulting instruction on a large front screen (or TV monitor). Here the user can choose which moves (and for how long), which music, and which instructor are desired for the workout. The session created by the user is then automatically generated and begins when the user enters the area in front of the screen (see Fig. 6).

The user periodically receives audio-visual feedback from the virtual instructor on his/her performance. To accomplish this, we use the silhouette form extracted by the IR system and use real-time computer vision techniques to recognize the aerobic movements of the user from the silhouette. Based upon the output of the vision system, the virtual instructor then responds accordingly (e.g "good job!" if the vision system recognizes that the user is performing the aerobic move correctly, or "follow me!" if the user is not performing the move correctly). When performing large-scale aerobic exercise movements, having a wireless interface (e.g. no wired body-suit) enables the experience to be more natural and desirable [2,15,12].

Fig. 6. Virtual PAT. A virtual personal aerobics trainer. Photo credit: Webb Chappell. Copyright: Webb Chappell 1998.

The underlying motivation for building the virtual aerobics system is that many forms of media that *pretend* to be interactive are in fact deaf, dumb, and blind. For example, many of the aerobics workout videos that one can buy or rent present an instructor that blindly expels verbal re-enforcements (e.g. "very good!") whether or not a person is doing the moves (or even is in the room!). There would be a substantial improvement if the room just knew whether or not a person was there moving in front of the screen. A feeling of awareness would then be associated with the system. And because of the repetitiveness of watching the same exercise videos, this "programmable" system heightens the interest of the user by allowing the design of specialized workouts (e.g. exercising only the upper body).

3.1 System Design

The PAT system is a modular design of media and vision components. All software[5] was written in C++ and run on SGI R10000 O2 computer systems (though we believe all the components could be placed within a much lower-end hardware setup). The output video of the system is sent to the frontal screen, as shown in Fig. 6, showing the instructor performing the moves. The feedback is routed through the audio channel. The music is currently in the form of MIDI files.

---

[5] All media components were developed using SGI's Digital Media utilities/libraries.

Fig. 7. Video output of virtual instructor (an Army Drill Sergeant).

Currently, a set of movie clips, showing a full view of the instructor, is used (see Fig. 7). In each clip (for each move), the instructor performs a single cycle of the move. This clip is looped for the duration of the time devoted for that move[6].

Each time a new aerobic move begins, a brief statement about the new move is given. For some moves, the comment may give the name of the move (e.g. "It's time for some jumping jacks") or for other moves explain their purpose (e.g. "This move is going to work the shoulders"). As for the feedback to the user, the system contains many *positive* comments (e.g. "good job!", "fantastic!") and many *negative* feedback comments (e.g. "get moving!", "concentrate!"). Whenever the system decides it is time for a feedback comment[7], it randomly picks and outputs a comment from the appropriate category. This way, one does not always here the same comment many times in a row or hear the same ordering of comments. There is an opportunity here to record very expressive comments for the system, which increases the entertainment value of the system as well as its usefulness.

---

[6] The speed of the current movie clip can be altered to be in synchronization with the MIDI music currently being played.

[7] The system checks every movement cycle to see if the user is complying. A *negative* comment is given immediately (every cycle) until the user performs the move correctly. If the user is performing the move, a *positive* comment is given at predetermined intervals (e.g. every few cycles or every few seconds).

Because the current version of the system uses real video clips it would be tedious to record all possible feedbacks during all possible moves. Therefore, the audio is decoupled from the video (e.g. the lips of the instructor do not move, as if speaking the lines). One could consider using a computer graphics model of the instructor. Here, the correct state of the instructor (e.g. doing jumping jacks while complementing the user) could be controlled and rendered at run-time. It might be fun to have virtual cartoonish-like characters as the instructors. Each character could have their own "attitude" and behavior [1], which would possibly increase the entertainment value of the system. But in this system, we chose to use stored movie and audio clips for simplicity.

3.2   Scripting

Since most instructional systems employ some underlying notion of event ordering, we can use this to allow the user to create and structure a personalized session. The system was designed so that each session is guided from a script which controls the flow of the session (as in [12]). Included in the script are the names for the workout moves, the time allotted for each move, the choice of music for the workout, and lastly the instructor to run the session. This allows the user to easily choose their own tailored workout. While we currently use only one instructor (a brash Army Drill Sergeant), the system is designed to have multiple instructors from which to choose. The program is instantly available upon instantiation of the system with a script, and is not generated off-line (not compiled). The system loads the script and initiates the program when the user enters the space. Currently the script is modified in a text editor, but its simple form would make the construction of a GUI script selector trivial.

3.3   Controller

A simple state-based controller was developed to run the workout script and act as a central node connecting the various modules. The controller consists of 7 states: Pause, Startup, Introduction, Workout, Closing, Shutdown, and Pre-Closing. The system begins in Pause mode, where it resides until a person enters the space. Then begins the Startup mode which opens windows and performs some system preparation. Next is the Introduction state, where a welcome and introduction is given by the instructor. After the brief introduction, the system loops in the Workout state (a loop for each move in the session) until all moves are completed. Then a Closing mode gives the final goodbye comments, followed by the Shutdown mode where the display is turned off and then system cleanup is initiated. There is an additional PreClosing state which is entered if the user prematurely leaves the space. Here, the instructor realizes the user is no longer there, and then starts a pause or shutdown of the system (the program will not continue if no one is there to participate). As previously stated, no hardcoding of media events is necessary, which makes this controller design much less complicated and easy to develop.

3.4   Recognizing Aerobic Movements with Computer Vision

Real-time computer vision techniques developed by the authors were used to "watch" the user and determine if he/she is performing the same move as the instructor.

The first task of the vision system is to monitor the area and make sure someone is actually present in the space. This is easily accomplished by looking for the presence of the person's silhouette generated by the IR system. The PAT system then starts-up when a person enters the space. Also, if the person prematurely leaves the area during the workout session, the system recognizes that the person has left and correspondingly shuts-down or pauses the session.

Recently, we have developed computer vision methods which show promising results in recognizing such large-scale aerobic exercise movements [4]. That work constructs temporally-collapsed motion templates of the participant's silhouette, and measures shape properties of that template to recognize various aerobic exercise (and other) movements in real-time. To show an example of such a motion template, Fig. 8 shows the templates generated from the IR silhouettes for the movements of left-arm-raise (left-side stretch) and fan-up-both-arms (deep-breathing exercise stretch). Training data of each of the moves executed by several users are collected to get a measure of variation which may be seen across different people. Statistical pattern recognition techniques are then employed for the recognition task. This approach easily extends to multiple camera views of the person. To ease in discussion here, we point the reader to [4] for details on the algorithm.

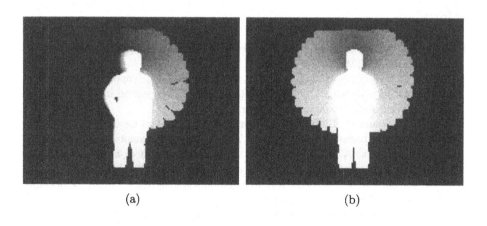

(a)   (b)

Fig. 8. Example motion templates for IR silhouettes. (a) Motion template for left-arm-raise (left-side stretch). (b) Motion template for fan-up-both-arms (deep-breathing exercise stretch).

4   Summary

In this paper we presented a simple and robust method for extracting a silhouette of a participant, overcoming the inherent problems associated with using traditional chroma-keying, background subtraction, and rear-light projection methods. The resulting system also makes available a new venue for multi-screen interaction by incorporating multiple video screens without requiring any special clothing or wired technology. We showed how a robust silhouette of the user can be extracted using specialized infrared lighting without making the underlying technology apparent to those interacting within the environment. To show an example application using the system, a virtual aerobics instructor was presented. The aerobics system applies special computer vision methods to the infrared silhouette to recognize the movements of the user. This then guides its interaction with the participant. The infrared sensing framework itself is a portable system which can act as a re-usable infrastructure for many interactive projects.

5   Acknowledgments

We first would like to acknowledge discussions with Joe Paradiso and Thad Starner for their helpful advice regarding the use of infrared light. We also would like to thank Andy Lippman for playing out the role of the Army Drill Sergeant in the virtual aerobics application. We lastly acknowledge the support of the Digital Life Consortium at the MIT Media Laboratory for this project.

References

1. Blumberg, B., "Old tricks, new dogs: ethology and interactive creatures," PhD dissertation, MIT Media Lab (1996)
2. Bobick, A., Intille, S., Davis, J., Baird, F., Campbell, L., Ivanov, Y., Pinhanez, C., Schutte, A., Wilson, A., "The KidsRoom: action recognition in an interactive story environment," *Presence* (to appear)
3. Darrell, T., Maes, P., Blumberg, B., Pentland, A., "A novel environment for situated vision and behavior," *IEEE Workshop for Visual Behaviors* (1994)
4. Davis, J., Bobick, A., "The representation and recognition of human movement using temporal templates," *Comp. Vis. and Pattern Rec.* (1997) 928–934
5. Davis, J., Bobick, A., "Virtual PAT: a virtual personal aerobics trainer," *Workshop on Perceptual User Interfaces* (1998)
6. Gonzalez, R., Woods, E., *Digital image processing,* Addison-Wesley (1992)
7. Hogg, D., "Model-based vision: a paradigm to see a walking person," *Image and Vision Computing,* 1 (1983)
8. Ishii, H., Ullmer, B., "Tangible bits: towards seamless interfaces between people, bits and atoms," *Conference on Human Factors in Computing Systems* (1997) 234–241
9. Krueger, M., *Artificial reality II,* Addison-Wesley (1991)
10. Murray, J., *Hamlet on the holodeck,* The Free Press (1997)
11. Paradiso, J., "Electronic music interfaces," *IEEE Spectrum* 34 (1997) 18-30

12. Pinhanez, C., Mase, K., Bobick A., "Interval scripts: a design paradigm for story-based interactive systems," *Conference on Human Factors in Computing Systems* (1997) 287–294

13. Rekimoto, J., Matsushita, N., "Perceptual surfaces: towards a human and object sensitive interactive display," *Workshop on Perceptual User Interfaces* (1997) 30–32

14. Strickon, J., Paradiso, J., "Tracking hands above large interactive surfaces with a low-cost scanning laser rangefinder," *Conference on Human Factors in Computing Systems*, (1998) 231–232

15. Wren, C., Azarbayejani, A., Darrell, T., Pentland, A., "Pfinder: real-time tracking of the human body," *SPIE Conference on Integration Issues in Large Commercial Media Delivery Systems*, (1995)

Local and Global Skeleton Fitting Techniques for Optical Motion Capture

Marius-Călin SILAGHI, Ralf PLÄNKERS, Ronan BOULIC, Pascal FUA, and
Daniel THALMANN

Computer Graphics Lab, Swiss Federal Institute of Technology Lausanne, CH-1015
Lausanne Switzerland
E-mail: silaghi@lia.di.epfl.ch, {plaenker, boulic, fua, thalmann}@lig.di.epfl.ch

Abstract. Identifying a precise anatomic skeleton is important in order to
ensure high quality motion capture. In this paper we discuss two skeleton fitting
techniques based on 3D optical marker data. First a local technique is proposed
based on relative marker trajectories. Then it is compared to a global
optimization of a skeleton model. Various proposals are made to handle the
skin deformation problem. Index Terms—skeleton fitting, motion capture,
optical markers

1   Introduction

As stressed in a recent production featuring many virtual humans, the most critical
element in their creation seems to be the replication of believable motion [1]. In most
productions optical motion capture is preferred due to its high precision measurement
of little reflective markers attached on some relevant body landmarks (**Fig. 1a**). The
movement of an artist is captured with two to eight calibrated cameras. For simple
motions the multiple views of markers allow the automatic reconstruction of their 3D
position. Once per session, a special calibration motion that highlights all the
necessary degrees of mobility allows to build or adjust a skeleton model (this motion
is further referred to as the *gym* motion). Then the skeleton model is used in a post-
processing phase to derive the angular trajectories of all the captured motions. Finally
animators often adjust angular data to adapt the motion to a virtual character that is
different from the artist (**Fig. 1d**).
Presently, the stage of automatic 3D reconstruction is often brought to a halt for
complex motions. Either some markers are obscured from camera view or the
algorithm confuses the trajectory of one marker with that of another. This requires
much manual intervention that severely reduces the productivity of the system. In the
framework of the MOCA ESPRIT project, we propose a motion capture methodology
based on an anatomic human model (**Fig. 1b**) [2]. This model encompasses a precise
anatomic description of the skeleton mobility [3] associated with an approximated
envelope. It has a double objective: by ensuring a high precision mechanical model
for the performer, we can predict accurately the 3D location and the visibility of
markers, thus reducing significantly the human intervention during the conversion

Nadia Magnenat-Thalmann, Daniel Thalmann (Eds.): CAPTECH'98, LNAI 1537, pp. 26-40, 1998.

process. In the present paper we discuss methods exploiting the gym motion to estimate the dimensions of the artist's skeleton.

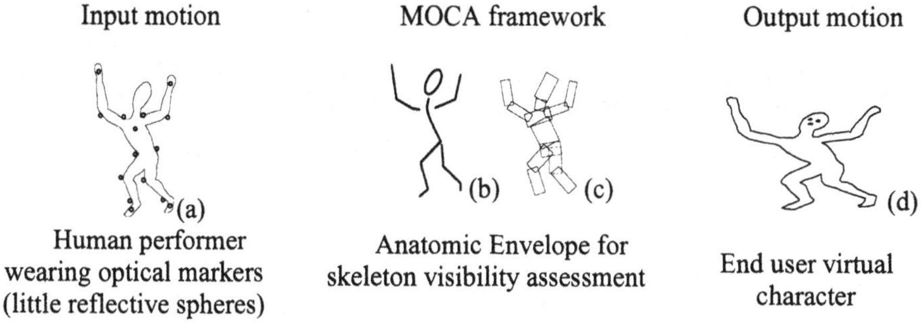

Input motion   MOCA framework   Output motion

Human performer
wearing optical markers
(little reflective spheres)

Anatomic Envelope for
skeleton visibility assessment

End user virtual
character

Fig. 1. Converting the human performer's motion (a) into the end-user character's motion (d) with the anatomic human body (skeleton (b) and approximated envelope (c))

In the next section we review skeleton identification approaches used in other motion capture techniques and in related fields. Then we propose a local skeleton fitting technique based on the relative marker trajectories. In the fourth section we develop a global fitting that adjusts simultaneously all the parameters of the skeleton. We conclude by reviewing our results and by making a comparison between the two proposed techniques.

2   Skeleton Fitting Techniques in Related Fields

Besides optical markers systems, other techniques exist that are based on magnetic trackers [5][9] or plain video sequences [4][6][8].

The main advantage of the magnetic trackers lies in the possible real-time acquisition and the unambiguous measurement of tracked points. However, its main drawback comes from a lower precision that is even worse when the magnetic field is perturbed by metallic objects or other magnetic fields. Regarding skeleton identification, in [5] it reduces to the scaling of a standard model to the size of the real human. Other important differences are estimated by manual measurements and reflected on the skeleton model.

The video-based motion capture techniques try to fit a human model to video sequences. Monocular or stereo video sequences may be used. The monocular case uses a planar projection [6] of a human body model. The parameters of the projection can model global scaling. The technique belongs to the image processing family of techniques and therefore the quality of the recording is strongly sensitive to noise. Another problem in this case is an undetermined direction. These drawbacks disappear when using stereo sequences. In [4] an arm recorded with a stereo system is being tracked by fitting a model built out of ellipsoids to the data. This way, the skeleton fitting is concomitant to the motion tracking. The complex body parts where the deformation of muscles has to be modeled as well, introduces a number of parameters that is proportional to the number of ellipsoids. The measures of the body are modeled by parameters of the ellipsoids and they are globally adjusted over all or selected frames of the sequence.

Other fields also rely on a precise identification of human features. In order to create virtual mannequins that behave exactly like the real human model for presenting garments, the body of the client has to be measured acceptably well [7]. To perform such measurements, two digital cameras capture frontal and side silhouette of customers. Although such an approach is efficient to build a suitable 3D envelope of the client, it fails to identify precisely the joint location [7].

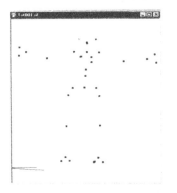   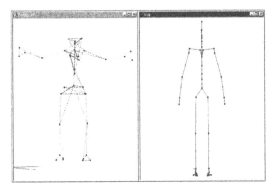

Fig. 2. A frame containing 3D optical markers from a gym sequence, used as input for the skeleton fitting

Fig. 3. Interface for correction and association of markers' sets with skeleton segments. Result of tuning the threshold (left). Skeleton model template (right)

The use of optical markers (**Fig. 2**) simplifies the human model without loss of precision, increasing significantly the speed of the computations while avoiding all the aforementioned problems. A problem lies in the possibility of loosing occluded markers during complex motions. This is the point where the rigorous fitting of an anatomic skeleton proves to be especially important. Using it, accurate prediction of the artist's posture can be made and integrated in the marker identification procedure. It supports suitable decisions in discarding hidden markers out of the alternatives of important choices at the 2D level of a camera view.

3   Local Technique

When looking for the position of the bones of a person, a first observation is that the relative distance of markers attached to one limb is almost constant. The biggest deviations occur when markers are attached on parts that suffer maximal deformation during the movement as around the joints or on massive muscles (e.g. on the thigh). Our approach handles this context by decomposing the problem into three stages developed in the following subsections:
- Partitioning the markers into rigid segment sets
- Estimating the position of joints
- Deriving the corresponding skeleton dimensions

3.1   Partitioning

We have to specify which marker belongs to which segment. This can be done manually by using an anatomic skeleton and making associations. Nevertheless, an automatic tool is welcomed (**Fig. 3**). We propose an algorithm that computes the distances between markers at each frame of the gym motion (**Fig. 4**). It selects the biggest sets of markers in which all distance variations between all pairs of markers are under a certain threshold. This condition defines a rigid segment set. The system may look for the expected number of partitions or the user can interactively tune this threshold (**Fig. 3**).

We call *partition* such a rigid segment set. Its formal definition is the following: we define a relationship R over the set of markers. The relationship R determines a cover C over the set of markers M.

$$C = \{P \mid P \subset M, \forall m_1, m_2 \in P, m_1 \neq m_2 \Rightarrow R(m_1, m_2)\} \tag{1}$$

where

$$R(m_1, m_2) \equiv (m_1, m_2) \in R \tag{2}$$

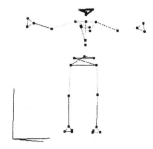

Fig. 5. Maximal Partitions after corrections and association with segments of the template

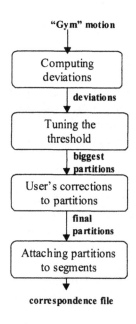

Fig. 4. Steps followed in partitioning

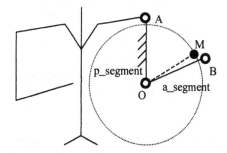

Fig. 6. The trajectory of a marker M around an adjacent segment OA

Now we define the cover $\Re$ over M as:

$$\Re = \{P | P \in C, \forall Q \in C, Q \neq P \Rightarrow P \not\subset Q\} \qquad (3)$$

We call $\Re$ "the set of biggest partitions of markers found in the relationship R".
In our case two markers m_1 and m_2 are in the relation R if, over all frames, the difference between the longest and shortest distances $d(m_1, m_2)$ between the markers, passes below a threshold θ. Thus R is the set:

$$\left\{ (m_1, m_2) | \max_{frames} d(m_1, m_2) - \min_{frames} d(m_1, m_2) < \theta \right\} \qquad (4)$$

We intend to further develop this tool using information based on the angles formed by the markers. Corrections can be done manually. After computing the sets in $\Re$ we need to establish a relationship between each of such set (**Fig. 5**) and a segment of the skeleton model. In the current stage we are doing this association manually, using an interactive graphical interface (**Fig. 3**). We will try AI learning techniques based on the motion of the local systems of coordinates to accomplish it (see section 3.3).
We define the *attachment weight* of a marker to a segment as a normalized measure of the rigidity of its attachment to that segment. By default, all the attachment weights have a value of 1.0.

3.2   Using the Relative Trajectories of the Markers

If we consider a referential bound to a bone represented by a segment e.g. OA (**Fig. 6**), the markers that are attached on adjacent segments (e.g. OB) theoretically move on a sphere centered on the joint that links the two segments (here joint O). This comes from the hypothesis of constant distance between markers and joints.
The position of a segment in space is completely defined by three points. Thus, if we have a minimum of three markers on a segment, we can define the position and orientation of that segment in space. Afterwards, we compute the movement of the markers on adjacent segments in the referential established by these markers and we estimate their centers of rotation (**Fig. 10**). The centers of rotations correspond to the joints. From their position in space we can compute the lengths of the segments as the distances between them. For example, in **Fig. 6** we can compute the position of the joints A and O in space and we get the distance $\|AO\|$.
Due to the deformations suffered by the skin during the motion, the markers attached on a limb change their position with respect to the bone. As long as the deformation is only due to a twisting rotation, it is filtered out by its property of maintaining the distance to the joints. However, a deformation that is changing the distance to the bone (e.g. due to muscles such as biceps) or one that changes the position along the bone induces unknown errors. Markers suffering such deformation errors are further said to belong to the *noisy class*. We deal with these errors by introducing a LSQ computation of the center of rotation. We use a modified version of the Levenberg-Marquardt method [10] for all of our least squares computations. Depending on the complexity of the movements, the errors sum up or compensate each other, the worst cases being presented in [12].

3.3   Segment Referential

Due to skin deformations, during motion the markers may change their position with respect to the underlying bones. This induces errors in computing a referential bound to a segment. The biggest errors result from the displacement that may affect the origin of the system of coordinates. In order to filter out such errors we assign little weights to the markers that belong to the noisy class, and we choose the origin as the *center of mass* of the weighted markers. In order to improve the stability of the direction of the axis, we first choose the farthest marker from the origin for the direction of one axis. In our case we compute this way the Ox axis. This marker is then marked during the whole video sequence. Then we define the plan xOy as the plan that contains the marker situated at the biggest distance from the axis Ox. All the distances used in comparisons are multiplied with the attachment weight because the increase in reliability is proportional to the distance.

The choice of the two important markers that determine the referential is done only once. The calibration frame is the first frame of the sequence in which all the markers attached to the reference segment (*p_segment* in the formula) are visible. They are used for computing the referential in all the frames. The user manually specifies the weights. We provide an interactive display that allows checking the effect of the weights (**Fig. 11** and **Fig. 12**).

3.4   Center of Rotation

In the p_segment referential we compute all the centers of rotation for all the markers of an adjacent segment *a_segment* (**Fig. 6**). The center of rotation is estimated as the result of the function:

$$\arg\min_{r, x_0, y_0, z_0 \ trajectory} \sum (d(r, x, y, z) \times weight(r, x, y, z))^2 \tag{5}$$

corresponding to the LSQ minimization [10] of the function:

$$d(r, x, y, z) \times weight(r, x, y, z) \tag{6}$$

where:

$$d(r, x, y, z) = \sqrt{(x - x_0)^2 + (y - y_0)^2 + (z - z_0)^2} - r \tag{7}$$

and the function $weight(r, x, y, z)$ is described in the section 3.6.

Then we estimate the joint position as the center of mass of the centers of rotation weighted by the associated marker weight and the radius of the sphere that they describe (**Fig. 7**).

$$weight_{center} = \frac{weight(mrk, a\_segment)}{radius(mrk, p\_segment)} \tag{8}$$

We have conjectured that the precision of the center estimation is related to the radius of the rotation and empirically we have used the previous formula. However, the relation between precision and radius proved, as shown in [12], not to be very tight.

Take as an example **Fig. 7**. After defining the system of coordinates bound to S_1, we estimate the center of rotation J of S_2 in this referential. In order to do this we estimate the center of rotation $\bar{x}_J$ of each of the markers M, N and P. Then we compute the mass center of the centers of rotation for M, N and P using the weights computed with the previous formula:

$$\bar{x}_J = \frac{\sum_{centers}(\bar{x}_{center} \times weight_{center})}{\sum_{centers} weight_{center}} \qquad (9)$$

There is a case where the trajectory of a marker describes a circle and not a sphere, due to reduced degree of freedom for a certain joint (e.g. elbow). We would project this trajectory in the plan that best contains it. This plan can be found by using a LSQ that minimizes the distance between it and the points on the trajectory (**Fig. 9**).

A certain attention has to be paid to the case where we have less than three attached markers on a segment. This case occurs often in our experiments (**Fig. 12**). Currently we solve it with two markers if the adjacent joints can be acceptably modeled as having only one rotational degree of freedom. In this case we determine the system of coordinates by the plane that contains the two markers of the base segment and the marker whose trajectory is being tracked. The center of rotation is computed in this plane and then retransferred into the global referential. There, we compute the center of mass of all the centers of rotation computed for all the markers on a neighbor segment in order to find an estimate for the position of the joint.

Afterwards, we perform as usually. For example (**Fig. 6**) we compute all the rotation centers of the markers on OA around OB, and all the rotation centers of the markers on OB around OA. Then we compute the center of mass using the weights of the considered markers and the inverse of the radius of the circles or spheres described by them during their motion.

3.5   Getting the Resulting Skeleton

By applying the previously described procedures we get finally a set of joints estimates for each frame. The next step is to compute the length of each bone in the anatomical skeleton so that the previously computed joints can be in the estimated position in each frame.

One trivial approach is to estimate the length as the average distance between the estimated joints. A more elaborated one is to compute the length that minimizes the square of deviations.

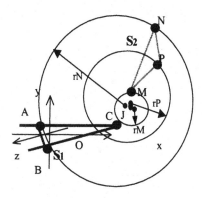

Fig. 7. Weighting centers of rotation for different markers on segment S_2

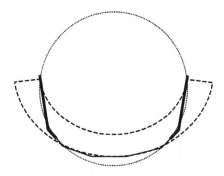

Fig. 8. Case where the lack of proper weighting would induce a bigger error than the ones described in the presented theory. The thickness of the continuous lines represents the density of the points in the trajectory

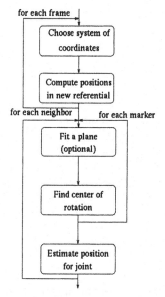

Fig. 9. Algorithm used to estimate the position of the joints for all the frames of the gym motion

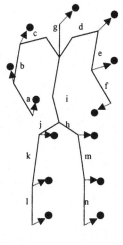

Fig. 10. Each segment length is multiplied with a coefficient (one of "a" to "n") and the degrees of freedom are modified in order to bring the model skeleton in the estimated position in each frame, marked here by the black circles

Currently we use a global adjustment of the lengths that minimizes the distance between the joints of a model and the estimated joints in each frame, adjusting in the same step all the other degrees of freedom of the model (**Fig. 10**). The same technique as the one presented in section 4.2 is employed.

We provide also the possibility of constraining the estimation of a symmetrical skeleton. This constraint can be set very easily in the context of using the global LSQ procedure mentioned above. The only change that has to be done in computations is to use the same coefficients for the adjustment of the symmetric lengths. For example, in **Fig. 10** we would have:

$$i \equiv h, k \equiv m, l \equiv n, i \equiv h, a \equiv f, b \equiv e, c \equiv d$$

Fig. 11. Estimating the center of rotation of a marker around a segment determined by several

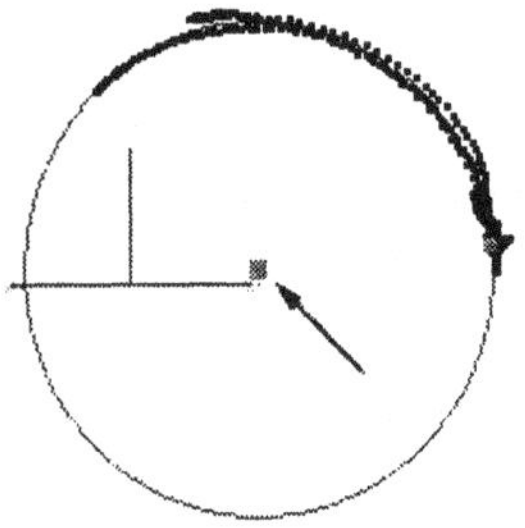

Fig. 12. Right upper arm. Example of a case where the segment can be determined by only 2 markers

3.6   Errors, Advantages, and Drawbacks

In order to restrict the errors of the previously shown type we weight the points on the trajectories. The weight is the inverse of the densities of these points in a region of the space. We compute this densities by first dividing the space in a set of parallelepipeds in which we count the number of points. First we compute automatically the minimal box containing all the points of the trajectory and we divide it, dividing each direction by a factor of 5 or 10. This increases the importance of poorly populated regions of the space representing extremities of the values of the degrees of freedom. Usually, the artist keeps for very short time such postures. Such an inverse density weight diminishes strong noise as the one in the **Fig. 8**.

As it is proved in 12, if

$$\varepsilon \ll R, \tag{10}$$

where R is the shortest possible distance between the joint and the marker while ε is the maximum deviation of this distance, then we can approximate the error x:

$$x \cong \frac{\varepsilon}{1 - \cos(\frac{\alpha}{2})} \geq \frac{\varepsilon}{2} \tag{11}$$

The last formula shows the maximum precision of the estimation of the position of a joint in a given direction. It is a function of the maximum angle α of the arc described by the marker in a plane determined by the joint and that direction vector. The maximum precision is less than half of the maximum deviation of the distance between marker and joint.

4   Global Technique

We now present a different approach to fitting a skeleton to motion capture data. It is called *global* skeleton fitting and here it is used to refine the results of the local technique of section 3. *Global* means, that we consider the whole skeleton at once, whereas the local approach fits one limb at a time, ignoring relations between remote limbs. A thorough description of the global method can be found in [4].

Since this method depends heavily on the underlying skeleton structure, we first give a brief description of the used skeleton.

4.1   Modeling the Skeleton

As mentioned in the introduction, the skeleton of a body model is defined as a set of articulations connected by rigid segments [3]. The model's topology is defined by a hierarchy tree and may be of humanoid, animal or any other shape which allows for tree-like representation of the connected articulations. A "template" defines the translations and rotations that have to be affected to get from an articulation to its parent articulation in the hierarchy. This template describes the initial state of the skeleton. It may vary between different instances of a model, i.e. different characters or actors, but it is fixed for each instance during animation. Here, the local transformation matrix of a joint is multiplied by a "motion matrix", i.e. the matrix of the rotation around this particular joint which represents the model's motion.

Thus, the state of the skeleton is described by the state vector $P_{body} = \left[P_{skel}, P_{motion}\right]$.

The initial state of the skeleton P_{skel} consists of the rotations and translations from each joint to its parent. It is fixed for a given body model. The variable state vector P_{motion} contains the actual values for each DOF. They reflect the position of the body with respect to its rest position.

For any given limb or body part a partial state vector for its parent joint can be written as $P_{part} = \left[P_{pre}, Q_i\right]$, where P_{pre} is the state vector of the preceding joint in the hierarchy, and Q_i is the rotation angle of this DOF.

The position of joints in a global or world referential is obtained by multiplying the local coordinates with a transformation matrix. This matrix is computed recursively by multiplying all the transformation matrices that correspond to the preceding joints in the body hierarchy:

$$X_w = \prod_i D_i(P) \times X_l, \tag{12}$$

with $X_{l,w}$ being local, resp. world, coordinates and the transformation matrices D_i, which depend on the state vector P, ranging from the root articulation's first to the reference articulation's last joint.

The articulations may consist of several joints, each having its own transformation matrix $D = D_{rot} \times D_{ini}$. Take as example the elbow which has the two DOFs flex and twist: $D_{elbow} = D_{rot}^{twist} \times D_{ini}^{twist} \times D_{rot}^{flex} \times D_{ini}^{flex}$. The "initial transformation"

$D_{ini}^{k} = R \times X + pT$, $k = \{flex, twist, ...\}$ is a matrix directly taken from the LIG skeleton. It translates by the bone length and rotates the local coordinate system from this joint to its parent. The matrix entries are calculated with the values of the state vector P_{skel}. The variable coefficient $p \in P_{skel}$ is necessary because we don't know the exact size of the person's limbs yet. For the first joint of an articulation this matrix is usually dense but the other joints have no translation and the rotational part usually consists only of a permutation of the axes to ensure that the DOF rotates around the local z-axis.

4.2   Fitting the Skeleton to Observations in a Global Approach

Optical motion capture delivers accurate 3D positions of markers in world coordinates. We fit a model to these markers by minimizing a certain error function, which penalizes the distance between real marker position and the position predicted by the model. The employed model is depicted by **Fig. 14**. In order to be able to measure a distance, both "marker observations" need to be in the same referential. Thus, we transform the local coordinates of the modeled marker positions into world coordinates by multiplying them with the recursive transformation matrix $D(p)$.

The fitting is then done by minimizing the error ε over all frames and all DOFs in the following equation:

$$\sum \|Obs - X_w\|^2 - \varepsilon = 0 \tag{13}$$

where X_w depends on the state vector P, as explained in the previous paragraph. To minimize the error, we employ the same LSQ algorithm as in section 3.2.

In other words, the global fitting searches optimal values for the DOFs and the lengths of the limbs by taking all frames into account.

4.3   Practical Constraints versus Modeling Real Deformations

Usually, the markers are modeled as being rigidly attached to the skin. But in reality they are effected by skin deformations. Those deformations are depicted by **Fig. 13**. We see that, due to the muscles (e.g. biceps), skin deformation at the joints and twisting, the markers are free to move in all directions. Allowing all those deformations in our model, even with limiting constraints, would lead to overparameterization. However we may consider that a certain position is the normal one while the others are unstable and less probable.

In this case, the fact itself that we use a LSQ technique models such deformations. Besides, some deformations are easily avoided by not attaching markers in noisy places. Usually markers are not attached on biceps or similar places so that the corresponding degree of freedom is sufficiently well modeled by the LSQ method. The deformation of the skin along the bones is important only on the joints. Several characteristics such as the attachment weight of markers (section 3.1) can be used. The deformations of the skin in transversal directions on the bones, due to twisting, are sometimes important. A limit may still be set on the extent of the deformation from one frame to another.

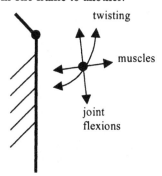

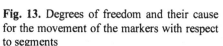

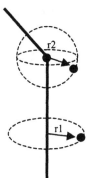

Fig. 13. Degrees of freedom and their cause for the movement of the markers with respect to segments

Fig. 14. The model of the markers on the segments

4.4 Computational Issues

The biggest drawback of the LSQ approach is that it gets stuck in local minima. The best solution to this problem is to ensure a good initialization. The random initialization is therefore avoided.

Taking into account the flexibility of the global approach regarding the models for the attachment of the markers on the limbs, we find it interesting to use the result of the local technique as the initialization of the global one. This way, as long as the model for the global LSQ is enough constraining, we are sure of improving the previously found result. The only condition is that the model should be more constraining than the local one, respectively the movement of the markers on circles around segments and weighted with attachment weights at joint proximity. The twisting model can be improved, eliminating the errors that come in the local technique from the computation of the referential.

4.5 Considered Models, Errors, Advantages, and Drawbacks

A model of the markers on the limbs being currently considered is presented in the **Fig. 14.** The markers that are secured to only one segment are modeled as moving on a circle around the segment. The exact position as well as the radius of the circle is computed as a result of the LSQ optimization (section 4.2) in which these parameters are global over all frames. This approach allows the modeling of the markers attached at different distance on the same bone.

The markers secured very close to joints are modeled as moving on a sphere around the joint. The radii of these spheres are also globally optimized. We intend to research the effects of additional constraints regarding the parallel and meridian of the sphere on which the marker can be found as a function of the current values of the degrees of freedom.

Additional frame to frame constraints may be added in order to improve the convergence of the LSQ technique while taking into account the position of the marker on the corresponding circle or sphere.

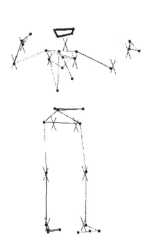 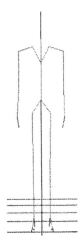 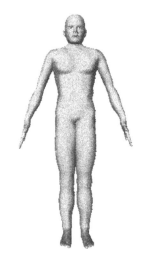

Fig. 15. Crosses show the position of some joints estimated using the local fitting technique

Fig. 16. Skeleton obtained by using a global adjustment of an anatomic skeleton to the positions of the joints estimated using the local algorithm

Fig. 17. Body obtained by covering the obtained skeleton with muscles and skin

5   Results and Experiments

We have tested the previously described algorithms on some "gym" motions. In **Fig. 15** we present the computed positions in space for the joints using the technique presented in section 3. Out of these positions estimated in all the frames of the sequence we obtain the skeleton in **Fig. 16** by applying the algorithm of section 3.5.

In addition to this skeleton we compute estimates of the position of the markers on the limbs. This estimation can be used in further improving the marker tracking and the analysis of the motion. After covering the computed skeleton with muscles and skin we obtain the skeleton of **Fig. 17**.

6   Local versus Global Approaches

Until now we have encountered some problems with the convergence of the global LSQ. The main reason is that we have not used all the frames for the global technique, and because of this, the possibility of introducing frame to frame constraints was also reduced. Another reason is that the conversion of the results of the local technique into the needed parameters for the initialization of the global LSQ was done using yet another LSQ. We intend to further do this analytically. One promising direction is to set multiple priorities levels [11] instead of looking for one global compromise in the posture adjustment phase.

Two complementary validation campaigns are also planned. First recording optical marker data on an articulated structure with known dimensions (e.g. a robot). Second to exploit a set of simple human motions isolating various degrees of mobility in complex regions as the shoulder. The analysis of these data should lead to a better understanding of the markers optimal positioning.

A comparison between the two approaches is summarized in the next table:

Local	Global
Complex algorithm	Simple algorithm
Low computational cost (high speed)	High computational cost (slow speed)
The manually specified weights are important	The importance of the values of the weights depends on the employed model.
The model of the markers on the limbs cannot be modified easily.	The model of the markers on the body is flexible.
Robustness within the limits of the quality of the input	May easily get stuck in local minima

7 Conclusion

We have proposed a new approach to fitting a skeleton to motion capture data. It is based on two different, yet complementary techniques: a local and a global one. The local technique consists of the analysis of the relative trajectories of the markers. It proves to be very fast but good results are dependent on the quality of the gym motion. Also, its output is a set of independent 3D positions of the joints which still have to be assimilated to a skeleton. The global technique employs expensive computations for the simultaneous estimation of all parameters. In order to succeed it needs an already close initialization and a good constraining model, otherwise it gets stuck in local minima. However, it is less sensitive to incomplete motions and can better handle skin deformation. Its output is a complete articulated skeleton structure, ready to be used for animation purposes.

The combination of both techniques eliminates the problems each of them has on its own: the local technique serves as initialization to the global one, which delivers the fitted skeleton.

Acknowledgements

We thank our MOCA partner, ACTISYSTEM, for their help in providing test data files as well as our colleagues in LIG for their technical help. The MOCA project is sponsored by the European ESPRIT program. This work is also partly supported by the Swiss Federal Institute of Technology, Lausanne.

References

1. Cinefex 72, Titanic special reprint, 98 pp, P.O. Box 20027, Riverside, CA 92516, USA, December 97
2. R. Boulic, P. Fua, L. Herda, M. Silaghi, J.-S. Monzani, L. Nedel and D. Thalmann "An Anatomic Human Body for Motion Capture" to appear in Proceedings of EMMSEC '98, Bordeaux
3. R. Boulic, L. Nedel, W. Maurel and T. Molet "Anatomic BODY Model, Kinematics", ESPRIT Project 25513 MOCA, D. Thalmann EPFL Project Director, 22 pages, December 1997
4. P. Fua, A. Grün, R. Plänkers, N. D'Apuzzo and D. Thalmann "Human Body Modeling and Motion Analysis From Video Sequences" International Symposium on Real Time Imaging and Dynamic Analysis, June 2--5, 1998, Hakodate, Japan.
5. Molet T., Boulic R., Thalmann D. "A Real-Time Anatomical Converter for Human Motion Capture" 7th EUROGRAPHICS Int. Workshop on Computer Animation and Simulation'96, Poitier, France, G. Hegron and R. Boulic eds., ISBN 3-211-828-850, Springer-Verlag Wien, pp 79-94.
6. S.Wachter, H.-H. Nagel "Tracking of persons in Monocular Image Sequences" Proceedings, IEEE Nonrigid and Articulated Motion Workshop, June 16,1997, San Juan, Puerto Rico.
7. Stephen Gray "Virtual Fashion" IEEE Spectrum, Feb. 98.
8. J.K. Aggarwal and Q. Cai "Human Motion Analysis: A Review" Proceedings, IEEE Nonrigid and Articulated Motion Workshop, June 16,1997, San Juan, Puerto Rico.
9. B. Bodenheimer, C. Rose, S. Rosenthal, J. Pella "The Process of Motion Capture: Dealing with data" 8th EUROGRAPHICS Int. Workshop on Computer Animation and Simulation'96, Poitier, Hungary, D. Thalmann and M. van de Panne eds., ISBN 3-211-83048-0, Springer-Verlag Wien, pp 3-18.
10. W.H. Press, B.P. Flannery, S.A. Teukolsky, and W.T. Vetterling "Numerical Recipices, the Art of Scientific Computing" Cambridge U. Press, Cambridge, MA, 1986.
11. P.Baerlocher, R.Boulic "Task-Priority Formulations for the Kinematic Control of Highly Redundant Articulated Structures" To appear in Proceedings of IROS '98, Victoria Oct. 98
12. M.-C.Silaghi, R.Plànkers, R.Boulic, P.Fua and D.Thalmann"Local and Global Skeleton Fitting Techniques for Optical Motion Capture" Technical Report, LIG, EPFL, Sept. 98

3D Part Recognition Method for Human Motion Analysis

Carlos Yániz, Jairo Rocha, and Francisco Perales

University of the Balearic Islands
07071 Palma de Mallorca, SPAIN
carlos@anim.uib.es, jairo@ipc4.uib.es, dmifpl0@ps.uib.es

Abstract. A method for matching sequences from two perspective views of a moving person silhouette is presented. Regular (approximate uniform thickness) parts are detected on an image and a skeleton is generated. A 3D regular region graph is defined to gather possible poses based on the two 2D-regular regions, one for each view, at a given frame. The matching process of 3D graphs with a model graph results in interpretations of the human motion in the scene. The objective of this system is to reconstruct human motion parameters and use the analytical information for synthesis. Experimental results and error analysis are explained when the system is used to drive an avatar.

1 Introduction

Human motion analysis and synthesis are of major interest in a variety of disciplines: sport analysis, dancer training and choreography, scientific simulation, 3D animation, medical rehabilitation, virtual reality and entertainment. Systems based on computer vision capture the motion parameters from images and these systems are called kinematics analysis systems. Other systems, called dynamics based systems, are aimed to model the motion using Physics laws. In general, it is also possible to combine both perspectives to complement the final reconstructions and reach adequate analysis and synthesis human motion systems. For full details see, for example, [12, 2]. The system we propose is based on kinematics analysis and is non-invasive.

The approaches to human motion analysis include top-down methods based on model guided analysis, and bottom-up methods based on understanding of low level features. In the former methods, the human body model is composed of a number of parts that allows movement among them, so that reconstruction of the human body motion should calculate shape and joint angle parameters. The main difficulties are related to modeling humans and to the expensive search procedure for the recovery of shape and motion parameters. Some recent work in this kind of approach are [14, 8, 4, 10].

The alternative approaches involve the extraction of the flow field, and then segmenting it into piecewise-smooth surfaces. These surfaces are then grouped and recognized as human parts, maybe using other type of features. Unfortunatly, optical flow segmentation methods are rarely sufficiently general, and the

Nadia Magnenat-Thalmann, Daniel Thalmann (Eds.): CAPTECH'98, LNAI 1537, pp. 41–54, 1998.
© Springer-Verlag Berlin Heidelberg 1998

recognition process may involve prohibitive search procedures. See for example [3, 15, 9, 6]. We do not intend to review all previous works here. The reader is referred to [1] for reviews on the area of human motion analysis.

The system we propose in this paper calculates human motion in three steps, starting with silhouettes from two orthogonally positioned cameras, in a bottom-up fashion. First, the boundary of the smooth body surface is used to recover candidate human parts, from both perspectives. Then, 3D part positions hypotheses are carried out, and finally, constrained matching with a model gives the best interpretation. The process is able to interpret human silhouette sequences and to give an approximate description of part movements. We found a new optimal search to fit a general human shape model into a 3D regular region graph, obtained from the perspectives.

This line of work is important because is within the new trend for animation of humanoids that uses analytical information from real subjects in addition to synthetic motion models. We present a framework in which the subject could be *any* human wearing tight clothes, and the type of motion is *any* motion in which the subject appendages are visible most of the time in the silhouette.

Our approach starts with a general and simple model of the human body and two orthogonal images sequences, and gives as a result a rough estimation of the body part sizes and their motion displayed by an avatar. Although the precision of the position is not high, it recognizes all parts, and their respective movements, with few assumptions.

The reader may wonder whether to find the silhouettes is difficult in real environments. There are systems [15] which are already able to find human part blobs on an arbitrarily learned background. The major restriction of our method is that the human parts ought to be elongated and approximately conical, which prevents the recognition of people with more or less normal clothing. Our research efforts are concentrated on detecting elongated textures in motion through flow analysis.

Section 2 introduces briefly the assumptions about the subject and the camera settings. Section 3 defines the 3D regular part graph concept. Section 4 includes the matching with a human model. Section 5 shows some results and we present in Section 6 some conclusions and current work.

2   Regular Region Extraction

Suppose we have two calibrated cameras placed so that their projection planes are orthogonal. We call the views *Frontal* (*F*) and *Lateral* (*L*). The perspective view from each camera contains a person silhouette in black moving on a simple background. See Figure 1.

The silhouette skeleton is found using an algorithm which decomposes the shape into regular and singular regions [13]. Regular regions correspond to elongated regions limited by opposite contour pieces. These are quasi-parallel and near to each other. Therefore, arms, legs, head and trunk are easily identified as regular regions. Regions which are not regular are considered singular. They

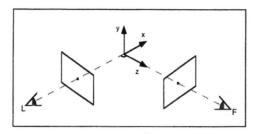

Fig. 1. Experimental set-up

are parts of the shape which connect or terminate the regular regions, such as, shoulders, heap, regions where arms cross each other, feet tips, etc. Thus, the human shape can be represented as a graph, in which nodes correspond to singular regions and edges correspond to regular regions.

The skeleton of a regular region is its middle line (its axis), which is divided into a number of rectilinear segments. In contrast, singular regions have no skeleton, they only connect skeleton lines of regular regions. A 2D skeleton is a graph where nodes are singular regions or corners between two segments and edges are rectilinear skeleton segments. The average width of a regular region is associated with its corresponding edge. A geometric point is associated with each graph node: a node is positioned at its singular region's centre of mass. In Figure 2 it should be noticed that regular regions may not touch each other. They are outwardly disconnected but in fact the node captures the adjacency relations among them. Circles represent the extent of the singular regions and set node positions.

3   The 3D Skeleton Graph

We assume that human parts (head, trunk, arms, legs) are elongated and approximately conical. In other words, each part is symmetrical with respect to an axis. The human parts considered are explained in Section 4. When parts are put together in space, they create connection regions which are not as regular as the original parts. There are also regions which are still regular because they are not affected by the connections, so they preserve their symmetry. We attempt to recover these regular regions, and also the connection regions.

For each frame, there are two skeletons, one for each view. They have complementary information which we capture in the following way. Each point on the skeleton in F has an epipolar line in L, and, the same is true interchanging L for F. The line equation can be calculated using the camera calibration parameters (focal distance and camera positions).

Most of the time, a 2D skeleton point is a projection of a 3D point located on a conic part axis. There are three cases:

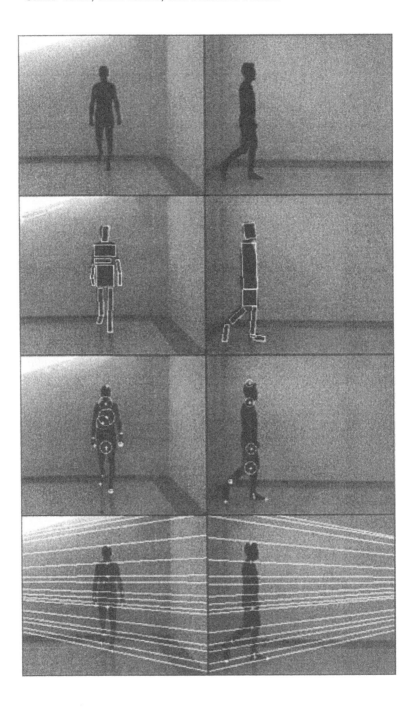

Fig. 2. 2D Processing (*from top to bottom*): (a) original images; (b) regular regions (graph edges); (c) centres of singular regions (graph nodes); (d) epipolar lines of graph nodes

- if this conic part is viewed as a regular region in the other view, the 3D point is projected on the 2D skeleton of the part. Therefore, intersections of the epipolar line of the original point with the other view skeleton are good candidates for its corresponding point.
- if a subpart of this conic part is viewed as a singular region in the other view, we can say that the point is somewhere on this singular region. Since we know that we do not have a good estimation of the point position, we do not generate candidate points. It should be noticed that singular regions are usually small.
- if the conic part is occluded in the other view, then the position of the point cannot be recovered with precision. In this case, we can only say that the point is somewhere hidden by another part and we represent its possible position on the axis of the occluding part, due to lack of more information.

Therefore, possible positions of a skeleton point in F are the intersections of its epipolar line in L with the skeleton in L. However, we keep in mind that the true candidate may not be one of them.

The idea is to find the possible positions of a skeleton segment in a view, in the other view. For this purpose, it is sufficient to obtain the possible positions of the segment endings. We also have to position the singular regions, i.e., the nodes of the graph.

For each node point in the F graph, the intersection of its epipolar line with the skeleton in L is found. A new node is inserted in the L graph, for each intersection of the line with skeleton segments. The new node divides a segment into two parts, so neither a geometrical nor a topological change is carried out on the graph. A similar process is applied to the L graph.

There is an important case we need to remark. The epipolar line may intersect a segment in more than one point, i.e., the segment may be on the line. In this case, no new nodes are inserted.

Moreover, we assume that for each node of F, the intersection of its epipolar line with the skeleton in L is not empty. If a node does not have a corresponding node in the other view, it is removed from the graph, together with its adjacent edges. A similar process is applied to the L graph.

After the above two processes are applied to the graphs, it is required that for each segment in F, the epipolar line of at least one point should intersect at least a segment in L. Otherwise, the segment is removed. A similar process is applied to the L graph.

The resulting graphs are defined below.

Definition 1 (alignment). *Let G_F and G_L be two skeleton graphs of F and L views, respectively. They are in alignment if the following conditions are satisfied:*

- *The epipolar plane which crosses each node in G_F intersects G_L only in positions of the nodes, e.g., it does not cross any segment of G_L. When a segment is in the epipolar plane, we say that the plane does not cross the segment.*

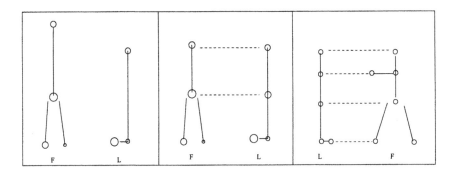

Fig. 3. Example of alignment of two graphs (*from left to right*): (a) original graphs; (b) graphs in alignment; (c) one segment is on the epipolar line of its endings

- *The epipolar plane which crosses each node in G_F intersects G_L in at least one node.*
- *For each segment in G_F, the epipolar plane of at least one of its points crosses a segment or a node of G_L.*
- *The same above conditions, when F is interchanged for L.*

Example 1. Figure 3(b) shows the new nodes inserted so the graphs in (a) are in alignment.

Example 2. When a segment is totally on the epipolar line of its endings, we say that the segment is *facing* the camera. Figure 3(c) shows that when the epipolar line of a node in one view intersects a segment which is facing the camera, no new nodes are inserted. Later on, we will see that this assumes that the 3D position of the node can be only on the segment endings in the other view.

After new nodes are inserted and nodes and edges without corresponding ones in the other view are removed from the graphs to guaranty alignment, we define a subgraph of the cross product of the two graphs. V and E represent vertices and edges, respectively. Graphs are assumed reflexive: $(a, a) \in E$ for each $a \in V$.

Definition 2 (3D Skeleton). *Given two graphs $G_F = (V_F, E_F)$ and $G_L = (V_L, E_L)$ in alignment, the 3D Skeleton is a graph $G = (V, E)$ where*

$$V = \{(a, a') \mid a \in V_F, a' \in V_L, a \text{ and } a' \text{ are in the same epipolar plane } \}, \text{ and}$$

$$E = \{((a, a'), (b, b')) \mid (a, b) \in E_F \text{ and } (a', b') \in E_L\}.$$

When nodes $a \in V_F$, and $b \in V_L$, are in the same epipolar plane, they define a unique 3D position. The 3D graph is constructed so that there is a

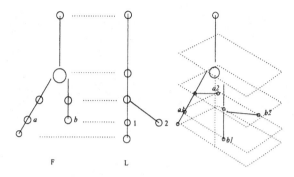

Fig. 4. Scheme of the 3D skeleton of two graphs

3D-edge between two 3D positions when on both projections there is evidence of its existence, e.g., when the 3D-edge projections are edges in the 2D graphs. To describe the exact geometry of the 3D-edge $((a, a'), (b, b'))$, its ending coordinates are calculated so that their projections are on the segments (a, b) and (a', b').

Example 3. Figure 5(b) displays two 3D skeleton graphs. A 3D graph edge is represented as a cylinder, where its radius depends on the observed widths of the 2D edges. On the left part of the figure, there are four legs because those are all the possible positions generated by the views. See also the scheme in Figure 4, where point a could be at point 1 or 2, in the other view. For simplicity, nodes drawn at the same height are assumed to be in the same epipolar plane.

Example 4. When segments are on the epipolar line of a point, there is a lot of ambiguity, because the segment of a view is reduced to a point in the other view. If there are several segments on the same plane, several alternatives are considered, as shown in Figure 6. It should be noticed that if the segments are human arms, the diagram includes several poses which one or two arms could generate.

If edge coordinate endings coincide with their adjacent nodes, i.e., when there is no gap between an edge ending and a node centre, the following statement is true.

Proposition 1. *Let G_F and G_L be the frontal and lateral skeletons of an image, in alignment. The frontal perspective projection of the 3D skeleton of G_F and G_L is G_F. The same is true for the lateral view.*

Proof: Let G be the 3D skeleton of G_F and G_L. It is easy to see that the frontal projection of G is contained in G_F. Conversely, let us show that any node and edge of G_F are in the projection.

Let a be a node in G_F. Since the graph is in alignment with G_L, there is a node a' in G_L on the same epipolar plane. Therefore, the node (a, a') is in G and its projection is a.

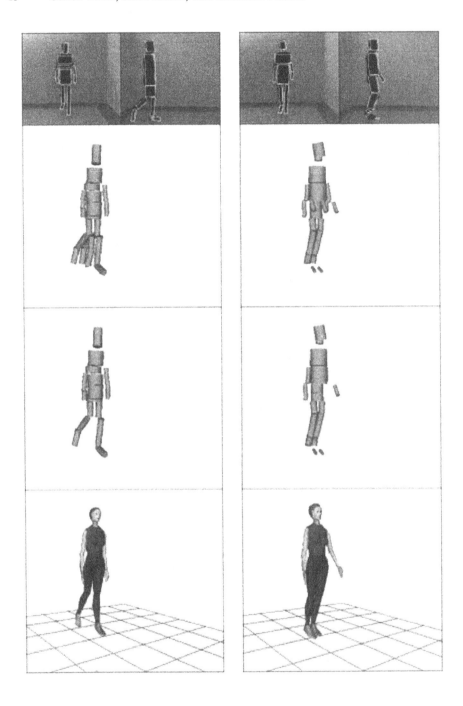

Fig. 5. Motion recovery of frames 3 and 6 (*from top to bottom*): (a) original frames with regular regions; (b) 3D graph; (c) 3D subgraph matched with the model; (d) recognition result driving *Nancy*

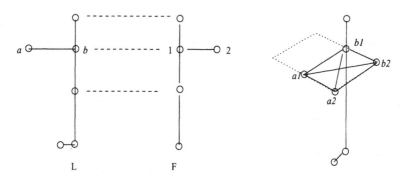

Fig. 6. The 3D skeleton of two graphs with segments on epipolar planes

Let (a, b) be an edge on G_F. Assume that the epipolar plane for a and the epipolar plane for b are not the same. The planes intersect the graphs only on nodes, and there are not any nodes between the planes. The middle point of the segment (a, b) intersects at least one segment (a', b') in G_L, where a' is on the plane for a, and b' on the plane for b. Therefore, (a, a') and (b, b') are nodes in G, $((a, a'), (b, b'))$ is an edge in G, and its projection is (a, b).

If (a, b) is on a single epipolar plane, it must intersect at least a node a' in G_L. Therefore, the nodes (a, a') and (b, a'), and the edge $((a, a'), (b, a'))$ are in G, using the graph reflexivity. Thus (a, b) is the projection of a node in G. This proves the statement.

The proposition above says that from the 3D graph G, it is possible to recover the information in both views (except information about parts that do not have counterpart in the other view). Hence, in one graph we compile the two projection graphs.

On the actual implementation, in order to generate a 3D-node, nodes do not have to be exactly on the same epipolar line, but some small deviation is allowed. Thus, fewer additional nodes are inserted during the alignment process, and the result is more stable to noise.

Any subgraph of G such that its projections are the original view graphs is a valid 3D interpretation of the views. Valid interpretations should also respect the human model structure and mechanics. Therefore, a subgraph which matches a human model and projects onto the views gives a 3D pose for the views. When this process is applied to each frame, a sequence of 3D graphs is generated.

4 Matching with a Model Graph

Each 3D graph contains segments for all possible positions (except for segments facing the camera) of 2D skeleton graphs. To choose one interpretation, knowledge of the human structure is used throughout a graph model which defines the parts of a person, and some quantitative relations among their lengths and widths. The human model considered is a graph which consists of 17 parts connected accordingly,the same number of parts that compound the humanoid skeleton used for displaying theresults.Hogg [7] is the first one that builds a system to recognize a complex movement, such as walking. He used a cylindrical model that is fit into the images by comparing directly the 2D model contours for walking to the grey-value edge points of real images. We instead compare, according to their width and length, whole 3D regions previously extracted from the image. The model we use is similar to Hogg's. It is structurally matched with the 3D graph and the numerical relationships are used to constrain the possible matchings. There are three types of constraints: aspect constraints (relate maximal length to the width of a part), width constraints among parts, and maximal length with respect to a previously defined part length (in our case, the trunk). All constraints are very relaxed to cover the sizes of most humans but avoid considering matchings which are not possible. Hence, the system is designed to recognize any person.

The process matches groups (paths) of segments in the 3D graph with each model part, matching as much as possible and rejecting the matching not satisfying the constraints. A branch-and-bound algorithm is implemented and applied to each 3D graph of the frame sequence.

The grouping into segment paths is required since several segments in the graph can form a single part, and vice versa, several model parts can appear as a single segment. A path generation process finds approximate collinear paths (sequences of adjacent edges) which are as long as possible and are called *maximal paths*. Next, for each maximal path, it generates *all* possible sub-paths, which will be called simply *paths* of the graph, since no other graph paths will be considered in this paper. This is a procedure which allows the future grouping of segments which actually belong to the same human part. Two paths which do not share segments are called *compatible*.

Let P and P_H be path sets. Given $G(V, E, P)$ and $H(V_H, E_H, P_H)$, a 3D graph and a model graph, respectively, an *interpretation*

$$\Phi : P_H \rightarrow P$$

is a partial one-to-one mapping such that

- the domain and the range consist of compatible paths, and
- it respects the path relations, so that if two paths in H are related in certain locations, their images in G are also related in the same locations.

If Φ is an interpretation of H in G, we also say that Φ is a *shape instance* of H in G.

The conditions ensure that paths are mapped into paths at the same relative positions. Therefore, an interpretation has the same flavour of *homeomorphic* subgraphs [5], but it is a more relaxed concept.

The best matching in each frame is chosen. Algorithm A^* is used to find the optimal solution provided that an *admissible* heuristic function is defined [11]. The details are out of the scope of this paper. The matchings recognize the human parts in the sequence.

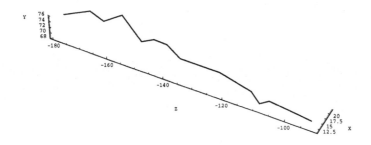

Fig. 7. Motion of the head centre

5   Experimental Results

Several sequences were filmed by two cameras. We show here the results on a walking man sequence. Each 288×216 frame view was filtered to remove background and noise and converted into a bilevel image. 2D skeletons from each view were converted into 3D graphs, which were matched against a human model. Angles between the recognized parts are given to an avatar, so that the results are displayed with the aid of a virtual humanoid, named *Nancy*. All parts are positioned relatively to its parent part, and only the first one, the trunk, has the absolute 3D position and orientation calculated for the 3D graph.

Nancy is a standard VRML humanoid developed at *3Name3D Inc.* It follows the specifications of the Humanoid Animation Working Group (H-ANIM).

Due to paper limitations, we only show the first 12 frames separated approximately $\frac{1}{8}$ s. from each other. See Figures 8 and 9.

5.1   Recognition Performance

Figure 7 shows the 3D coordinates of the head centre, as calculated by the system. There is no ground truth available for any position, except the fact that the subject walked following a line parallel to the Z-axis. Therefore, we assume that the head followed approximately a line, and we measure the deviation of the points from a line.

Using Principal Component Analysis the Root Mean Squared (RMS) error in the 3D space is 2.87 units, out of 292 of the subject height (1 unit = 0.6 cm approx.) and the angle between the best line and the Z-axis is 4.27 degrees. The head apparently moves to and fro due to lack of precision of the regular region analysis. We expect to apply a Kalman filter to smooth the Nancy driving data.

From the figures, a qualitative evaluation can be carried out. Most of the part orientations are correct and the humanoid seems to walk normally. However, the leg's poses are recovered better than the arms' because they are less affected by occlusion in this sequence. We plan to use optical flow to guide the matching more precisely and obtain more robustness.

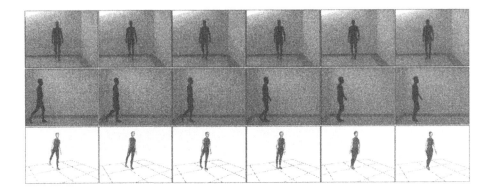

Fig. 8. Recognition result of 12 frames driving *Nancy* (*from top to bottom*): original frontal view sequence, lateral sequence, and Nancy's one view sequence

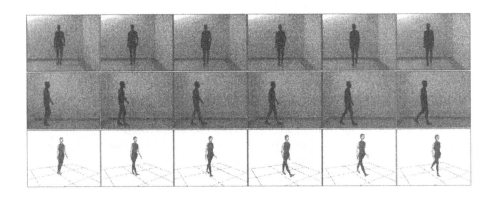

Fig. 9. Recognition result of 12 frames (*cont.*)

5.2   Computational Performance

In the image processing and skeleton extraction are lineal with respect to the number of pixels. The 3D graph calculation is lineal with respect to the number of segments in both views. In contrast, the matching procedure is exponential in the size of the graphs in the worst case. In practice, real graphs are small and the constrains considerably prune the search.

The system performs in batch. Half of the computational time is spent by the matching procedure. The experiment was performed using the C programming language on a SUN SPARCstation IPX and it takes 1.2 cpu seconds per frame. Up to date no effort has been made to optimize the program for speed.

6   Conclusions and Future Work

An analysis vision system for human motion detection is presented in this paper. The global system analyses the two-view input image sequence to discover the 3D spatial information in each image frame. The subject could be *any* human wearing tight clothes, and the type of motion is *any* in which the users' appendages are most of the time visible on the silhouette. No other assumptions are made with respect to the subject or the type of motion. Currently, our method is limited by the fact that we assume the person is moving in front of a simple background.

The level of error obtained is low given the roughness of the skeleton extraction process. Therefore, we claim that we could recover motion without the use of detailed subject information.

Our research is nowadays concentrated on using optical flow to propagate through the sequence the recognition results, and to make an overall reduction of the computational time. Future research includes the use of colour to segment arbitrary images, management of complex backgrounds and combination with a synthesis process to improve the position of the limbs.

Acknowledgements. We would like to thank Ms. Cindy Reed-Ballreich from *3Name3D Inc.* for kindly making the humanoid Nancy available to us. This work is supported in part by the grant CICYT TIC96-0528.

References

[1] J K. Aggarwal and Q. Cai. Human motion analysis: A Review. In *Proceedings of IEEE Non-Rigid and Articulated Motion Workshop*, pages 90–103, Puerto Rico, USA, 1997.

[2] N. I. Badler, C. B. Phillips, and B.L. Webber. *Simulating Humans.* Oxford University Press, 1993.

[3] A. Bottino, A. Laurentini, and P. Zuccone. Toward non-intrusive motion capture. *Computer Vision-ACCV'98*, 1352:416–423, 1998.

[4] D. M. Gravila and L.S. Davis. 3-d model-based tracking of humans in actions: a multi-view approach. In *IEEE Conf. on CVPR*, pages 73–80, San Francisco, USA, 1996.

[5] F. Harary. *Graph Theory*. Addison-Wesley, 1972.

[6] I. Haritauglu, D. Harwood, and L. Davis. w^4s: A real-time system for detecting and tracking people in $2\frac{1}{2}$d. *Computer Vision- ECCV'98*, 1406:877–892, 1998.

[7] D. Hogg. Model-based vision: A program to see a walking person. *IVC*, 1(1):5–20, 1983.

[8] E. Hunter, P. Kelly, and R. Jain. Estimation of articulated motion using kinematically constrained mixture densities. In *Proceedings of IEEE Non-Rigid and Articulated Motion Workshop*, pages 10–17, Puerto Rico, USA, 1997.

[9] S. Ju, M. Black, and Y. Yacoob. Carboard People: A Parameterized model of articulated image motion. In *2nd International Conference on FAce and Gesture Analysis*, pages 38–44, Vermont, USA, 1996.

[10] I. A. Kakadiaris and D. Metaxas. Model based estimation of 3d human motion with occlusion based on active multi-viewpoint selection. In *Proceedings of the*

IEEE Computer Society Conference on Computer Vision and Pattern Recognition, pages 81–87, San Francisco, CA, USA, 1996.

[11] J. Pearl. *Heuristics: Intelligent Search Strategies for Computer Problem Solving.* Addison-Wesley, Paris, France, 1984.

[12] Boulic R., N. Thalmann, and D. Thalmman. A global human walking model with real-time kinematic personification. *CThe Visual Computer*, 6:244–358, 1990.

[13] T. Suzuki and S. Mori. Structural description of line images by the cross section sequence graph. *Int. J. PRAI*, 7(5):1055–1076, 1993.

[14] S. Wachter and H. Nagel. Tracking of persons in monocular image sequences. In *Proceedings of IEEE Non-Rigid and Articulated Motion Workshop*, pages 2–9, Puerto Rico, USA, 1997.

[15] C. Wren, A. Azarbayejani, T. Darrel, and A. Pentland. Pfinder: Real-time tracking of the human body. *IEEE trans. on PAMI*, 19(7):780–785, July 1997.

Motion Capture Data Manipulation and Reuse via B-splines

Sandra Sudarsky[1] and Donald House[2]

[1] Computer Science Dept., Texas A&M University
sudarsky@cs.tamu.edu
[2] Visualization Laboratory, Texas A&M University
house@viz.tamu.edu

Abstract. This paper presents an integrated set of tools to facilitate the manipulation and reuse of motion capture data. A functional representation in terms of nonuniform B-splines provides a compact and efficient description of motion sequences. A collection of B-spline curves attached to a hierarchical structure is used to represent the animation of articulated figures. A set of primitive operators acting on these curves and their application to motion editing is presented. We have successfully used these primitives to generate smooth transitions between motion sequences, motion interpolation and motion cyclification.

1   Introduction

Motion capture is the process of recording motion data in real time from live actors and mapping it into computer characters. Motion capture systems include mechanical, magnetic and optical devices that directly or indirectly track the actor's movements.

During the past decade, motion capture has become increasingly popular as a tool to speed up the computer animation process. It has been used to produce high quality animations in relatively short amounts of time[10]. The major drawback of this technique is the lack of tools to efficiently edit the captured data. In fact, often the whole acquisition process needs to be repeated in order to modify sections of a motion sequence[5].

Motion capture techniques can also be used to build a database of basic motions ([4], [13], [2]) to be used in interactive 3D character animation applications. In such environments, characters are controlled by the user and should move accordingly. Since only a small subset of all possible motions that the user may select can be stored, the challenging task is to design tools that allow reusing these sequences to generate new animations.

Our purpose is to present an integrated set of tools to facilitate the manipulation and reuse of motion capture-based animation data. The design of these tools is based on the following requirements:

- Data reduction. The data generated by motion capture systems consists of a value for each degree of freedom at every sampled frame. A compact representation with a reduced number of parameters to be adjusted is essential

Nadia Magnenat-Thalmann, Daniel Thalmann (Eds.): CAPTECH'98, LNAI 1537, pp. 55–69, 1998.
© Springer-Verlag Berlin Heidelberg 1998

to facilitate motion editing and reuse. This representation can also be used to reduce storage and transmission costs.

- Data smoothing. The sensitivity of magnetic and optical devices to metals and lights introduces some noise in the captured data. In addition, the post-processing step to generate three dimensional data and the occlusion problem related to optical systems can add extra artifacts. Some type of filtering mechanism needs to be incorporated to automatically produce smooth motion sequences. Editing operations, such as transitions between two existing motion sequences, must guarantee smoothness of the resulting motion.
- Computational efficiency. Interactive speeds are required for the system to be of practical use.
- Animator Control. One of the major limitations of motion capture is the lack of animator control. High level editing operations together with direct manipulation of the motion parameters need to be provided.
- Easy integration. The tools need to be easily integrated with traditional computer animation techniques such as keyframing, forward and inverse kinematics.

The basis of our approach is the use of nonuniform B-splines to provide a compact and efficient representation of motion sequences. A set of operators is then applied to these spline curves to support the creation of new animations from previously recorded motion data.

The rest of this paper is organized as follows. Section 2 summarizes related previous work. Section 3 describes our approach, presenting a curve fitting technique based on B-splines and its application to noise reduction. It also describes a set of primitive operators designed to manipulate spline curves. Section 4 demonstrates the usefulness of our approach for the adaptation and reuse of motion sequences. Section 5 summarizes the work and proposes potential enhancements.

2   Related Work

Most of the early editing methods for motion capture-based animation relied on keyframing [5]. However, the large amount of data involved makes this approach undesirable. In what follows, we describe more recently proposed techniques from the computer graphics literature.

Using the principle of motion warping introduced simultaneously by Witkin and Popovic [14] and Bruderlin and Williams [4], new motions can be generated from a given motion sequence and a specified set of positional (or time) constraints. Gleicher [9] combined motion warping techniques with spacetime constraints to edit motion sequences. As in previous motion warping techniques, the user specifies a set of kinematic constraints that must be satisfied by the edited motion. These constraints together with an objective function describe the spacetime constraint problem. In contrast to other spacetime constraints techniques, interactive speeds are achieved by simplifying the objective function. While these methods allow the interactive creation of new animations they do not provide tools for the automatic generation of new sequences.

Bruderlin and Williams [4] applied multiresolution techniques well known in the areas of image and signal processing to edit motion sequences. They use a multiresolution filtering method to transform the motion into frequency bands. Adjusting the amplitude of these bands produces interesting effects on the motion. Other techniques presented in [4] include waveshaping, which is useful to enforce joint limits of articulated figures, and multitarget motion interpolation that allows the blending of two motion sequences.

In the Fourier interpolation approach of Unuma et al. [13], the motion of the joints of an articulated figure are represented by their corresponding Fourier series expansion. Using this representation, they describe a method to interpolate *periodic* motions of articulated figures and to extract certain characteristics of human behavior. In contrast to this technique, our approach is not based on the frequency domain and therefore it is not restricted to periodic motions.

Rose et al. [11] applied spacetime and inverse kinematic constraints to generate smooth and dynamically plausible transitions between sequences of human body motions. Although physically correct, these transitions can not be generated in real time. Recently, Rose et al. [2] proposed a technique for real-time interpolation of motion sequences. Their approach closely relates to our own, it represents the motion of each degree of freedom as a function through time in terms of B-splines. An important distinction in our work is the use of *nonuniform* splines which provide more flexibility during the curve fitting process (see section 3.2).

3 Approach

The motion of an object can be described as a collection of curves in time. When dealing with articulated figures, these curves represent the trajectories followed by the joints. Motion capture systems transform these curves into discrete-time signals by sampling the position and/or orientation of selected joints at regular time intervals. We use a curve fitting technique based on nonuniform B-splines to reconstruct continuous-time curves from the sampled data. These provide a compact representation of motion sequences and allow us to design a set of primitive operators that act on these curves to provide efficient tools to edit the motion.

3.1 Hierarchical Model

The captured data is transformed into anatomical rotations corresponding to an articulated figure ([1], [3]). Our model has six degrees of freedom at the root (typically the hips) which allow us to translate and rotate the entire model. The rest of the hierarchy is modeled as a set of revolute joints, each with three rotational degrees of freedom. A typical model with fifteen joints and 48 degrees of freedom is shown in Figure 1.

Fig. 1. Hierarchical model with 48 degrees of freedom.

3.2   Curve Fitting and Noise Reduction

Let $\{(x_0, t_0), \ldots, (x_r, t_r)\}$ be the set of data points generated for a particular degree of freedom, where x_i is the data value at time t_i. We use a least squares approach to fit a spline curve $Q(t) = \sum_{i=1}^{n} c_i B_{i,k,\tau}(t)$ to the data, where $B_{i,k,\tau}$ is the ith B-spline basis function of order k associated with the knots $\tau_i \ldots \tau_{i+k}$ and c_i is a weighting coefficient. The values of the coefficients $\mathbf{c} = \{c_1, \ldots, c_n\}$ of $Q(t)$ are found by minimizing the expression

$$E = \sum_{j=0}^{r} (Q(t_j) - x_j)^2. \tag{1}$$

The least squares solution of (1) can be found by solving a linear system of the form

$$A\mathbf{c} = r, \tag{2}$$

where A is a positive definite, symmetric and sparse matrix. The system (2) can be solved efficiently using the Cholesky decomposition method [8].

The curve fitting problem described above assumes a fixed knot vector τ. In the case that the position of knots are left as variables the problem becomes a constrained optimization problem. A number of algorithms to solve this problem have been proposed (see [7] for a good review). The success of these algorithms depends on the choice of the initial position of the knots and they suffer from the existence of many stationary points.

For efficiency purposes, we select the knot vector prior to solving the least squares problem. The straight forward approach of using a uniform knot vector has several shortcomings. First, in order to refine a spline defined in terms of a uniform knot sequence, a knot must be inserted at the midpoint between every pair of existing knots. This restriction forces the addition of knots along the whole curve when only portions of the curve may require refinement. Second, discontinuities can not be represented in terms of uniform knots since the addition of knots with multiplicities greater than one is required. Third, a nonuniform representation usually provides a better approximation when the geometry of the data is "used" to determine the knot placement. Our approach consists of selecting the knot vectors according to the following heuristics:

- Add knots in regions of high curvature
- Avoid knots in regions of noise
- Add multiple knots to represent geometric discontinuities of the input data

Figure 2 shows 1578 data points describing the position of the hips along the Y axis during a dancing sequence. The corresponding approximating spline defined in terms of only 218 control points is shown in figure 3. The B-spline representation not only provides a compact representation, but also offers local control.

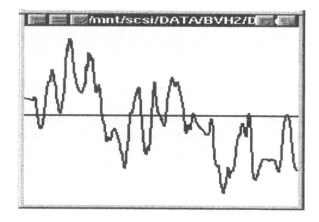

Fig. 2. Motion capture data-hips-1578 data points.

Although in practice these heuristics produce good results, the curves can always be refined by introducing extra knots in regions where the data exceeds a specified tolerance and solving smaller least squares problems. During the curve fitting process, some of the noise inherent to the motion capture data can be filtered out by introducing a weighting factor $\frac{1}{w_j+1}$ in equation (1),

$$E = \sum_{j=0}^{r} (\frac{1}{w_j + 1}(Q(t_j) - x_j))^2. \tag{3}$$

The weight w_j represents how much deviation exists between the parameter value x_j and the average value for that parameter around the neighborhood of

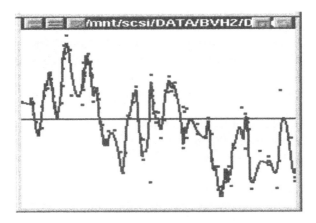

Fig. 3. Approximating spline curve-hips-218 control points.

t_j. The larger the deviation, the less influence that point has over the fitting process. We use

$$w_j = [x_{j-2}, x_{j+1}] - [x_{j-w}, x_{j+w-1}],$$

where $[x_{j-a}, x_{j+b}] = \frac{\sum_{k=j-a}^{j+b} |x_{k+1}-x_k|}{1+b-a}$ and $2 * w$ is the width of a window centered at t_j.

Figure 4 shows the original data representing the rotation of the upper leg during a running sequence. The result of applying the noise reduction approach to approximate this data is shown in Figure 5 (the control points are omitted for readability).

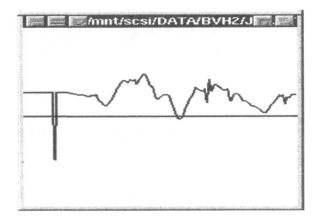

Fig. 4. Motion capture data-Upper leg.

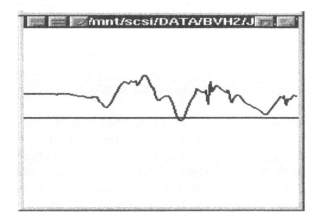

Fig. 5. Approximating spline with noise reduction.

3.3   Primitive Motion Operators

We treat motion curves as objects which can be manipulated by a set of primitive operators. Below we describe some of these operators and their application to motion capture-based data manipulation.

The first set of operators acts on individual curves. Let $Q(t) = \sum_{i=1}^{n} c_i B_{i,k,\tau}(t)$ be a spline curve defined by a set of control points $c_1, \ldots, c_n$ and a knot vector τ of size $n + k$, where k is the order of the spline.

Curve Cyclification. Assume that $Q(t)$ describes a periodic motion (with period δ) for a particular parameter. The cyclification operation generates a new spline $S(t)$ such that $S^{(l)}(t) = S^{(l)}(t + \delta)$, for $l = 1, \ldots, k - 2$.

Given the knot vector $\tau = \tau_1, \ldots, \tau_{n+k}$ of the original spline, we generate the knot vector $\Pi = \pi_1, \ldots, \pi_{2*n+k}$ as follows:

$$\pi_j = \begin{cases} \tau_j & 1 \leq j \leq n+k \\ \pi_{j-1} + \gamma_j & n+k+1 \leq j \leq 2*n+k \end{cases}$$

where $\gamma_j = \tau_{j-n} - \tau_{j-n-1}$. Similarly, given the coefficients $c_1, \ldots, c_n$ of the original spline, the coefficients for the resulting spline $d_1, \ldots, d_{2*n}$ are given by:

$$d_j = \begin{cases} c_j & 1 \leq j \leq n \\ c_{j-n} & n+1 \leq j \leq 2*n. \end{cases}$$

This process can be repeated to generate spline curves of arbitrary length. Note that in the case where the motion is not exactly periodic, the blending operators described below can be used to smooth out the transitions.

Knot Adjustment. Splines provide a parametric curve representation whose length can be controlled by changing the knot vector appropriately. The knot vector can be used to adjust the timing within a sequence or to synchronize two or more motion sequences. For example, we can change the starting time of the animation by shifting the entire knot vector by a constant. Slower and faster animations can be generated by scaling the distance between every pair of knots by a constant factor.

Motion synchronization is very important when blending motion sequences together in order to guarantee that important events coincide in time. Suppose $\{t_1, \ldots, t_m\}$ and $\{T_1, \ldots, T_m\}$ represent two sets of time instances specifying corresponding key events on two motion sequences. We can view each pair (t_i, T_i) as a time constraint specifying the time T_i at which the value associated with time t_i should occur. This problem is equivalent to the time warping problem described in [14] and [2]. However, instead of transforming the raw data to satisfy the time-constraints, we transform the knot vector τ to a new knot sequence π as follows. For $\tau_j \in [t_i, t_{i+1}]$, the corresponding knot π_j is given by

$$\pi_j = T_i + \frac{(T_{i+1} - T_i)}{(t_{i+1} - t_i)} * (\tau_j - t_i).$$

Translation. Translating the curve $Q(t)$ by a constant δ is equivalent to translating the control points by δ and computing the spline using the new vertices. The translated curve is given by

$$Q_T(t) = \sum_{i=0}^{n} (c_i + \delta) B_{i,k,\tau}(t).$$

Scale. Let S be a scaling factor. Then, the scaled curve can be written as

$$Q_s(t) = \sum_{i=0}^{n} (Sc_i) B_{i,k,\tau}(t) = SQ(t).$$

The next set of operators takes as input two spline curves and generate a new curve. Let $Q_1(t) = \sum_{i=0}^{n} c_i B_{i,k,\tau_1}(t)$ and $Q_2(t) = \sum_{i=0}^{m} b_i B_{i,k,\tau_2}(t)$ be two spline curves defined on the knot vectors τ_1 and τ_2 respectively. A new spline curve $Q_3(t)$ can be generated in two steps. First, the two original curves are represented with respect to the *same* knot vector $\tau_3 = \tau_1 \cup \tau_2$ via the Oslo algorithm [6], i.e. $Q_1(t) = \sum_{i=0}^{n+m} c_i^* B_{i,k,\tau_3}(t)$ and $Q_2(t) = \sum_{i=0}^{n+m} b_i^* B_{i,k,\tau_3}(t)$, where $\{b_i^*\}$ and $\{c_i^*\}$ stand for the coefficients under the refined representation. Second, we construct the new curve $Q_3(t) = \sum_{i=0}^{n+m} d_i^* B_{i,k,\tau_3}(t)$ in terms of the knot vector τ_3. The coefficients of the new curve $\{d_i^*\}$ are computed according to the desired operation. We describe below several operators by specifying how the new coefficients are computed.

Uniform Blending. This operation consists of a convex combination of the spline coefficients,

$$d_i^* = ub_i^* + (1 - u)c_i^*, \quad 0 \le u \le 1.$$

It generates a curve that lies somewhere in between the two original curves, according to the parameter u. Figure 6 shows a uniform blending of two splines curves. When this operation is applied to each pair of curves representing the motion of two articulated figures, a new animation that corresponds to an interpolant between the two original ones is generated.

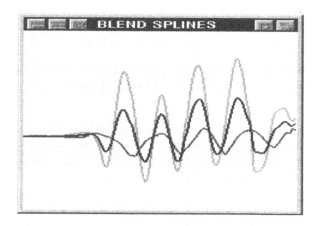

Fig. 6. Two spline curves (one light gray, the other thin dark gray) and the result of applying the uniform blending operator (shown in black) with $u = 0.5$.

General Blending. A general blending operation results when the coefficients for the new spline are generated by combining the original coefficients according to a blending function $0 \le f(t) \le 1$,

$$d_i^* = f(t_i)b_i^* + (1 - f(t_i))c_i^*,$$

where t_i corresponds to the value of the ith entry of the knot vector τ_3. Figure 7 shows the result of blending two motion curves using

$$f(t) = 2(\tfrac{t-a}{b-a})^3 - 3(\tfrac{t-a}{b-a})^2 + 1,$$

where a and b correspond to the value of the first and last knots of τ_3. The above blending function provides smooth changes at the initial and final stages (slow-in/slow-out) and almost constant rate of change in the middle. Note that the resulting spline (shown in black) slowly transitions from one input spline to the next.

We can control the interval during which the blending takes place by supplying two real numbers t_0 and t_1. In this case, the new curve $Q_3(t)$ is identical to

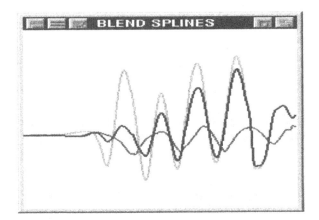

Fig. 7. Two spline curves (one light gray, the other thin dark gray) and the result (shown in black) of applying the blending operator.

$Q_1(t)$ for $t \leq t_0$; it corresponds to a smooth transition between Q_1 and Q_2 for $t_0 \leq t \leq t_1$ and it matches Q_2 for $t > t_1$. Note that the curves $Q_1(t)$ and $Q_2(t)$ must be refined to share the same knot vector only in the interval $[t_0, t_f]$. The coefficients for the new curve are given by

$$d_i^* = f(t_i, t_0, t_f)b_i^* + (1 - f(t_i, t_0, t_f))c_i^*,$$

where t_i corresponds to the value of the ith entry of the knot vector τ_3. As an example of a blending function let

$$f(t, t_0, t_f) = \begin{cases} 1 & t < t_0 \\ 2(\frac{t-t_0}{t_f-t_0})^3 - 3(\frac{t-t_0}{t_f-t_0})^2 + 1 & t_0 \leq t \leq tf \\ 0 & tf < t. \end{cases}$$

Figure 8 shows two original spline curves and the resulting curve after the blending operation is applied using a short interval $[t_0, t_1]$.

These blending operators can be used to generate smooth transitions between motion sequences.

Difference. The difference (addition) between two curves is found by subtracting (adding) their coefficients,

$$d_i^* = b_i^* \pm c_i^*.$$

Motion Warping. The technique described in [14] and [4] can be easily extended to work with B-spline curves. Given a curve $Q_1(t)$ and a set of displacements $d_i(t_k) = p_k$ for $i = 1, \ldots, m$, we find a new B-spline curve $Q_3(t)$ by

$$Q_3(t) = Q_1(t) + Q_2(t),$$

where $Q_2(t)$ is a B-spline curve interpolating the displacements.

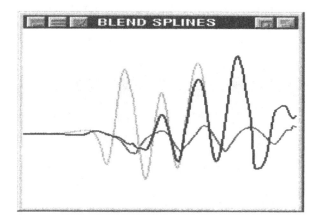

Fig. 8. Two spline curves (one light gray, the other thin dark gray) and the result (shown in black) of applying the blending operator with a specified blending interval.

When applying these operators to the curves describing the motion of articulated figures, we must guarantee that joint limits are maintained and kinematic constraints are enforced. Due to the convexity and locality property of B-splines, joint limits can be violated only on the local interval controlled by a control point whose value exceeds the limit. In this case, we force the curve to reach the limiting value via motion warping. Kinematic constraints can be enforced via inverse kinematics. Once the joint angles are known, the motion curves for those joints can again be modified via motion warping techniques.

4   Results

A prototype [12] is being implemented to serve as a testbed for the application of these operators to the manipulation and reuse of motion capture-based animation data. Figures 9 and 10 show original walking and running sequences. Motion is from right to left, with the stick figures representing the character's pose at discrete uniform time steps. Note the greater distance between successive poses in the running sequence, as well as the more extreme swings of arms and legs. Figure 11 shows a smooth transition from one sequence to the other. This new sequence is generated in three steps: First, the starting time of the running sequence is updated by shifting every knot vector defining the motion curves by a constant factor. Second, the spline curves representing the position of the hip during the running sequence (root of the hierarchy) are translated so that the position of the hip at the beginning of the running sequence closely matches the position of the hip at the end of the walking sequence. The final step consists of blending (with a carefully chosen interval $[t_0, t_f]$) every corresponding pair of splines representing the motion of the two articulated figures. Note that the interval $[t_0, t_f]$ defines how fast the transition should occur.

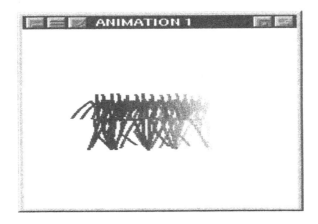

Fig. 9. Walk sequence.

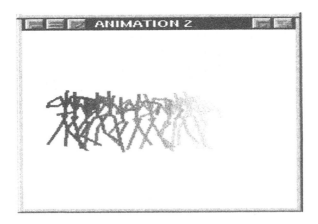

Fig. 10. Running sequence.

The uniform blending operation (with $u = 0.5$) applied to the walking and running sequences of figures 9 and 10 generates the accelerated walk shown in Figure 12. This corresponds to an interpolation between the two original sequences.

Motion cyclification is achieved by applying the curve cyclification operation to every motion curve describing the animation of a periodic motion (except for

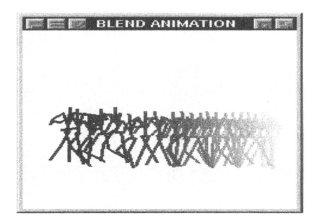

Fig. 11. Smooth transition from walking to running.

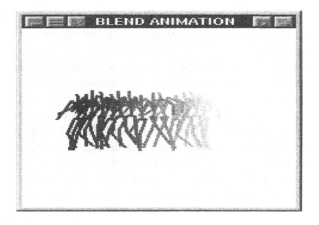

Fig. 12. Uniform blending of a walk and a run sequence.

the curves describing the position of the hips along the X-Z plane which can specified by an arbitrary path). Figure 13 shows an original sequence of running steps (in dark gray) and the result of applying the cyclification operation (in light gray). This operation applied repeatedly can be used to generate animations of arbitrary length.

5 Conclusions

We mention in closing how the proposed approach allowed us to achieve the desired objectives.

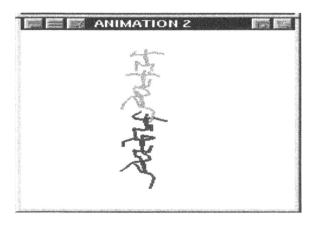

Fig. 13. Motion Cyclification.

- Data reduction. Nonuniform B-splines provide a compact representation since the number of control points is usually far less than the number of input data points.
- Data smoothing. The use of cubic B-splines allow us to generate smooth curves having positional, first and second derivative continuity everywhere except at multiple knots. The incorporation of a filtering mechanism during the curve fitting step reduces some of the noise inherent to the data.
- Computational efficiency. The development of efficient heuristics for finding "good" knot vectors is an important algorithmic improvement, since currently existing spline fitting methods are very efficient once a "good" knot vector is provided. The efficiency of the editing primitives relies on the fact that the operators are applied directly to the control points.
- Animator control. The primitive motion operators provide the animator with tools for motion curve manipulation and reuse. In addition, the local support property inherent to B-splines permits direct and local manipulation of motion curves via control points.
- Easy integration. The adoption of a standard hierarchical model to represent articulated figures simplifies the process of incorporating our tools with traditional computer animation algorithms based on forward and inverse kinematics. The techniques described in this paper were applied to motion capture data but they are equally applicable to motion gathered in other ways. Some possibilities include the evaluation of spline curves in a keyframe system or data generated by procedural algorithms.

The use of the operators described in this paper facilitates the creation of complex motions from simple animations. We are currently exploring the use of these techniques to design other operators that allow the incorporation of cartoon-like effects such as exaggeration and squash and stretch into previously recorded motion sequences.

Acknowledgments

The authors would like to thank LambSoft for access to motion capture data. They are also grateful to James Abello and Jeff Trinkle for their suggestions and discussions. Special thanks to Susan Van Baerle and Jeff Thingvold for their continuous support.

References

1. Bodenheimer, B., Rose, C., Rosental, S., Pella, J., The process of Motion Capture: Dealing with the Data, *Computer Animation and Simulation'97*, Eurographics Animation Workshop, D. Thalmann and M. van de Panne, eds., Springer-Verlag, New York, Sept. 1997, pp. 3-18.
2. Bodenheimer, B., Rose, C., Cohen, M., Verbs and Adverbs: Multidimensional Motion Interpolation, *IEEE Computer Graphics and Applications*, Sept. 1998, pp. 32-40.
3. Molet, T., Boulic, R., Thalmann, D., A Real-Time Anatomical Converter for Human Motion Capture, In *Computer Animation and Simulation'96*, Eurographics Animation Workshop, G. Hegron and R. Boulic eds., Springer-Verlag, 1996, pp. 79-94.
4. Bruderlin, A., Williams, L. Motion Signal Processing. In *Computer Graphics (SIGGRAPH'95 Proceedings)*, Aug. 1995, pp. 97-104.
5. Character Motion Systems. In *Computer Graphics* (SIGGRAPH'93), Course no. 01.
6. Cohen, E., Lyche, T., Riesenfeld, R., Discrete B-splines and Subdivision Techniques in Computer-Aided Geometric Design and Computer Graphics. *Computer Graphics and Image Processing*, 14(2), Oct. 1980, pp 87-111.
7. Dierckx, P., *Curve and Surface Fitting with Splines*. Oxford University Press, New York, 1993.
8. George, A., Liu, J., *Computer Solution of Large Sparse Definite Systems*. Prentice-Hall Inc., 1981.
9. Gleicher, M., Motion editing with space-time constraints, In Michael Cohen and David Zeltzer, editors, *Proceedings 1997 Symposium on Interactive 3D Graphics*, Apr. 1997, pp. 139-148.
10. Motion Capture in Practice. In *Computer Graphics* (SIGGRAPH'97) Course no. 01.
11. Rose, C., Guenter, B., Bodenheimer, B., and Cohen, M., Efficient Generation of Motion Transitions using Spacetime Constraints. In *Computer Graphics (SIGGRAPH'96 Proceedings)*, Aug. 1996, pp. 147-154.
12. Sandra Sudarsky, *Manipulation and Reuse of Motion Data via B-Splines*, Ph.D. thesis, Texas A&M University, in preparation.
13. Unuma, M., Anjyo, K., Takeuchi, R. Fourier Principles for Emotion-based Human Figure Animation. In *Computer Graphics (SIGGRAPH'95 Proceedings)*, Aug. 1995, pp. 91-96.
14. Witkin, A., Popovic, Z., Motion Warping. In *Computer Graphics (SIGGRAPH'95 Proceedings)*, Aug. 1995, pp. 105-108.

Motion Abstraction and Mapping with Spatial Constraints

Rama Bindiganavale and Norman I. Badler

Computer and Information Science Department
University of Pennsylvania, PA 19104-6389, USA

Abstract. A new technique is introduced to abstract and edit motion capture data with spatial constraints. Spatial proximities of end-effectors with tagged objects during zero-crossings in acceleration space are used to isolate significant events and abstract constraints from an agent's action. The abstracted data is edited and applied to another agent of a different anthropometric size and a similar action is executed while maintaining the constraints. This technique is specifically useful for actions involving interactions of a human agent with itself and other objects.

1 Introduction

When one person mimics the actions of another, the two actions may be similar but not exact. The dissimilarities are mainly due to the differences in sizes between the two people, as well as individual performance or stylistic variations. In this paper, we address the first of these issues, namely, controlling virtual humans of various sizes who imitate the action of a motion captured subject.

A subject, called the *primary agent*, is motion captured executing a specific action. We are mainly interested in movements involving interactions with other objects (*e.g.*, drinking from a cup, digging with a shovel, etc.). The imitators, referred to as *secondary agents*, try to execute the same action by interacting with the objects in a similar fashion. As the body sizes and segment lengths of the primary and secondary agents are likely to differ, the motion imitation may not be successful or satisfactory. The thesis of this paper is that *relationships between the world, the body, and the end-effectors (hands, eyes) of the primary agent have been overlooked and are of considerable importance in reconstructing correctly scaled motions.* Often the objects being held are simply wielded for effect, such as holding a shield or slashing with a sword. Keeping feet in contact with the ground plane is one frequently encountered problem, but usually only vertical displacements are moderated: the actual horizontal step position may be input to inverse kinematics procedures to keep the body from floating or sinking. The issue of changing the step locations is related to the motion mimicry problem, but we do not address it here. In this paper, we assume that maintaining spatial constraints for hands and eyes – such as grasping a cup at the correct place and bringing it to the mouth for a drink – is more important than maintaining a similar trajectory or motion style between the various spatial constraints. Style integration will be considered in subsequent efforts.

Nadia Magnenat-Thalmann, Daniel Thalmann (Eds.): CAPTECH'98, LNAI 1537, pp. 70–82, 1998.
© Springer-Verlag Berlin Heidelberg 1998

Several types of motion editing techniques have been developed in the past few years for different purposes. Some of the techniques [1, 7, 21, 23] use signal processing methods to edit and modify the actions for the same agent. A few techniques [6, 15, 18, 19, 22] try to replicate the motions of a person on different sized avatars in real time. The techniques described in [9, 11] use optimization methods to modify the original motions in the presence of space-time constraints. As explained in [9], space-time refers to "the set of all DOF (joint angles and figure position) over the entire animation sequence." In [17], a new set of transition motions are created between two basis motions using space-time constraints. All these techniques treat the problems of mapping motions to other agents, of modifying the nature or style of the motions, and of modifying the motions while maintaining space-time or spatial constraints as separate problems and solve them individually. In [13], constraint based motions are adapted to other agents, but they do not consider interactions between objects and self. In [12], optimization techniques are used to retarget the motions to other agents during object interaction. But a very simple human model is used and the problem of visual constraints is not considered. In this paper, we introduce a technique to automatically recognize such spatial and visual alignment constraints from captured motions. Maintaining these constraints is the basis of motion mapping from the primary agent to secondary agents.

The problem of recognizing motion events directly from (synthetic) image sequences was first studied by Badler [4]. We update these notions to abstract information about significant events and spatial constraints from 3D motion captured data. We begin by generating motion for the primary agent from the motion capture data by using real-time optimization techniques [20, 24] to solve for the kinematic constraints imposed by the data itself. During the execution of the action, we use the concepts of *zero-crossing* and *co-occuring spatial proximities of end-effectors with interacting objects* to recognize the spatial constraints. We then modify the original motion to fit another agent of a different size while maintaining the same spatial constraints. We also abstract the line of attention of the primary agent during significant events. We then impose this as an additional spatial constraint to be solved during motion generation for the secondary agents. This alignment constraint forces the secondary agent to *look at* the same objects. This provides a very natural affect as, in general, people tend to look at an object while interacting with it [8].

The rest of the paper is organized as follows. Section 2 describes the human body model and the technique used to derive the motions for the primary agent from the motion capture data. Section 3 describes the technique to recognize the spatial constraints and Section 4 explains the method to compute the locations of the constraints. Section 5 describes the technique to map the motions to other agents and Section 6 describes a simple technique to recognize the visual attention of the primary agent. Section 7 presents the results and Section 8 discusses the impact of this approach.

2   Deriving Motions from Motion Capture Data

We have implemented this technique completely within the Transom *Jack*®[3] software. The human model we use is highly articulated and has 68 joints and 135 degrees of freedom.

The technique introduced in this paper can be applied to data from any source - motion capture, keyframe or procedural. We have chosen to use only motion captured data. We use the CyberGlove from Virtual Technologies and the MotionStar system from Ascension Technology. The CyberGlove has 24 sensors and generates the joint angles for all the fingers. The MotionStar system consists of one Extended Range Controller (ERC), one Extended Range Transmitter, and 12 Bird units, each controlling a single receiver (referred to as a sensor in the remainder of this paper). The two systems are calibrated separately but synchronized together to generate data at a frequency of 60Hz.

As a preliminary, off-line step in deriving motions from motion capture data for the primary agent, an avatar is built to the size of the subject and is calibrated by placing one of the sensors of the MotionStar system on the lower back of the subject roughly corresponding to the $L5$ segment of the spine (sacro-iliac). In the human model, a corresponding site[1] (FOBpelvic) is created in the $L5$ segment of the spine. The transformations between the MotionStar reference frame and the Jack reference frame are calculated by positioning the pelvic sensor at the FOBpelvic site. All the sensors are then mapped correctly onto the human model in the Jack environment. Next, using the data from all the sensors for the first frame, the human model is postured correctly to match the initial posture of the subject. Finally, sites are automatically created within the human model at the locations where the sensors lie on the body.

To generate the motions, kinematic constraints are established between the newly created sites corresponding to the sensor positions on the model and the sensors themselves. As the sensors move, the human model moves with them along trajectories computed subject to the constraints [5]. This process easily creates motions in real-time while interacting with an object for a similarly-sized avatar. To recreate the same motions for a different-sized agent while maintaining the spatial constraints, we first need to post-process the data to recognize the spatial constraints and map the newly derived data to the secondary agents.

3   Recognition of Spatial Constraints

During interactions with objects, the spatial constraints between the agent and the objects are in general defined by the proximities of the end-effectors and the objects. End-effectors correspond to sites in the human model that are constrained to follow the sensors in the motion capture system. Hence, assuming that the inverse kinematic routines solve the constraints exactly, the sensors themselves can be used to keep track of end-effector locations.

---

[1] Sites are oriented co-ordinate triples.

One method for recognizing spatial constraints is to use fast collision detection methods [10, 14] between different objects in the environment to compute the exact time of initial contact. An alternative method (which we use here) is to compute the spatial proximities of each of the end-effectors with the different objects in the environment. A spatial constraint is recognized when the objects first come in contact with each other (in the collision detection method) or when the computed proximal distance is less than some pre-specified value, ϵ. It would be possible, though computationally inefficient, to compute these collisions or proximities at every frame of the animation. In this section, we describe the various computational simplifications that we use while still being able to derive all the necessary information to recognize the spatial constraints.

3.1   Zero-Crossing

In computer vision, zero-crossings of the second derivative are commonly used for edge detection [16] in static images. For example, the Marr-Hildreth operator uses the zero-crossings of the Laplacian of the Gaussian and the Canny operator uses the zero-crossings of the second directional derivative.

In motion analysis, we can use the zero-crossings of the second derivative of the motion data to detect significant changes in the motion. The zero-crossing point in a trajectory implies changes in motion such as starting from rest, coming to a stop, or changing the velocity direction. These events were noted to have descriptive significance in [4]. When the zero-crossing point also coincides with an end-effector being proximal to another object, it implies contact of the end-effector with the object. In motion studies, this further implies that the primary agent came in contact with the object and suggests creating a spatial constraint to mark this occurrence. We record the corresponding global location of the sensor and mark it as a constraint point for the corresponding end-effector of a secondary agent. The zero-crossings enable us to compute the proximities only at *possibly relevant* frames.

3.2   Tracking Sensors

For an action, it is not necessary to track the zero-crossings of all the sensors on the human model. So, for each action, the user can specify the few specific sensors that need to be tracked. For example, in *drink from a mug*, only the sensor on the hand needs to be tracked for zero-crossings. In all actions, the sensor on the head is used as a tracking sensor for capturing the primary agent's attention.

3.3   Tag Objects

For an action, it is again not necessary to compute proximities of the tracking sensors with all the objects in the environment. As this entire technique is done as a post-process of the motion-capture session, the specific objects that are involved in the action are already known. Using this knowledge, the user can specify the few objects in the environment that need to be used for computing the proximities. To use these, we introduce *tag objects*.

A *tag object* is associated with a site, figure, type and status. A 3D object in our environment can have a number of sites defined on it for various purposes. Each *tag object* has a *tag site* associated with it which is actually used for computing the proximities to the end-effectors. The tag figures refer to the 3D object (or parts of the 3D object) itself. This enables us to have tag sites which are not associated with the tag figure. For example, in the action of *touch the table*, the tag site may be a site on the sensor used to obtain the position on the table. But the tag figure would refer to the table itself. We can define *tag objects* on parts of the human model, thus allowing us to track body/self interactions. For example, in *drink from a mug*, one of the *tag objects* would refer to the mug with a tag site defined on the handle of the mug, and another *tag object* would refer to the head of the human model with the corresponding tag site defined at the mouth.

The *tag objects* may be of different types:

SELF: The tag figure is a part of the human model itself - *e.g.*, head.

FIXED: The tag figure does not move in the environment - *e.g.*, table.

MOBILE: The tag figure can be moved in the environment. *e.g.*, mug.

In examples considered here involving mobile objects, we assume that the agent interacts with them by grasping or holding them and moving them to another place. In other words, for at least part of the action, the mobile object is constrained to move with an end-effector of the agent. In such cases, the status flag of the *tag object* indicates if the tag object is CONSTRAINED to the agent or if it is FREE.

3.4   Spatial Constraint

The process of automatically recognizing a spatial constraint can be summarized as follows: For each tracking sensor, Euclidean distances are computed, at every zero-crossing frame, between the tracking sensors and each of the tag sites. If any of these distances is less than some predefined value, ϵ, a spatial constraint is said to exist between the tracking sensor and the corresponding tag object. The exact location of the spatial constraint to be used for another agent depends on the type of the tag object and its status (if it is a mobile object). This is discussed in detail in the next section. Figure 1 shows the trajectory of the hand tracking sensor for the example *touch the table* and Figure 2 shows the corresponding plots of the distance between the tracking sensor and a tag site (sensor on the table) and the zero-crossings of the accelerations. It can be clearly seen that a spatial constraint is established when the zero-crossings coincide with the close proximity of the tracking sensor and a tag object.

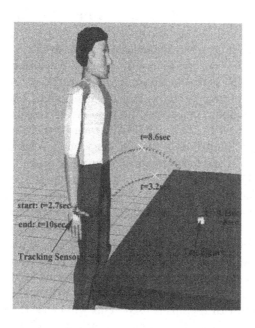

Fig. 1. Trajectory of the tracking sensor in the example *Touch the Table*

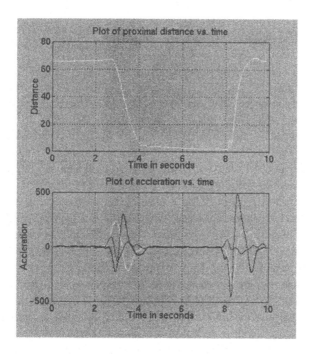

Fig. 2. Plots of spatial proximity and zero-crossings

4   Determination of Spatial Locations of Constraints

The spatial proximity of each tracking sensor from each tag site is computed at the zero-crossings of the tracking sensor. If a spatial constraint is recognized as outlined above, then the global locations of the constraint need to be used as a constraint location during the secondary agent's action. The global location of the constraint is computed based on the type of the associated *tag object*. If the *tag object* is of type FIXED or MOBILE, then it refers to an external 3D object and the absolute location of the tracking sensor is used as the location of the constraint. But, if the *tag object* is of type SELF, then the relative global location of the tracking sensor is used as the location of the constraint. The relative global location is computed by taking into account the size (lengths of the different segments) of the secondary agent. For example, in *drink from a mug*, for the first spatial constraint established during grasping the mug to pick it up, the absolute global location of the hand sensor at the time of first contact with the mug is used as the location of the constraint. For the second spatial constraint (of the same action) established during holding and bringing the mug to the mouth, the relative global location of the hand sensor when the mug comes in contact with the lips is used. This will cause the secondary agent to grasp the mug at the same location as the primary agent but will hold the mug to his mouth correctly, which may be at a different global location based on the difference in sizes between the two agents.

5   Mapping Motions to Other Agents

Once the locations of the spatial constraints are determined, a combination of different techniques may be employed to generate the movements for the secondary agent. To generate efficient motions, the optimization techniques described in [9, 13, 12] may be used. Here, we describe a simple technique to generate the motions. We decompose the joints in the human body into different kinematic joint chains (Fig. 3). We consider each joint chain separately. For the set of joints which are not contained in the same hierarchical chain as any of the tracking sensors, the joint angles computed for the primary agent may be proportionally mapped to the secondary agent. This is possible as they do not have additional constraints imposed on them. All the other joints are driven by the new spatial constraints computed above. As each joint chain is treated separately, it is very important to achieve global synchronization between the different joint chains during the entire action. To do this, we preserve the same timing information *i.e.*, the second agent takes the same amount of time as the primary agent to complete the action. In an effort to maintain the same action style (frame-wise variations in the angular velocity), we modify the speed transform method used in [1].

To solve for the new spatial constraints, a trajectory has to be traced for each joint in the chain containing the tracking sensors. For this, we first use inverse kinematics [20] to solve for the spatial constraints at each of the zero-crossing

Fig. 3. Sets of joint chains defined in the human model

proximal frames. We then do a linear or spherical linear interpolation in the joint angle space for each *time period* defined between any two successive zero-crossing proximal frames. The interpolating factor $\hat{s}$ is derived by computing the normalized distance moved in the joint space by the primary agent at each frame during the corresponding *time period*:

$$s = \int_0^t |\dot{\theta}(\tau)| d\tau \tag{1}$$

where t is time, s is the angular distance moved along the trajectory, and $\dot{\theta}(t)$ is the velocity vector of the joint. The data is normalized along the trajectory:

$$\hat{s} = \frac{\int_0^t |\dot{\theta}(\tau)| d\tau}{\int_0^{t_{end}} |\dot{\theta}(\tau)| d\tau} \tag{2}$$

where t_{end} is the duration of the basic period. These interpolating values help maintain the angular velocity profile of the primary agent during the course of the action and is independent of the difference in spatial distance covered during each *time period* by the two agents.

6   Visual Attention Tracking

Capturing and maintaining visual attention is very important for movement realism in the secondary agent. Without it, actions appear unnatural even if all the other constraints are correctly satisfied. For example, while picking up an object, the secondary agent would look extremely unnatural if she looked at some other point in space. Here, we use the above technique to easily address the visual attention constraint.

During interaction with objects, we tend to always look at the object that we are interacting with (at least when we first come in contact with it). This direction is automatically captured for the primary agent by the sensors on the head. If we naively map head motions of the primary agent to a different secondary agent, this gaze direction will be lost and *cannot be re-captured by simple signal processing techniques*. Instead, we define the sensor on the head as a *tracking sensor*. The zero-crossings in the acceleration space of the head sensor indicate a change in gaze direction or indicate gaze at a specific point in space. During these zero-crossings, we check for visual attention constraints by using the line of sight of the agent. For efficiency, we compute the intersections of the line of sight with the bounding boxes of the tag objects only. If there is any tagged object in the direction of the line of sight, the global location of the point of attention is calculated and used as the visual (alignment) constraint for the secondary agent during its motion computation. We use a head-eye tracking model to solve for the joint angles in the eyes, head, and neck at the gaze direction zero crossing frames. For the remainder of the frames, we use joint angle interpolation while maintaining the angular velocity profile as outlined above.

7   Results

We have tested this technique by mapping the actions of an adult to the virtual model of a nine year old child. We have captured *touching a table* which involves only a FIXED tag object and *drinking from a mug* which involves a MOBILE object. In both cases, we were able to successfully recognize the spatial constraints and map the motions correctly to the second agent. Of these, the example of *drink from mug* is more complicated and we discuss this in detail here.

In the example of *drink from mug*, the primary agent bends over, picks up a mug from the table, drinks from it and places it back on the table. Figure 4 shows the the plots of the trajectories of the hand end-effector of the secondary agent before and after abstraction. Before abstraction, the trajectory obtained is the result of direct mapping of the joint angles of the primary agent to the child model. It can be clearly seen that the constraint of picking the mug cannot be satisfied. But after the automatic recognition of spatial constraints and subsequent remapping of the motions as outlined in this paper, the motion of the secondary agent is corrected as can be seen by the modified trajectory.

Figure 5 shows the various stages of the drinking motion as captured for the primary agent. Figure 6 shows the various stages of the drinking motion after abstraction and mapping have been applied.

Fig. 4. Trajectory plots of the secondary agent's hand end-effector (corresponding to the tracking sensor on the hand of the adult) before and after abstraction

8   Conclusion

We have presented a new technique to automatically recognize and map spatial and visual constraints to other different sized virtual humans. This could be the basis of a very useful tool for motion capture and animation that enables automatic *semantically consistent* modification of captured data involving interactions with space and self. The potential exists for extending this technique to real-time (on-line) execution.

We have used simple interpolation techniques to generate the trajectories. We currently do not consider collisions of the new trajectory with other objects in the environment. For example, there is a possibility of collision of the secondary agent's hand with the table while reaching for the mug although there was no collision in the path of the primary agent's reach. This could be easily modified by imposing additional constraints during the trajectory generation [2].

Acknowledgments

We would like to specifically thank Harold Sun for his help in capturing all the data and Christian Vogler for building all the necessary drivers.

This research is partially supported by the following grants: Office of Naval Research K-5-55043/3916-1552793, DURIP N0001497-1-0396, and AASERTs N00014-97-1-0603 and N0014-97-1-0605, Army Research Lab HRED DAAL01-97-M-0198, DARPA SB-MDA-97-2951001, NSF IRI95-04372, NASA NRA NAG

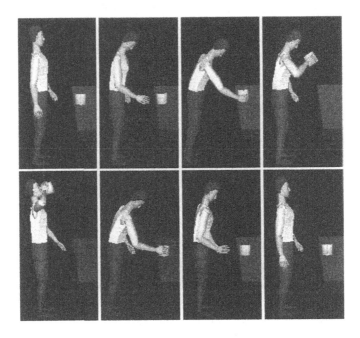

Fig. 5. Different stages in *drink from mug* of the primary agent (adult male)

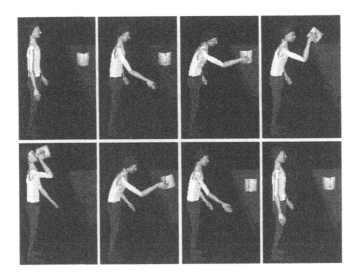

Fig. 6. Different stages in *drink from mug* of the secondary agent (a nine year old child) - after mapping

5-3990, National Institute of Standards and Technology 60 NANB6D0149 and 60 NANB7D0058, and JustSystem Japan.

References

[1] Kenji Amaya, Armin Bruderlin, and Tom Calvert. Emotion from motion. In *Graphics Interface*, pages 222–229, 1996.

[2] N. Badler, R. Bindiganavale, J. Granieri, S. Wei, and X. Zhao. Posture interpolation with collision avoidance. In *Proc. Computer Animation*, pages 13–20, Los Alamitos, CA,, 1994. IEEE Computer Society Press.

[3] N. Badler, C. Phillips, and B. Webber. *Simulating Humans: Computer Graphics, Animation and Control*. Oxford University Press, New York, NY, 1993.

[4] Norman Badler. *Temporal Scene Analysis: Conceptual descriptions of object movements*. PhD thesis, CS, University of Toronto, 1975.

[5] Norman Badler, Michael Hollick, and John Granieri. Real-time control of a virtual human using minimal sensors. *Presence Journal*, 2(1):82–86, 1993.

[6] Joshua Bers. A body model server for human motion capture and representation. *Presence*, 5(4):381–392, 1996.

[7] Armin Bruderlin and Lance Williams. Motion signal processing. In *Computer Graphics Proceedings*, pages 97–104. SIGGRAPH, 1995.

[8] Sonu Chopra. Where to look? automating some visual attending behaviors of human characters. Technical Report IRCS-98-17, University of Pennsylvania, 1998.

[9] Michael Cohen. Interactive spacetime control for animation. In *Computer Graphics Proceedings*, volume 26, pages 294–302. SIGGRAPH, ACM, 1992.

[10] D.W. Johnson E. G. Gilbert and S.S Kerthi. A fast procedure for computing the distance between objects in three dimensional space. *IEEE Journal on Robotics and Automation*, RA-4:193–203, 1988.

[11] Michael Gleicher. Motion editing with spacetime constraints. In *Symposium on Interactive 3D Graphics*, pages 139–148. ACM, ACM, 1997.

[12] Michael Gleicher. Retargetting motion to new characters. In *Computer Graphics Proceedings*, pages 33–42. SIGGRAPH, ACM, 1998.

[13] Michael Gleicher and Peter Litwinowicz. Constraint-based motion adaptation. *The Journal of Visualization and Computer Animation*, 9(2):65–94, 1998.

[14] Thomas C. Hudson, Ming C. Lin, Jonathan Cohen, Stefan Gottschalk, and Dinesh Manocha. V-collide: Accelerated collision detection for vrml. In *Proceedings of VRML*, 1997.

[15] Tom Molet, Ronan Boulic, and Daniel Thalmann. A real time anatomical converter for human motion capture. In *Eurographics Workshop on Computer Animation and Simulation*, pages 79–94, 1996.

[16] Vishvjit S. Nalwa. *A Guided Tour of Computer Vision*. Addison-Wesley Publishing Company, 1993.

[17] Charles Rose, Brian Guenter, Bobby Bodenheimer, and Michael Cohen. Efficient generation of motion transitions using spacetime constraints. In *Computer Graphics Proceedings*, volume 30, pages 147–154. SIGGRAPH, ACM, 1996.

[18] Sudhanshu Semwal, Ron Hightower, and Sharon Stansfield. Closed form and geometric algorithms for real-time control of an avatar. In *Proceedings of VRAIS*, pages 177–184, 1996.

[19] Sudhanshu Semwal, Ron Hightower, and Sharon Stansfield. Mapping algorithms for real-time control of an avatar using eight sensors. *Presence*, 7(1):1–21, February 1998.

[20] Deepak Tolani. *An inverse kinematics toolkit for human modeling and simulation.* PhD thesis, CS, University of Pennsylvania, 1998. In preparation.

[21] Munetoshi Unuma, Ken Anjyo, and Ryozo Takeuchi. Fourier principles for emotion-based human figure animation. In *Computer Graphics Proceedings*, pages 91–96. SIGGRAPH, ACM, 1995.

[22] Douglas Wiley and James Hahn. Interpolation synthesis of articulated figure motion. *IEEE Computer Graphics and Applications*, pages 39–45, November/December 1997.

[23] Andrew Witkin and Zoran Popovic. Motion warping. In *Computer Graphics Proceedings*, pages 105–108. SIGGRAPH, ACM, 1995.

[24] Jianmin Zhao and Norman Badler. Inverse kinematics positioning using nonlinear programming for highly articulated figures. *ACM Transactions on Graphics*, 13(4):313–336, 1994.

Artificial Neural Networks for Motion Emulation in Virtual Environments

Y. Bellan[1], M. Costa[1], G. Ferrigno[2], F. Lombardi[3], L. Macchiarulo[1], A. Montuori[3],
E. Pasero[1], C. Rigotti[2]

[1] Dept. of Electronics , Politecnico di Torino, Italy
pasero@polito.it
[2] Dept. of Bio-Engineering, Politecnico di Milano, Italy
ferrigno@regolo.cbi.polimi.it
[3] Dept. of Manufacturing Systems and Economics, Politecnico di Torino, Italy
lombardi@athena.polito.it

Abstract. Simulation of natural human movement has proven to be a challenging problem, difficult to be solved by more or less traditional bio-inspired strategies. In opposition to several existing solutions, mainly based upon deterministic algorithms, a data-driven approach is presented herewith, which is able to grasp not only the natural essence of human movements, but also their intrinsic variability, the latter being a necessary feature for many ergonomic applications. For these purposes a recurrent Artificial Neural Network with some novel features (recurrent RPROP, state neurons, weighted cost function) has been adopted and combined with an original pre-processing step on experimental data, resulting in a new hybrid approach for data aggregation. Encouraging results on human hand reaching movements are also presented.

1   Introduction

Human interaction with such complex systems as working places, driving seats, or cockpits is more and more asking for designers to face both the human-machine compatibility ("industrial ergonomics"), and the efficiency of the overall engineering system. Because of the rising costs in product development, the market is issuing a growing demand for advanced CAE / CAPE tools, capable to assist the product designer in evaluating the human behaviour under several perspectives. In particular, the correct simulation of pseudo-human movements in virtual environments could help designers to assess the suitable ergonomic variables and their influence on some product features. This gives the opportunity to avoid both the construction of physical mock-ups and the execution of long experimental runs on real people at an early design stage.

Some commercial software packages are able to perform pseudo-human movements that fulfil visual requirements on the computer screen. They usually rely upon deterministic algorithms, mainly based on cost/energy strategies [9]][15], in order to control the related kinematics and/or dynamics. These approaches, however,

Nadia Magnenat-Thalmann, Daniel Thalmann (Eds.): CAPTECH'98, LNAI 1537, pp. 83-99, 1998.
© Springer-Verlag Berlin Heidelberg 1998

cannot match several requirements for industrial ergonomics because of two main drawbacks:

⇒ firstly, the intrinsic variability of human tasks, as well as its dependency on relevant ergonomic factors, are very hard to be modelled by means of a deterministic approach;
⇒ secondly, the reliability of higher-order inferences based on virtual movements should rely on some experimental evidence, together with a suitable error metrics.

For the above reasons, this work proposes a methodology based on the inference of each pseudo-human (i.e. virtual) movement, starting from a sample database of real ones, previously logged by means of a dedicated data acquisition system, described in paragraph 3.

The nature of the problem suggested a two step methodology. In fact raw data are affected by a variability which has a twofold source:

a) an implicit component - related to the intrinsic variability of human behaviour in the accomplishment of the same task - and also affected by "ergonomic" factors, i.e. physical and mental ones alike.
b) an explicit component (independent from psychophysical factors), mainly related to changes in anthropometrical quantities among different individuals.

As to the latter point, it is clear that different samples can be gathered into a unique experimental evidence, provided that a standard mannequin is adopted. Therefore, each real movement is not directly fed to the ANN, but it is previously transformed into a set (or sequence) of instantaneous states (or postures) of a parametric biomechanical model. The transformation procedure at the basis of the adopted methodology also allows to estimate the uncertainty associated to the biomechanical model parameters. These topics are described in paragraph 4.

As to the former point, an artificial neural network (ANN) with some novel features (resilient propagation – RPROP -, state neurons, weighted training) is adopted to learn the way humans perform elementary tasks.

An application of this data driven approach to a simple experimental case is also given, which proves that the proposed data analysis could be afforded without any underlying hypotheses about the human dynamics. In fact, data collected from a series of trials concerning point-to-point reaches performed by a single person are examined, and elaborated according to the presented methodology. Results are showed in paragraph 6.

2   The Hybrid Methodology

In case of complex systems it is hard to adopt detailed models describing every feature of the former. Even more difficult might be to assess all the system parameters by means of a set of direct and independent measurements, as the specific context could affect any identification methodology of the very parameters.

In principle, raw data could be completely interpreted by means of an ANN: the latter could learn structural (i.e. anthropometrical) relations among raw data, as well as general cinematic behaviour and their dependency from environmental and ergonomic factors. Anyway the two faces of the same problem should better be decoupled upon availability of an explicit model for cinematic relations only [3]. This hybrid approach is justified by a set of reasons, listed below.

The ultimate purpose of this work is to reproduce a realistic simulation of human movement by means of a virtual mannequin implemented in a CAD environment, in order to perform several analyses (working space, postures, collisions, etc.). The mannequin obviously imposes its own geometric relations, thus giving rise to unavoidable discrepancies between the mannequin movements and the information got back by the ANN (based on raw data, whatever real test they may represent).

Since the biomechanical features of the person under test are known in advance, there is no use to make recourse to neural computation in order to determine those constraints imposed by geometric relations among the marker locations, which – in case of tests performed on a single person – are fixed throughout the whole set of experiments. Otherwise, the ANN would be indirectly charged with the target of modelling those time-invariant relations that have a different nature from other time-dependent relations and factors mentioned above.

Another reason arises from the fact that, in case of tests performed on more individuals, relative raw data cannot be directly compared and used to train the same ANN: as a matter of fact, the constraints imposed by geometric relations among the marker locations would be different from person to person, and would ask for further integration to the neural computation.

For both cases, given any other set of conditions, a demand for wider integration would negatively reflect on the total uncertainty of the ANN prediction.

As to what has been stated above the sampled raw data are first used to evaluate the parameters of an explicit model for the structural relations among marker locations. The fitting model is used to define a referring posture at every time step, which in its turn is identified by the set of model state variables (i.e. angular values of rotational joints). In such a way, raw data are transformed into a sequence of values for such variables, representing the information quota strictly related to the dynamic characteristics of human movements.

3   The Data Acquisition System

In order to get the human kinematics data, we adopted the ELITE® system [7] which allows, through real time processing, to automatically detect small retro-reflective markers arranged onto human subjects. This TV camera-based motion capture system guarantees very high accuracy even if small markers are used (1/3000 of the field of view over all the working volume and 1/20000 of the field of view locally). The following paragraphs describe the system and how it is operated.

3.1   ELITE System

The innovative feature of the ELITE system is the marker detection hardware, which utilises the shape and size of the markers rather than only their brightness. This characteristic makes the system easy to use, with respect to others, even in sunlight and is the reason for ELITE's very high measurement accuracy. The architecture of the system is hierarchically organised on two levels.

The lower or first level includes the Interface to the Environment (ITE) and the Fast Processor for Shape Recognition (FPSR). The higher or second level is implemented on a personal computer (IBM AT compatible with 386, 486 or Pentium processors).

First level
The ITE normally includes passive markers of dimensions selected according to the field of view (about 5 mm on a 2 m field of view), composed of a thin film of retro-reflective paper on plastic hemispheres. Moreover, ELITE system gives possible to acquire surface features with great accuracy by a laser beam; the reflection/scattering of the laser on the body is recognised by the system as a marker. Pointing the beam, the surface is completely explored; assuming that the surface is stationary, all the collected co-ordinates are used to describe mathematically the surface.

The TV cameras (solid state CCDs which allow the best definition of the images) with a sampling rate of 100 Hz also belong to the ITE.

The second block of the first level, the FPSR, constitutes the core of the system and performs the recognition of the markers and the computation of their co-ordinates. The FPSR computes in real time a two-dimensional cross-correlation between the incoming digitised signal and a reference mask and drives the ITE with synchronisation signals. The mask is a 6x6 pixel matrix and is designed to achieve a high correlation with the marker shape and a low one with the background [6].

After correlation, the first level sends to the computer the 2D co-ordinates of the over threshold pixels as recorded during the acquisition of the subject

Second level
The second level performs a high level processing: 2D calibration (camera calibration), 3D intersection and further processing such as filtering, derivatives computing, modelling, etc. Between the first and the second level (albeit software implemented in the computer) a further step is carried out. By using a co-ordinate enhancement algorithm, taking into account the cross-correlation function, the 2D resolution is increased to 1/65000 of the field of view [5]. This is achieved by computing the centre of gravity (x_c and y_c) of the over-threshold pixels (of co-ordinates $x_{i,j}$ and $y_{i,j}$) belonging to the same marker weighted by the cross-correlation value ($R_{i,j}$). This processing relies on the fact that the closer it is the pixel to the true marker centre; the higher is the value of the cross-correlation function.

System calibration
The system calibration consists of two steps required to achieve 3D reconstruction (space intersection): camera calibration and space resection (localisation of cameras in space). The accuracy in this phase is very important as it influences the subsequent processing of the acquired data. The co-linearity equations represent a mathematical model of the cameras, which relates the 2D target co-ordinates of marker projection, the 3D co-ordinates of the marker in the space and the stereogrammetric parameters [17] (the six spatial camera co-ordinates and its three internal parameters):

$$x - x_0 = -c \; \frac{m_{11} (X - X) + m_{12} (Y - Y_0) + m_{13} (Z - Z_0)}{m_{31} (X - X_0) + m_{32} (Y - Y_0) + m_{33} (Z - Z_0)} \tag{1a}$$

$$y - y_0 = -c \; \frac{m_{21} (X - X_0) + m_{22} (Y - Y_0) + m_{23} (Z - Z_0)}{m_{31} (X - X_0) + m_{32} (Y - Y_0) + m_{33} (Z - Z_0)} \tag{1b}$$

with:

X_0, Y_0, Z_0 - TV camera location (3D co-ordinates of the perspective centre);

$m_{i,j}$ - nine director cosines, which are function of the camera rotation angles with respect to an absolute reference system: Ω, Φ, K (pitch, yaw, roll);

x_0, y_0 - TV camera principal point co-ordinates (intersection of optical axis and image plane);

c - focal length;

X, Y, Z - 3D co-ordinates of the surveyed point;

x, y - 2D target co-ordinates of its projection.

X_0, Y_0, Z_0, Ω, Φ, K are named external geometrical parameters; x_0, y_0 and c inner parameters.

In the real situation the quantisation stochastic error, introduced by the measuring system and optical distortions (systematic error), has to be considered.

The approach to space resection, to determine the geometrical parameters in equations (1a) (1b), is based on the classical iterative least-squares estimation extended to the inner parameters which allows the maximum freedom in TV cameras positioning and setting. By surveying a set of points of known co-ordinates (control points of co-ordinates X, Y, Z), it is possible to write the couple of equations (1a) and (1b) for each of them. All these 2N equations (with N equal to the number of control points) can be arranged in a non linear system, which can be solved after a linearisation around a suitable starting point. In order to obtain the number of control points required (at least 5 not lying on a plane), without having to spend much time to compute their 3D co-ordinates, the control points have been located on a plane grid, which is shifted according to reference locations placed on the floor. Very precise measurements are required only once, when the markers are put on the grid and the references on the floor are located, so every time that the system set-up has to be changed, little time is required to calibrate it.

The determination of the parameters for the correction of the optical distortion errors is realised with the acquisition of a grid of markers located on a plane, which is parallel to the sensor and at such a distance to fill it. By the deformation of the meshes of the grid, the coefficients of suitable quadratic functions are computed. These functions applied to the points of each mesh compensate the deformation [7].

This type of calibration can be referred as virtual rather than physical; in fact the distance between the grid and the camera, grid dimension and focal length need not to be known. The co-ordinates are expressed in pixels and not in target physical units.

Once the stereogrammetric parameters have been estimated, space intersection can be carried out. The two straight lines conveyed through the cameras perspective centres (c_i) and 2D image projection (x_i, y_i) are considered; the co-ordinates of the middle point of the minimum distance segment between the lines are assumed to be the co-ordinates of the reconstructed point (X, Y, Z).

The system local accuracy has been evaluated and the maximum error found with respect to the true value was 1/24000 of the diagonal [12] of the calibrated volume.

4   The Generalized Biomechanical Model

The proposed structural model, in its overall form, consists of a cinematic chain with G segments and M joints, and with a total number of D degrees of freedom (DoFs).

A local reference system (LRS) is attached to each segment S_j in order to reconstruct its position and orientation in the space.

Denote with L_j and L_w the LRSs corresponding to two consecutive segments, respectively S_j (descendent) and S_w (parent). If $\mathbf{P}_k^j$ is a column vector specifying the homogeneous co-ordinates of a generic point k in L_j, the vector $\mathbf{P}_k^w$, specifying the homogeneous co-ordinates of the same point in L_w, can be calculated as:

$$\mathbf{P}_k^w = \mathbf{A}_j^w \mathbf{P}_k^j = \begin{bmatrix} & & & x_j \\ & \mathbf{R}_j^w & & y_j \\ & & & z_j \\ 0 & 0 & 0 & 1 \end{bmatrix} \mathbf{P}_k^j \qquad (2)$$

where (x_j, y_j, z_j) are the co-ordinates of the origin of L_j with respect to L_w and $\mathbf{R}_j^w$ is the rotation matrix of L_j with respect to L_w.

By identifying the origin of each LRS with the rotation joint centre that links the current segment with its parent, the co-ordinates (x_j, y_j, z_j) allow for the straight recover of the distances between joint centres, that is the anthropometrical lengths or structural parameters of the biomechanical model.

Now denote with $S_0 \, S_x \, S_y \, ... \, S_w \, S_j$ the polygonal that belongs to the cinematic chain starting from the root, up to the segment S_j, where the elements of the polygonal are selected according to the topology of the current chain. The laboratory homogeneous co-ordinates $\mathbf{T}_k$ of a checkpoint k integral to the anatomical segment S_j, can be recovered starting from its local homogeneous co-ordinates $\mathbf{P}_k^j$, with respect to L_j, as follows:

$$\mathbf{T}_k = \mathbf{A}_x^0 \mathbf{A}_y^x ... \mathbf{A}_j^w \mathbf{P}_k^j \qquad (3)$$

where the elements in eq. (3) are again selected according to the topology of the current chain. From the homogeneous co-ordinates $\mathbf{T}_k$ it's easy to obtain the laboratory co-ordinates $\mathbf{t}_k$ by selecting the first three elements of the array.

The biomechanical model establishes clear-cut hypotheses as to the nature of raw data before processing takes place. That is:

1. All the checkpoint positions measured on the same individual during the same experimental session derive from the same instance of the biomechanical model, which means that the model structural parameters are time-invariant i.e. the anthropometrical lengths and the local markers position cannot vary among frames of the same movement.

2. For this reason the fitting procedure performs an *inter-frame* estimation treating each movement as a whole; however *intra-frame* estimates, coming from the acquisition process, are used as initial guess to speed up convergence.

No hypothesis about the position of the joint rotation centres is needed.

Discrepancies between measured and virtual markers' positions are mainly owed to random errors affecting the measuring system.

Of course the biomechanical model is not perfectly faithful. Strictly speaking there exist no "true" values of its structural parameters and DoFs. However "optimal" (i.e. maximum likelihood) values can be found through a suitable fitting procedure provided that a noise model is given.

4.1 Model Fitting

Given the checkpoint trajectories, the problem of solving the biomechanical model structural parameters and states is tackled as a statistical inference problem. The model is characterised by G free structural parameters h_j (segments lengths: pelvis, trunk, clavicles, arms, legs,...), M joints and D degrees of freedom $\omega_{i,l}$ (rotation computed for G reference systems angles and translation co-ordinates of the LRS *attached* to the root with respect to the laboratory system). Further unknowns are the locations p_k of the checkpoints with respect to the LRSs.

By denoting i as the posture index, k as the marker index, $t_{i,k}$ as the laboratory co-ordinates of a checkpoint k in the posture (calculated by means of eq. (3)), the expected value $E(y_{i,k})$ of the measured data $y_{i,k}$ is related to the quantity $t_{i,k}$ as follows:

$$E(y_{i,k}) = t_{i,k} \qquad (4)$$

If the errors $(y_{i,k} - t_{i,k})$ are independent and normally distributed with a standard deviation $\sigma_{i,k}$, the statistical process can be stated as an optimisation of the likelihood function expressed by the following relationship:

$$L = \frac{1}{\prod_{i,k} \sqrt{2\pi} \cdot \sigma_{i,k}} \cdot \exp\left(-\frac{\sum_i \sum_k \|y_{i,k} - t_{i,k}\|^2}{2\sigma_{i,k}^2}\right) \qquad (5)$$

Three kinds of parameters (i.e. quantities whose optimal values have to be found through the fitting procedure) are included therein:

1. Lengths of anatomical segments h_j.
2. Checkpoint positions $\mathbf{p}_k$ in each LRS.
3. Rotation angles and translation co-ordinates $\omega_{i,l}$.

By denoting with λ_i a generic parameter included in the previous listed class (hereafter denoted with Λ), the set of values $\Lambda^o = \lambda_1^o,...,\lambda_i^o,...,\lambda_n^o$ that maximise the cost function L represent the set of maximum likelihood estimates for the set of parameters Λ.

However, most elements of the roto-translation matrices are set in advance. Their values fix additional structural constraints. For example, some joints have less than 3 associated DoFs. Moreover, some critical checkpoints are used to identify reference frames of relative reference systems. In this way such critical frames - associated to critical checkpoints - are time-invariant. Provided that such critical checkpoints are carefully positioned on the body, the same "physical" meaning of joint angles could be preserved also across different individuals.

After the fitting phase checkpoint positions loose their usefulness. The relevant informations inherited from the original experimental evidence, together with the structural hypotheses, are summarised into the optimal values of all the other parameters.

To optimise the cost function L an iterative algorithm has been used, i.e. given trial values for the parameters, a procedure that improves the trial solution has been developed.

At each step, the searching direction is obtained by using the Levenberg and Marquardt's method [11], to proceed smoothly between the extremes of the *inverse-Hessian* method and the *steepest descent* method [13].

4.2 Uncertainty Estimation

The proposed approach is intended to supply, together with the anthropometrical parameters and joint angle estimates, the probability distribution of the estimators and then the data training uncertainties, linking the data acquisition phase with the neural processing in a consistent way.

In fact, without training data uncertainty estimation we incur in several drawbacks. The main are:

The learning procedure cannot weigh in a suitable way the information that data carry with them.

We could not estimate neural network performances because the output data uncertainty depends on data training uncertainty.

Denoting with λ_r, λ_s two generic parameters belonging to the set Λ it's possible to define the elements of Fisher's matrix $\mathbf{F}$ as follows:

$$\mathbf{F}_{r,s} = -\mathrm{E}\left(\ell_{r,s}''\right) \tag{6}$$

where $\ell = \ln(L)$ is the logarithmic likelihood function and $\ell''_{r,s} = \dfrac{\partial^2 \ell}{\partial \lambda_r \lambda_s}$ are second

derivatives of ℓ computed in the maximum likelihood point Λ^o, $\forall \lambda_r, \lambda_s \in \Lambda$.

Using asymptotic properties of maximum likelihood estimators the covariance matrix of the estimates can be expressed [2] as $\mathbf{C} = \mathbf{F}^{-1}$, where:

$c_{i,k} = \mathrm{cov}(\lambda_i, \lambda_k)$ is the covariance between the estimated parameters λ_i and λ_k;

$c_{i,i} = \sigma^2(\lambda_i)$ is the variance of the estimated parameter λ_i.

5   The Neural Network

Contrary to previous works, which rely on explicit assumptions about some relevant features of movement [4][8][15], our neural model is essentially based on the mere description of the problem itself.

We can represent the desired network behaviour as a discrete-time mapping:

$$\mathbf{x}_n = F(\mathbf{x}_{n-1}, \mathbf{x}_{n-2}, ..., \mathbf{x}_{n-i}, \mathbf{y}) \tag{7}$$

being $\mathbf{x}_n$ the position of the anatomical point of interest at the n-th time step, F a generic non-linear function; i the number of previous positions to be taken into account; $\mathbf{y}$ the set of "exogenous" inputs that describe the task to be performed; that is, for reaching movement, the desired initial and final positions of the forefinger tip, together with the duration T of the movement of the effector.

In this way we allow the network to learn how duration affects the shape of the trajectory as well as the velocity profile. This reformulation of the problem, that is the determination of the appropriate mapping F, finds its immediate neural counterpart in a recurrent autoregressive network. Supervised training can then be accomplished by means of - for instance - the popular BackPropagation Through Time (BPTT) algorithm [16]. A second-order regression scheme (i.e. with $i = 2$) allows the network to "sense" both the velocity and the acceleration of the marker. This leads to an almost complete definition of the outer architecture. The insertion of a single hidden layer with full connectivity simply meet a parsimony requisite (Fig.1).

This kind of network could easily learn more general (i.e. non time-invariant) mappings. To this purpose some "floating" **state neurons** are added to the output layer; their responses are fed back to the hidden layer according to the same second-order scheme.

During the training phase the recurrent network has to be unfolded in time in order to compute the error signals coming from all the points of the trajectory. It therefore becomes like a huge multi-layer perceptron with massive weight sharing, whose depth depends on the duration of the movement. Because of that gradient components are likely to span a very large dynamic range both across weights and training epochs.

We therefore adopted an advanced weight updating policy known as Resilient PROPagation (RPROP) [14]. Here each weight has its own adaptive learning rate. Moreover, whenever a weight is updated, the corresponding gradient determines only the sign of the change, whose absolute amount is instead completely dictated by the learning rate itself.

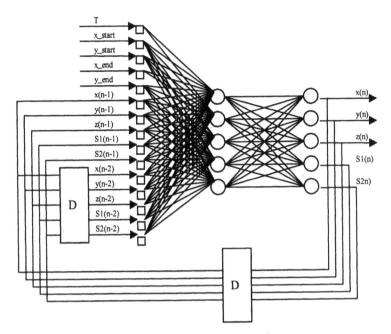

Fig. 1. Neural network topology

6   Experimental Tests

The first step to be taken in order to test the feasibility and reliability of our methodology was obviously to design a simple but meaningful experimental case. A great deal of work has been carried out on point-to-point reaching movements, so that deep insight has been gained in their main cinematic features [4][15]. We chose our test case accordingly, while adding some constraints to make it both more complex and closer to real working tasks: a subject sitting in front of a desk was required to touch 6 marked points lie on the table with his forefinger tip in a sequential fashion. We surveyed the behaviour of a dextrous individual belonging to the 50° percentile[1] male.

Unlike fully unconstrained reaches, the presence of the desk prevented the subject from moving his hand along a straight-line path, forcing him to perform three-dimensional paths.

We acquired through the ELITE system [7] the positions of 29 passive markers placed on the body partition upper from the pelvis. Figure 2 represents three-

---

[1] Generally speaking, in the ergonomic analysis, the population is supposed to be normally distributed with respect to the random variable height and subdivided in percentiles with the 1% of extension. Often the studied percentiles taken in account are the 95th and 50th male, the 5th female. For example, the 95th percentile male means that 95% of the male people are smaller than this model, and that 5% of the male are larger.

dimensional markers' trajectories in a stick model form; they were registered during an elementary left arm movement in a single test.

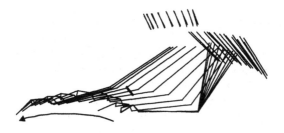

Fig. 2. Movement capture

About 200 elementary reaching point-to-point movements were sampled at a rate of 50 Hz.

6.1 The Adopted Biomechanical Model

A biomechanical model, i.e. the identification of anatomical district, the definition of local reference systems and the identification of the anthropometrical lengths of interest, was defined.

The proposed model included 11 anatomical district, 11 joints and 30 Dof (degrees of freedom). The 11 anatomical district were:

- the pelvis (1) characterised by 6 Dof (root of the bio-mechanical model);
- the trunk (2) characterised by 3 rotational Dof;
- the head (3) characterised by 3 rotational Dof;
- the clavicles (4, 5) characterised by 2 rotational Dof each;
- the arms (6, 7) characterised by 3 rotational Dof each;
- the forearms (8, 9) characterised by 1 rotational Dof each;
- the hands (10, 11) characterised by 3 rotational Dof each.

Each anatomical district was considered as a rigid body and, for each one of these, a LRS was defined.

The anthropometrical measures of interest were:

- the pelvis height: the distance between the pelvis and the trunk rotation centre.
- the trunk height: the distance between the trunk and head rotation centre.
- the right (left) clavicle length: the length of the segment between the neck and right (left) shoulder rotation centre.
- the right (left) arm length: the length of the segment between the right (left) shoulder and the right (left) elbow rotation centre.
- the right (left) forearm length: the length of the segment between the right (left) elbow and the right (left) wrist rotation centre.

To reduce the computational load and data processing effort, the designed model was recovered by using 26 markers.

6.2 Data Elaboration

Data provided from ELITE system were 3D co-ordinates of the markers placed on the body landmarks. In order to extract the quantities needed for the neural network training, an elaboration flow was designed.

The first step needed to properly condition raw data is strictly connected with the acquisition phase. By mean an intra-frame fitting procedure, preliminary values of the biomechanical parameters were carried out taking into account some heuristic about the nature of the task.

However the biomechanical model was not perfectly faithful to the human subject, a fitting procedure to determine its optimal parameters occurred. Starting from the previous guesses, by an inter-frame Maximum Likelihood estimation [3], we computed the value of the structural and angular quantities with the related uncertainty. This step of processing was based on the natural assumption that the measures acquired during a single experiment were drawn from a unique instance of the biomechanical model (time invariance of the anthropometrical length). The error introduced by the model was evaluated in terms of spatial distance among its "virtual" markers and the "real markers" placed on the surveyed subject; this discrepancy was assumed normally distributed.

The representation of the human body by means of an explicit cinematic model permitted to decouple the structural aspects of the movement from the proper underlying dynamics. Starting from the estimates carried out at the previous step, we consistently propagated this information to obtain the effector trajectory and its correspondent uncertainty at each time. However we forced the structural parameters to be equal to those identified, considering only joined probability distributions of the angular quantities.

Analysing the obtained movements we noticed that each one was surrounded by a random number of leading and trailing frames in which the subject was substantially still. Obviously, no autoregressive model could be expected to be robust against such unpredictable behaviour. It was therefore mandatory to identify the actual start and end frame, identifying at the same time the correct duration of the movement. We accomplished this in two different ways: that is, by imposing a threshold on velocities and by fitting bell-shaped time functions to both the trajectory and the velocity profile. The two approaches gave similar results.

Data **representation** turned to be another critical issue. We assumed that the initial posture determined the qualitative features of the movement. In order to take into account this aspect, which appeared biologically plausible, we expressed the effector position with respect to the initial position of the pelvis (root of the cinematic chain). On the contrary, the choice of expressing effector positions w.r.t. the moving pelvis gave rise to synchronisation problems between the movements and was experimentally proven to be subject-dependent, leading to convergence problems or unnatural constraints: for those reasons it was abandoned.

Moreover, in order to take into account the prior knowledge about the relationships between start and end point, we represented them by a two-dimensional reference system defined on the working bench.

Then we proceeded with an undersampling (down to 25 Hz) to substantially speed up training while keeping an adequate time resolution.

We finally performed a numerical normalisation to bring the values of the inputs and outputs within the range [0,1].

There was one sensible point pertaining to this process, as the different data sets should better be normalised with respect to themselves: this in turn brought to a clustering with two different classes, A and B, so divided: exogenous inputs (class A), recurrent inputs (class B), outputs (class B).

This dissection of input data takes into account the fact that recurrent inputs are ANN outputs, and therefore are not homogeneous with exogenous (contextual) inputs. We observed substantial differences between the performances of the nets trained with and without this distinction in mind.

6.3 Some Results

In order to test the whole methodology, differently from the past work [1] in which only raw data were involved, we decided to focus on the training problem in presence of a unique neural topology.

We adopted a topology with 5 hidden and 2 state neurons (5 outputs). Two networks were compared: the former was trained without taking into account the uncertainty of the effector trajectories, on the other hand the second one was trained weighting the learning set with its uncertainty. As it can be seen from figure 3 and figure 4, in both cases the learning behaviour showed a monotonic tendency, with a good error decrease. RPROP really boosted the convergence speed and relieved us from any careful tuning of learning parameters.

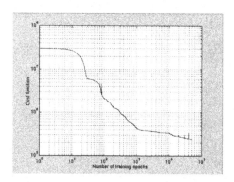 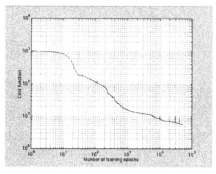

Fig. 3. Learning without uncertainty weighting   **Fig. 4.** Learning with uncertainty weighting

However, no simple numerical index is known to express how natural a movement is. A first qualitative test on the generated movements can be given by a comparison between the real recorded movements with the outputs of the nets: see, as examples of trajectories, figure 5 and figure 6. Dashed lines represent neural predictions.

Even though in principle the knowledge of movement duration allows to stop the production phase when needed, nevertheless this should not cause a sudden variation in velocity. In our networks, the movement really stops at the target endpoint (see velocity profiles: figure 5 and figure 6); on the base of the analysis of the state neurons' output we think this is due to a sort of "counting action" performed by them.

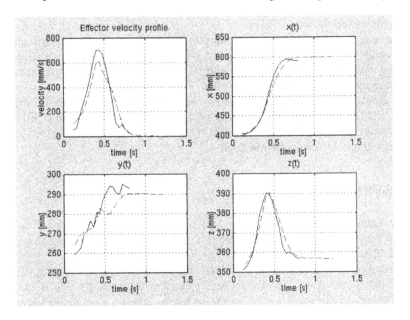

Fig. 5. Movement generation without uncertainty weighting

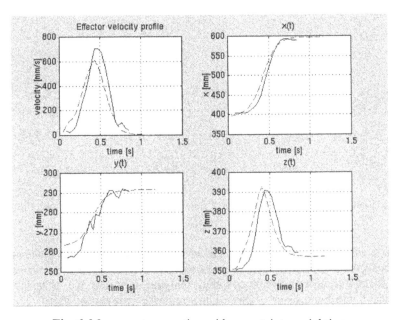

Fig. 6. Movement generation with uncertainty weighting

Due to data poorness, we used a "leave-one-out" strategy, validating the network with couples of movements extracted from the total training set. Apart from fluctuations fluctuations, most movements well validate the nets, giving about as twice the error as patterns in the respective training sets. Even more important than trajectory similarity, the velocity profiles (figure 5 and figure 6) are close to each other, and the learned profiles have the same bell-shaped feature reported in literature [10]. Therefore the nets have learned quite a lot of the features that other model-based approaches use as a criterion of good performances.

An important result clearly emerges comparing the predictions of the two nets together with the real markers' positions: even if sometime no-weighted training leads to a best fit of the natural data in Euclidean sense, the net trained with uncertainty estimates present always a more biologically plausible smooth behaviour. This fact put in evidence the capability of learning intrinsic features of human movement, even if in presence of the non-uniform noise introduced by the model and by the acquisition equipment.

7 Conclusions and Future Developments

In the field of neural network design scholars usually draw a crisp distinction between the Neurobiologic (i.e. bioinspired, neuromorphic) standpoint, where explicative models of neural computation are built, and the Engineering standpoint, more application-oriented, where ANNs are seen as tools to perform generic complex tasks. The same dichotomy can be extended to the study of human motion as well. In this case the usual "bioinspired" view of explicative and generative models (torques, sensorimotor integration) aims at gaining deeper insight in human motor behaviour. On the contrary, our work joins an application-oriented perspective; its main purpose is to take the intrinsic and irreducible variability of human movement as it is. This becomes a great source of information that allows to compute the value of any ergonomic index and, more generally, to draw any higher-order inferences.

Previous paragraphs show the reliability of our ANN data-driven approach to human movement generation. We fixed a methodology tailored to relieve ANN core from the burden of any kind of structural identification. This method appears more flexible and no model is embedded.

We use MLPs, checking the predictability of the movement in term of expectations. Good generalisation capabilities have to be remarked, even if in presence of data poorness.

Future perspectives mainly concern the opportunity of comparing different individuals of the same population. Therefore a normalisation procedure is needed in order to compare subjects of the same population. To normalise the movement produced by a human subject means to transform his movement in an equivalent movement for a "virtual average individual" (a biomechanical instance hereafter called *archetype*) of the tested population. The normalisation procedure should occur for every movement collected. The result of the normalisation procedure will give a set of angular position identifying the state of the anthropometrical model through a postural representation independent from the anthropometrical lengths of the fitted model.

In order to reduce uncertainty, the proposed methodology could include a clustering procedure of the performed test into anthropometrical classes gathering suitable percentiles of the overall population. Each class will be represented by its *archetype*. In this case the *archetype* will represent the overall individuals of each class.

Given an "experimental" instance of the biomechanical model, two closely related questions will arise:

1. To which class does the instance belong?
2. How much do residual discrepancies increase if the optimal lengths of anatomical segments are replaced by the standard values of the proper class?

The common answer is that the "right" class will be the one where residual discrepancies increase by the least amount.

If optimal lengths of anatomical segments will be affected by different uncertainties, the "right" class could not even be the one corresponding to the closest standard instance according to the Euclidean metrics. For these reasons the asymptotic properties of Maximum Likelihood estimates, uncertainties, or better the covariance matrix, will be essential to standardise any "experimental" instance in the correct way and, at the same time, to assess the degree of sub-optimality induced by the standardisation itself.

New involved aspects about the simulation of the postural behaviour became visible. The possibility of learning cinematic time sequences of clustered individuals, weighted by their joined uncertainties, appear very interesting.

8   Acknowledgements

The work has been partially supported by the EC Brite-EuRam project n. BE96-3433 "ANNIE: Application of Neural Networks to Integrated Ergonomics", for which specific tools based on this methodology have been implemented

References

[1]   Y. Bellan, M. Costa, L. Macchiarulo, E. Pasero, "Task-Oriented Estimation Of Trajectories in Human Reaches", *Proc. of the NN&B*, Beijing, CN, 1998.

[2]   S. Brandt, Statistical and Computational Methods in Data Analysis, North-Holland Publishing Company, Amsterdam, pp. 191-239, 1976.

[3]   M. Costa, F. Lombardi, A. Montuori, "A data driven methodology for the simulation of human movement in CAD environments", *Proc. of the CIRP International Seminar on Intelligent Computation in Manufacturing Engineering - ICME 98*, Capri (Naples), IT, 1998.

[4]   H. Cruse, "On the cost functions for the control of the human arm movement", *Biol. Cybernetics*, 62, pp. 519-528, 1990.

[5]   G. Ferrigno , A. Pedotti, "ELITE: a digital dedicated hardware system for movement analysis via real-time TV signal processing", *IEEE Trans. Biomed. Eng. (BME)*, 32, pp. 943-949, 1985.

[6]   G. Ferrigno, A. Pedotti, "Modularly expansible system for real-time processing of a TV display, useful in particular for the acquisition of coordinates of known shapes objects", *US Patent No. 4,706,296* (1987).

[7]   G. Ferrigno, N. A. Borgese, A. Pedotti, "Pattern recognition in 3D automatic human motion analysis", *ISPRS Journal of Photogrammetry and Remote Sensing*, 45, pp. 227-246, 1990.

[8]   J. C. Fiala, "A network for learning kinematics with application to human reaching models", *Proc. of the ICNN*, vol. 5, pp. 2759-2764, Orlando, FL, 1994.

[9]   T. Flash, N. Hogan, "The co-ordination of the arm movements: an experimentally confirmed mathematical model", *Journal of neuroscience,* 7, pp. 1688-1703, 1985.

[10]   J. M. Hollerbach, T. Flash, "Dynamic interactions between limb segments during planar movements", *Biol. Cybernetics*, 44, pp. 66-77, 1982.

[11]   D.W. Marquardt, *Journal of the Society for Industrial and Applied Mathematics*, vol. 11, 1963.

[12]   A. Pedotti, G. Ferrigno, "Opto-electronic based system", in *Three dimensional analysis of human movement*, P. Allard, I.A.F. Stokes and J.P. Bianchi, pp. 57-77, Human Kinetics Publishers, 1995.

[13]   W.H. Press, S.A. Teukolsky, W.T. Vetterling, B.P Flannery, Numerical Recipes in C: The Art of Scientific Computing , Cambridge University Press, pp. 681-688, 1988.

[14]   M. Riedmiller, H. Braun, "A Direct Adaptive Method for Faster Backpropagation Learning: The RPROP Algorithm", *Proc. of the ICNN*, San Francisco, CA, 1993.

[15]   Y. Uno, M. Kawato, R. Suzuki, "Formation and control of optimal trajectory in human arm movement", *Biol. Cybernetics*, 61, pp. 89-101, 1989.

[16]   P. J. Werbos, "Backpropagation Through Time: What It Does and How to Do It", *Proc. of the IEEE*, vol. 78, n. 10, 1990.

[17]   Wolf, "Elements of photogrammetry", McGraw-Hill, New York, 1974.

Synthesis of Human Motion Using Kalman Filter

ChangWhan Sul[1], SoonKi Jung[2], and Kwangyun Wohn[1] *

[1] Department of Computer Science, KAIST
(Korea Advanced Institute of Science and Technology)
373-1 Kusong-dong, Yusong-ku, Taejon 305-701, Korea,
{cwsul,wohn}@vr.kaist.ac.kr
[2] Department of Computer Engineering, Kyungpook National University,
1370 Sankyuk-dong, Puk-ku, Taegu 702-701, Korea,
skjung@kyungpook.ac.kr

Abstract. This paper is concerned with the post-processing of motion-captured data. The post-processing is needed for several reasons: jerky motions due to sensor noise, violation of body constraints such as extraneous joint D.O.Fs, generation of new motion by editing existing motion data, and application of a motion to different character models. In this paper, the process of generating animated motion is viewed as a dynamic system, which takes the captured motion as input. Within a single Kalman filter framework, we were able to handle the following problems effectively: satisfaction of physical constraints inherent to human body, user-specified kinematic constraints, motion transition, and noise reduction.

1 Introduction

Motion capture is a method of recording human body movement (or the movement of any articulated object) for immediate or delayed analysis and playback of the recorded motion sequence. Motion capture for computer character animation involves the application of human motion onto the computer character.

The captured motion data is usually represented by a sequence of sampled positions for each body part, or by a sequence of joint angle values (which is typically obtained from the sampled data through the inverse kinematics). Before applying the raw motion data to the computer character, one would like to edit the motion for several reasons.

First, a captured motion is subject to the sensor noise which results the jerky motions. Although most motion capture systems are equipped with some kind of smoothing filter [1], such filters hardly guarantee that the filtered motion is the exact replica of the actual motion, satisfying the physical constraints of human body.

---

* This work is partially supported by the Electronics & Telecommunications Research Institute (ETRI) under constract ETRI-8MG2600, and Center for AI Research (CAIR), KAIST.

Nadia Magnenat-Thalmann, Daniel Thalmann (Eds.): CAPTECH'98, LNAI 1537, pp. 100–112, 1998.
© Springer-Verlag Berlin Heidelberg 1998

Second, most captured motion data tends to add extraneous degrees of freedom which the actual motion would never have undergone, thereby producing a quite unnatural motion. This is due to the registration error and/or the modeling error. Rose *et. al.* attempted to remove the fictitious motions by an optimization procedure which minimized the angular and positional deviations between the internal human model and the captured data [2].

Third, there is the need for generating a various classes of motion from a set of pre-captured motion data, or the *clip-motions*. A new motion can be generated by concatenating, blending and altering the existing clip-motions. Several researchers have proposed the techniques for editing the captured motion [1, 2, 3, 4, 5, 6]. Witkin and Popovic represented the motion data with a set of *motion curves*, each giving the value of one of the model's parameters as a function of time [3]. They then proposed the so-called motion warping technique to warp each motion curve. Bruderlin and Williams proposed motion multi-resolution filtering, motivated by the following intuition: low frequencies contain general gross motion patterns, whereas high frequencies contain details, subtleties, and noises [1]. They treated the motion parameter as a sampled signal which represents the value for a particular D.O.F. too. As mentioned in [3], the techniques for editing the motion curves are purely geometric ones, not incorporating any knowledge of the physical motion. Consequently, the edited results are prone to violate the physical constraints of human body. Rose *et. al.* developed an algorithm that generated the motion transitions semi-automatically [2]. They used a combination of spacetime constraints and inverse kinematic constraints to generate the transitions between segments of animations. However, since the algorithm was formulated with a dynamics formulation to solve the spacetime constraint and inverse kinematic optimization, it could not generate the motion in real time.

Fourth and lastly, since each character model has different proportions, motion data should be compensated for geometric variations from one model to another [7]. This issue will not be treated in this paper even though the ability to adjust the motion data automatically is very important.

In this paper, we present a novel approach that handles the fore-mentioned problems effectively. Motion generation from the captured data is viewed as a dynamic system whose input is the captured motion data, and the output is the motion parameters to be used to activate the animated character. As such, noise removal (which is the primary reason that most dynamic system is designed for), motion constraint satisfaction and motion concatenation can be handled within a single, unified framework. Namely, in addition to handling the sensor noise, the proposed method allows an easy integration of physical constraints (such as the angle limitation and the D.O.F. of joints) into the system "filtering". In the course of processing the motion data, the predicted motion from dynamic model, the captured motion and the constraints all contribute to the resulting motion. Since our formulation enables the motion generation in real time, the method is not limited to off-line post-processing purposes. It could be useful for real-time applications such as digital puppetry.

The remainder of the paper is organized as follows: Section 2 describes the modeling of human body and instantaneous motion using the Kalman filter. Section 3 describes the motion resolution and motion transition with the multi-level control. In Section 4 we describe the results by using our preliminary optical motion capture. We conclude with a brief discussion of the method's advantages and limitations and directions for further work.

2   Kalman Filtering Human Body Motion

In this section, we describe the modeling of human motion under Kalman filter framework and how the framework is applied to post-processing of captured motion data. Kalman filter is a well-known tool suitable for modeling and controlling dynamic systems with inherent noise. The captured motion data contain noise caused by several reasons: electro-magnetic sensor-inherent noise, unstable marker attachment in optical motion capture process and errors from simplified human body modeling. The Kalman filter takes care of the noise systematically and enables us to integrate, in a single framework, those essential features in post-processing of motion data like motion smoothing, motion transition, and constraint satisfaction. The proposed model of human motion is influenced by both the unprocessed input motion data and the constraints included in the model in its update. We devised a method to control the relationship between the input motion, constraints and the output motion.

2.1   Human Body Model

The human body is approximately modeled by articulated object, which consists of rigid parts (segments) connected together by joints with kinematic constraints such as degree of freedom (D.O.F.). Articulated objects are represented by the *nested coordinate frame* forming the hierarchical tree. The pose of the each subpart is described by the relative posture with respect to the coordinate frame of its parent.

One example of the hierarchical model for articulated object is shown in Fig.1. Each subpart consists of a transformation node, a set of markers, a scale node, geometric shape information and a sub-tree link for its child nodes. The transformation node defines a coordinate system with respect to the parent coordinate system. In the case of root node, the transformation means a rotation and translation on the reference frame. On the contrary, other nodes have only the relative rotation for their parent. The constraints node includes the information of the kinematic constraints such as D.O.F. constraints and joint angle limitation. Note that the kinematic constraints are not embedded or hard-coded in our human model (the reason will be discussed in 2.4). The scale node adjusts the size of geometric shape for each subpart to handle variety of body proportions for different human models. The geometric shape node is defined with a surface model (a set of polygons).

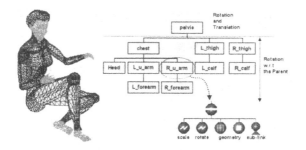

Fig. 1. A hierarchical human body model

2.2   Modeling of Human Motion

In Kalman filter framework, the *dynamic model* describes the time-varying behavior of the target, which is a human body in our problem. We describe the human body with pose (a snapshot configuration of the body model in 2.1) and its time derivative, such that its time-varying behavior means body motion.

The 3-D motion of a rigid segment has six degrees of freedom - three translation components and three rotational components. Translational kinematics is defined as the position, the velocity, the acceleration, etc., of the origin of the object-coordinate frame with respect to the reference frame. Rotational kinematics is defined as the object's angular position, velocity, acceleration, etc., of the origin.

Given a hierarchical model as in 2.1, only the root segment has both translational and rotational kinematics. In order to separate translational and rotational segments and treat them differently, we separate the root segment into the rotational and the translational segments.

Our simple dynamic model assumes *piecewise constant velocity motion*, i.e. the translational and angular velocity of any segments does not change in a short period of time when no external force exist. Based on this assumption, we specify the *state vector* for each rigid segment as follows.

The state of each segment is defined with the following variables, the position $\mathbf{p} = [p_x, p_y, p_z]^T$ and the velocity $\mathbf{v} = [v_x, v_y, v_z]^T$ for the translational segment, the angular position $\mathbf{q} = [q_w, q_x, q_y, q_z]^T$ and the angular velocity $\Omega = [\omega_x, \omega_y, \omega_z]^T$ for rotational segments.

The dynamic model that describes the time-varying behavior of human body in terms of state vector $\mathbf{s}_t^j$ for segment j is:

$$\hat{\mathbf{s}}_t^{j(-)} = \begin{cases} f_T(\hat{\mathbf{s}}_{t-1}^{j(+)}), & j = 0 \\ f_R(\hat{\mathbf{s}}_{t-1}^{j(+)}), & 1 \le j \le N \end{cases} \tag{1}$$

where $\mathbf{s}_t^{j(-)}$ is *a priori* state vector and $\mathbf{s}_t^{j(+)}$ is *a posteriori* value of $\mathbf{s}_t^j$, the superscript $j = 0$ means the translational segment, N is the number of segments, and $f_T(\cdot)$ or $f_R(\cdot)$ is a simple transition function with the piecewise constant velocity assumption.

Translational Segment The state vector is

$$s^0 = \begin{bmatrix} \mathbf{p}^T & \mathbf{v}^T \end{bmatrix}^T \tag{2}$$

where the variables are defined in the reference frame. The dynamic model is $\hat{s}_t^{0(-)} = F_T \cdot s_{t-1}^{0(+)}$. The state transition matrix is

$$F_T = \begin{bmatrix} \mathbf{I}_{33} & \mathbf{I}_{33} \\ \mathbf{0}_{33} & \mathbf{I}_{33} \end{bmatrix} \tag{3}$$

where $\mathbf{I}_{33}$ is a 3×3 identity matrix and $\mathbf{0}_{33}$ is a 3×3 zero matrix.

Note that F_T coincide with the assumption of piecewise constant velocity. We assume that the initial state is known (We use the first position of captured motion as the initial position), and the initial velocity is zero.

Rotational Segments The state vector is

$$s^j = \begin{bmatrix} \mathbf{q}^T & \Omega^T \end{bmatrix}^T \tag{4}$$

where the variables are defined in the parent coordinate system. The dynamic model is

$$\hat{s}_t^{j(-)} = f_R(s_{t-1}^{j(+)}) = \begin{bmatrix} \mathbf{w}_{t-1}^{j(+)} \otimes \mathbf{q}_{t-1}^{j(+)} \\ \Omega_{t-1}^{j(+)} \end{bmatrix},$$

$$\text{where} \quad \mathbf{w}_t^{j(+)} = \begin{bmatrix} \cos(|\Omega_t^{j(+)}|/2) \\ \frac{\sin(|\Omega_t^{j(+)}|/2)}{|\Omega_t^{j(+)}|} \Omega_t^{j(+)} \end{bmatrix} \tag{5}$$

and "$\otimes$" means quaternion multiplication [8].

Since the transition function $f_R(\cdot)$ is nonlinear, we need extended Kalman filter, which linearizes $f_R(\cdot)$ using its partial derivative matrix $F_R^j(t-1)$. (For the readability, we will abbreviate the segment term j from now on.)

$$F_R(t-1) = \left. \frac{\partial f_R(s)}{\partial s} \right|_{s=\hat{s}_{t-1}^{(+)}} = \begin{bmatrix} \frac{\partial \mathbf{q}'}{\partial \mathbf{q}} & \frac{\partial \mathbf{q}'}{\partial \Omega} \\ \mathbf{0}_{34} & \mathbf{I}_{33} \end{bmatrix} \tag{6}$$

where the partial derivatives for the rotational posture and the rotational velocity with respect to $\mathbf{q}_{t-1}$ and Ω_{t-1} are as follows:

$$\left. \frac{\partial \mathbf{q}'}{\partial \mathbf{q}} \right|_{\mathbf{q}_{t-1}^{(+)}, \Omega_{t-1}^{(+)}} = \cos(|\Omega_{t-1}^{(+)}|/2)\mathbf{I}_{44} + \frac{\sin(|\Omega_{t-1}^{(+)}|/2)}{|\Omega_{t-1}^{(+)}|} \overset{+(+)}{\Omega}_{t-1}, \tag{7}$$

$$\left. \frac{\partial \mathbf{q}'}{\partial \Omega} \right|_{\mathbf{q}_{t-1}^{(+)}, \Omega_{t-1}^{(+)}} = -\frac{\sin(|\Omega_{t-1}^{(+)}|/2)}{2|\Omega_{t-1}^{(+)}|} \mathbf{q}_{t-1}^{(+)} \Omega_{t-1}^{(+)T}$$

$$+ \left(\frac{\cos(|\Omega_{t-1}|/2)}{2|\Omega_{t-1}|^2} - \frac{\sin(|\Omega_{t-1}^{(+)}|/2)}{|\Omega_{t-1}^{(+)}|^3} \right) \overset{+(+)}{\Omega}_{t-1} \mathbf{q}_{t-1}^{(+)} \Omega_{t-1}^{(+)T} \tag{8}$$

$$+ \frac{\sin(|\Omega_{t-1}^{(+)}|/2)}{|\Omega_{t-1}^{(+)}|} \overset{-(+)}{\mathbf{q}}_{t-1}$$

and $\overset{+}{\alpha}$ and $\overset{-}{\alpha}$ are matrix representation for the quaternion multiplication (See [8]).

For all segments, the associated error covariance matrix is propagated to time t by the following equation:

$$P_t^{(-)} = F_{t-1} P_{t-1}^{(+)} F_{t-1}^T + Q_{t-1} \tag{9}$$

where F_t is $F_T(t)$ for the translational segment and $F_R(t)$ for the rotational segments, and Q_t is defined by

$$E[\mathbf{n}_k \mathbf{n}_i^T] \triangleq \begin{cases} Q_k & i = k \\ 0 & i \neq k \end{cases} .$$

2.3 Motion Update

The measurement model describes the relationship between observed measurements and the state vector, which can usually be expressed as:

$$\mathbf{z}_t = h(\mathbf{s}_t) + \eta_t \ , \tag{10}$$

where $h(\cdot)$ is a vector-valued function called the observation function and η represents the random noise contained in the measurements. In our problem of filtering captured motion data, we consider the captured motion data as the observation itself. That is, the measurement model is $\hat{\mathbf{z}}_t = H_t \cdot \hat{\mathbf{s}}_t^{(-)}$, where H_t is $H_T(t)$ for the translational segment and $H_R(t)$ for the rotational segments,

$$H_T(t) = \begin{bmatrix} \mathbf{I}_{33} & \mathbf{0}_{33} \end{bmatrix}, \quad H_R(t) = \begin{bmatrix} \mathbf{I}_{44} & \mathbf{0}_{43} \end{bmatrix} . \tag{11}$$

The measurement residual is defined as the difference between the predicted measurement by the dynamic model and the "measured" motion data. In the Kalman filter, the measurement residual is weighted by the Kalman gain matrix to generate a correction term and is added to the predicted state to form the updated state as:

$$\mathbf{s}_t^{(+)} = \hat{\mathbf{s}}_t^{(-)} + K_t(\mathbf{z}_t - H_t \hat{\mathbf{s}}_t^{(-)}) \ , \tag{12}$$

where the Kalman gain is computed as follows,

$$K_t = P_t^{(-)} H_t^T \Lambda_t^{-1} \tag{13}$$

and Λ_t is the associated error covariance matrix for the each measurement (its utilization is discussed in section 3.1). (12) indicates that the updated motion is affected by both the predicted motion driven by the dynamic model and the measurement that attracts the model to original motion data.

In order to reduce the problem space and enhance numerical stability, we assign a Kalman filter per each segment and apply Kalman filtering adaptively in an hierarchical manner [9]. In doing that, state vectors for all but current updating segment is assumed to be constant with the last estimated value.

2.4   Integrating Kinematic Constraints

Human bodies reveal their kinematic constraints between two connected segments. The constraints are simply modeled with error functions, which are minimized when the constraints are satisfied. We designed the error function for the
D.O.F. constraints and the joint angle limitation. By integrating the error functions for the kinematic constraints into the Kalman filter framework as special
kind of measurements with very low uncertainty, the filtered motion gets closer
to the direction of satisfying the kinematic constraints. Likewise, we can add
any type of constraints to the measurement, provided that the constraint and
its partial derivative are expressed as a function of state vector.

When a joint j has 2 D.O.F. and two directional cosine vectors are n_1 and
n_2 as shown in Fig.2(a), we obtain an orthonormal vector for two n_i given by

$$n_i \cdot v = 0, \quad \text{for } i = 1, 2 . \tag{14}$$

A quaternion q is represented by a rotational axis as follows:

$$w = \frac{\theta}{\sin(\theta/2)} q, \quad \text{where} \quad \theta = 2\arccos(q_w) \tag{15}$$

and q denotes the vector quaternion of q. The length of the rotational axis w
means the degree of the rotation and the direction of w is the rotational axis. An
arbitrary rotation is represented by a vector in 3-D space as shown in Fig.3(a).
In the case of the 2 D.O.F. joint, the error $E(w)$ is given by $w \cdot v$. As shown
in Fig.3(b), when the joint has the joint angle limitation between θ_1 and θ_2, the
error $E(w)$ can be defined as

$$E(w) = w \cdot v + \max\{0, \theta_1 - w \cdot n_i, w \cdot n_i - \theta_2\} . \tag{16}$$

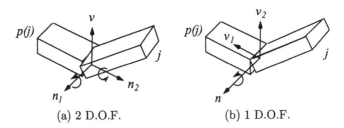

(a) 2 D.O.F.   (b) 1 D.O.F.

Fig. 2. The D.O.F. constraints between segments

Similarly when a joint has only 1 D.O.F., we can obtain two orthonormal
vectors. The error $E(w)$ is a 2 dimensional vector, and the value for each dimension is calculated by the same method to the 2 D.O.F. case. For the angular
velocity as well as the rotation, we define the constraints similarly.

The human body is not strict for the defined D.O.F. For example, we usually
give 1 D.O.F. for the elbow joint, but the lower arm has the limited roll motion.

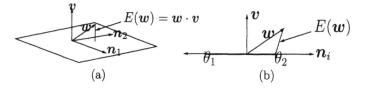

Fig. 3. A rotational axis w in 3-D space and D.O.F

The kinematic constraints are not embedded in our human model. Instead, we give each joint all the rotational D.O.F.(i.e. 3) and then impose the constraints as measurements with low uncertainties. Consequently the human body has the allowance for the rotational movement with respect to the restricted axis.

During the motion generation, the constraints are given as

$$E(w) = 0, \quad \text{and} \quad E(\Omega) = 0 . \tag{17}$$

Adding the constraints (17) as one of the "measurement" in the model has the effect of attracting the motion to the direction of satisfying those constraints when the motion is updated. The derivatives of (17) with respect to **s**, which is needed in Kalman filtering, are given by

$$\frac{\partial E(w)}{\partial \mathbf{s}} = \left[\frac{\theta \mathbf{q}_w - 2\sin(\theta/2)}{\sin^2(\theta/2)\sqrt{1 - \mathbf{q}_w^2}} q^T (v + \alpha) \quad \frac{\theta}{\sin(\theta/2)} (v + \alpha) \quad 0_3^T \right] , \tag{18}$$

$$\frac{\partial E(\Omega)}{\partial \mathbf{s}} = \left[0_4^T \quad v^T + \alpha \right] \tag{19}$$

where 0_n means zero vector with n rows and α is defined as follows,

$$\alpha = \begin{cases} 0_3 & \text{for } \theta_1 < w \cdot n_i < \theta_2 \\ n_i & \text{for } \theta_2 < w \cdot n_i \\ -n_i & \text{for } w \cdot n_i < \theta_1 \end{cases} .$$

Since we use the quaternion to represent the rotation, we also have added the constraint $\|\mathbf{q}\| = 1$, i.e., $\mathbf{q}^T \mathbf{q} - 1 = 0$ in the measurement model as the additional measurement. The derivative of $\mathbf{q}^T \mathbf{q} - 1$ with respect to **s** is given by

$$\frac{\partial}{\partial \mathbf{s}} (\mathbf{q}^T \mathbf{q} - 1) = \left[2\mathbf{q}^T \quad 0_3^T \right] . \tag{20}$$

3   Motion Generation

3.1   Motion Resolution Control

The Kalman filter formulated in the previous section acts like a smoothing filter. The dynamic model makes the motion have the inertia with the constant velocity. The measurements - in this case, the captured motion data and the kinematic constraints - function as an external force to update the state of human motion. As we can see from (13), the Kalman gain is inversely proportional to the uncertainty in the measurements. If the measurement is very uncertain, then the measurement residual is resulted mainly by the noise and little change in the state estimate should be made.

We control the motion resolution with the uncertainty of measurements. When the external force is weak (the measurement is very uncertain), the motion becomes smooth due to the dynamic model. Otherwise, the original captured motion has more influence to the resulting motion. Fig.4 shows the graph for one variable q_w of the chest during the human walking motion. As we can see from the graph, the original data has much jerky motion and the curve B follows very closely the original data. As the uncertainty is increased, the graph becomes smoother.

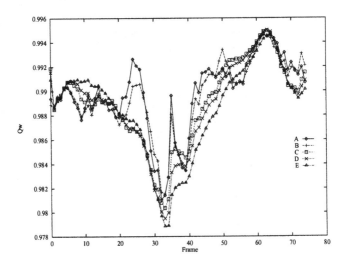

Fig. 4. The motion resolution for the different uncertainties - the plot of for chest segment in walking with the increasing uncertainty values from the curve A to E : A 0.0 (no filtering), B 0.001, C 0.1, D 0.2, E 0.5.

Similarly we control the strictness of the kinematic constraints with the norm of the normal vector v in (14). Table.1 shows the weighting factors for the kinematic constraints. Fig.5 shows the change of the variables q_x and q_y for the forearm which has only 1 D.O.F. and the rotational axis is y. As the weighting factor is increased, q_x (the error for D.O.F.) decreases while q_y representing legal D.O.F., has little change due to the normalization of the quaternion.

3.2   Motion Transition

Concatenating multiple segments of motion data together to obtain longer sequence is a basic operation in motion editing. In concatenating clip-motions, the motion data should seamlessly transit the boundaries from one motion clip

Table 1. The weighting factors for the kinematic constraints

Curve	Uncertainty	Weight
A	0.000 (No filtering)	-
B	0.1	0.1
C	0.1	0.5
D	0.1	1.0
E	0.1	2.0

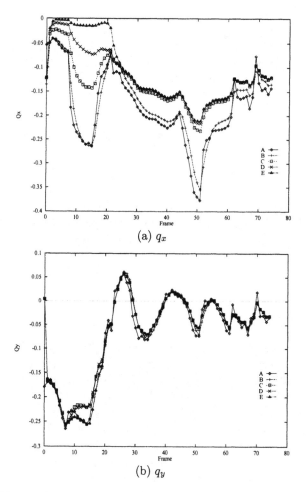

(a) q_x

(b) q_y

Fig. 5. The kinematic constraints with the weighting factor. (See Table.1 for weights)

to another. Our Kalman filtering framework can also be applied to the motion transition process. At first, we place different motion clips along the timeline and link corresponding D.O.F. by simple linear interpolation. Before processing, the motion data reveal abrupt changes at the boundaries. During the Kalman filtering process, the dynamic model handles the discontinuities at the boundaries and the updated motion smoothly connects different motion clips. Fig.6 shows an example of such process. Curve A shows discontinuous motion data before the Kalman filter is applied, whereas curve B shows the smoothed results while satisfying other kinematic constraints.

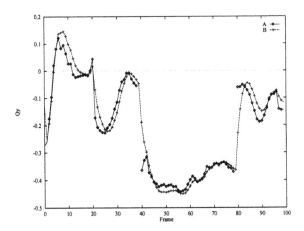

Fig. 6. Motion smoothing between clip-motion transition: We inserted 40 frames of the bending motion between the 40th and 41st frame of the walking motion. Before processing (curve A) and after processing (curve B).

4   Experiments

In the previous work [9], we have developed a preliminary optical motion capture system. The performer's motion is recorded using four video recorders and then captured off-line while playing back frame-by-frame. The system uses a Panasonic AG-DS850 video recorder and a Pentium PC for this process. The image sequences from multiple cameras are the input of our motion capture system which is implemented with C++ and Open Inventor Library on a SGI Onyx. The motion capture system processes the motion data and generates the motion results with a computer character on near real-time.

Fig.7 shows an example for the motion smoothing. In the captured motion, the left thigh and calf are twisted due to the error (the first row). The smoothing result shows that the error is removed (the second row).

Fig. 7. An example of the motion smoothing - 45th, 46th, 47th and 48th frame

5 Conclusions

In this paper we presented a simple but effective method for post-processing the captured motion data. The post-processing involves three operations: (i) smoothing the jerky motion due to the sensor noise, (ii) satisfying the kinematic constraints of the human body, and (iii) generating a seamless motion transition between motion segments. Instead of having different processes for each of three operations, we devised the Kalman-filter approach that handles these problems in a single, unified framework. Here, we control the motion resolution with the weighting factor of the kinematic constraints and the uncertainty variables of the measurement. Our algorithm is efficient enough to generate the animated motion in real-time.

We plan to extend our method to include dynamics of the human body model, which can be formulated in terms of another measurements. The automatic compensation of the motion data from model to model is another future direction.

References

[1] Armin Bruderlin and Lance Williams. Motion signal processing. In *ACM SIG-GRAPH '95*, pages 97–104, Los Angeles, CA, August 1995. ACM Press.
[2] C. Rose, B. Guenter, B. Bodenheimer, and M.F. Cohen. Efficient generation of motion transitions using spacetime constraints. In *ACM SIGGRAPH '96*, pages 147–154, New Orleans, LA, August 1996. ACM Press.
[3] Andrew Witkin and Zoran Popovic. Motion warping. In *ACM SIGGRAPH '95*, pages 105–108, Los Angeles, CA, August 1995. ACM Press.

[4] Ronan Boulic and D.Thalmann. Combined direct and inverse kinematic control for articulated figures motion editing. *Computer Graphics Forum*, 11(4):189–202, 1992.

[5] Munetoshi Unuma, Ken Anjyo, and Ryozo Takeuchi. Fourier principles for emotion-based human figure animation. In *ACM SIGGRAPH '95*, pages 91–96, Los Angeles, CA, 1995. ACM Press.

[6] Michael Gleicher. Motion editing with spacetime constraints. In *Symposium on Interactive 3D Graphics*, 1997.

[7] Michael Gleicher. Retargetting motion to new characters. In *ACM SIGGRAPH '98*, pages 33–42. ACM Press, 1998.

[8] J.C.K. Chou. Quaternion kinematic and dynamic differential equations. *IEEE Transactions on Robotics and Automation*, 8(1):53–64, February 1992.

[9] SoonKi Jung and KwangYun Wohn. Tracking and motion estimation of the articulated object : A hierarchical kalman filter approach. *Real-Time Imaging*, 3(6):415–432, 1997.

Real-Time Hand and Head Tracking for Virtual Environments Using Infrared Beacons

Klaus Dorfmüller and Hanno Wirth

ZGDV Computer Graphics Center, Visual Computing Department,
Rundeturmstr.6, D-64283 Darmstadt, Germany
Klaus.Dorfmueller@zgdv.de, Hanno.Wirth@zgdv.de
http://www.zgdv.de/www/zgdv-vc/

Abstract. In this paper, we introduce an optical tracking system for the use with virtual environments which is able to track the hand and the head of a user simultaneously and in real time. The system utilises infrared beacons instead of visible light, because of the special lighting conditions which must be met to employ the system together with a projection table. The working principle of a simple and fast three-step calibration process is described. The characteristics of the tracking system are described with regard to the hardware configuration needed, the software we developed, and the interface to virtual reality applications.

1 Introduction

Tracking user movements is one of the main low-level tasks which nearly every VR system needs. There are different methods how this tracking may be performed. Common tracking systems use magnetic or ultrasonic trackers in different variations as well as mechanical systems. All of these systems have drawbacks which are caused by their principles of work. With nearly all of these systems, the user has to be linked to a measurement instrument, either by cable or, even more restraining for the user, by a mechanical linkage. Furthermore, while mechanical tracking systems are extremely precise, magnetic and acoustic tracking systems suffer from different sources of distortions. For this reason, we are developing an optical tracking system, which should overcome many of the drawbacks of conventional tracking systems.

In the Visual Computing Lab at the ZGDV, we are using a BARCO BARON projection table to present virtual environments three-dimensionally and in a way which enables users to work in an environment they are accustomed to (see Fig. 1).

In cooperation with BMW, we are developing new video-based interaction techniques to plan assembly processes. In commercial systems like RobCad[1], the definition of insertion and extraction paths has to be done in a trial-and-error way by explicitly indicating the translation and rotation parameters. Our assumption is that depth perception of a virtual scene, direct manipulation with grab and

---

[1] RobCad is a product of Tecnomatix Digital Factory^{TM}

Nadia Magnenat-Thalmann, Daniel Thalmann (Eds.): CAPTECH'98, LNAI 1537, pp. 113–127, 1998.
© Springer-Verlag Berlin Heidelberg 1998

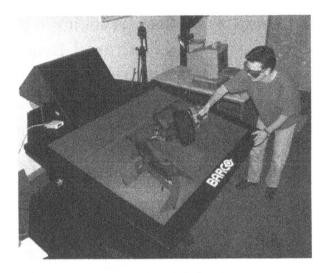

Fig. 1. Virtual assembly using video-based interaction techniques

release gestures and head tracking will overcome many disadvantages currently used applications to plan assemblies and dismantling of hardware have. Using a horizontal or tilted workspace is a well known environment many professionals like engineers, architects, and physicians are familiar with. The perspective of the image projected on the display surface is calculated such that the user perceives the objects as being above the display surface. To move away from a display-only of objects and to enable the user to interact directly with the 3-D objects rendered by the computer (i.e. the virtual environment), user actions need to be tracked. Apart from the movements of the user's hand, his or her head has to be tracked so the computer can calculate the correct perspective projection for the two viewpoints. Per frame, the computer renders two pictures for the left and the right eye, respectively. The images are displayed in sequence and are synchronised with shutter glasses the user has to wear. These glasses are equipped with an infrared emitter to be able to track them and are see-through so the user perceives the virtual environment as being integrated in his or her normal environment.

We started working with the projection table using a magnetic tracking system (Polhemus FASTRACK), with which we encountered severe calibration and distortion problems (mainly caused by the metal in the table and electro-magnetic emissions of the projector). As currently available acoustic trackers do not have a sufficient range to track the whole area of a projection table like the BARON, we started developing the optical tracking system described in this paper. One further reason for us to consider an optical tracking system was the fact that the calibration of an optical tracking system may be mostly automated, as described below. Opposed to this, the calibration of a magnetic tracking system is a time-consuming, and, if not performed very carefully, error-prone task.

As described by Zachmann [Zach97], measurements have to be taken with the tracking system where the tracker is positioned at specific positions in space to get known reference coordinates on the basis of which the correction may be calculated. Even with this system, the minimal error in a volume like the CAVE was 4cm with the average error being 7cm.

2   Previous Work

A precise measurement of the 3-D position and orientation is necessary for many virtual and augmented reality applications. In order to get no linkage restrictions and an absolute position, more recently developed systems are based on optical tracking using CCD cameras. Heap and Hogg [HH96] have introduced their hand tracking system running on a Silicon Graphics Indy with a standard Indy camera. They are able to get depth information of the user's hand in relation to the hand size in previous frames, but the system is not able to supply absolute positions as long as only one camera captures the user's hand. A stereo video system for hand tracking with 27 degrees-of-freedom has been introduced by Rehg and Kanade [RK93], [RK94]. They are able to build a cylindric model of the human hand with regard to the hand's kinematic properties. The hand is restricted to a movement in front of a black background to make the segmentation with grayscale video images easier to handle. In order to fulfil real-time requirements, special hardware is necessary. Wren et al. described a real-time system for tracking and interpretation of people [WADP96]. Later publications [AP95b], [AP96] about this system mentioned the employment of two video cameras for position estimation. Their system is able to perform the camera calibration by tracking a moving person. An optical beacon tracking system has been introduced by Madritsch and Gervautz [MG96]. Their hardware system consists of two Silicon Graphics Indy workstations with CCD-cameras and infrared LEDs. They applied a classical calibration like Tsai's technique [Tsa86] with radial lens distortion parameters which is suitable under laboratory conditions only. Our work is closely related to previous research of Pentland et al. at the Media Lab of the MIT. Our system is using a stereo camera system, too, and we are interested in automatic calibration processes like the one described later in this paper. But in contrast, we do not have the same conditions and restrictions imposed by our application environment, as described later.

3   The Real-Time Tracking System

The operation of the tracking system is, on the one hand, defined by the physical constraints the projection table imposes on the system. The table itself is about $2m * 2m$ large and $1.2m$ high, the display surface is about $1,36m * 1,02m$ large. That means that a volume of about $3m * 3m * 1.5m$ above and in front of the table (*width * depth * height*) has to be observed.

The lighting conditions around the projection table have to be subdued as the brightness of the projection itself is limited. This limits an optical tracking system to using infrared light, where one has two possibilities to choose from: either the system may use active infrared beacons or the tracking area has to be illuminated with infrared light while the objects to be tracked are fitted with reflective markers. We chose the first approach because it was easier to realise for our prototype.

As we wanted to enable the users to walk around three sides of the projection table, the camera positions were restricted to the far side of the table, to the left and to the right of the projector. Mounting the cameras closer together (e.g. both on top of the projector cover) would create accuracy problems as the 3-D position of the beacon can be best calculated when the cameras are arranged with convergence angle of between 60 and 120 degrees between them. While a small angle between the cameras yields a good correlation between the images and thus facilitates segmentation, the angle used in our setup yields better 3-D position reconstruction and minimises occlusion problems.

Another requirement was that the system should work with minimal mechanical calibration, i.e. the camera position should not be restricted to specific mounting points as it is not always possible to use these and keep them aligned all the time, like, for example, when transporting the table. The accuracy of the system should be less than 1 cm, as otherwise display errors (distortions of the perspective) would be too big and precise interaction with objects displayed on the projection table would not be possible.

3.1 System Setup

To fulfil the constraints described before, we chose to use wide-angle lenses of $4.8mm$ with the video cameras. To avoid errors introduced by taking left and right images used to determine the beacon positions asynchronously, we are using externally synchronised cameras from which the left and right images are acquired at the same time, minimising the error introduced by the motion of the user's hand. As we do not use colour information, we are able to use a single framegrabber card where the cameras are connected to different colour channels[2]. The synchronisation logic for the two cameras is present on the framegrabber card. This system is much cheaper and easier to synchronise than using two separate framegrabber cards. The cameras used are sensitive for infrared as well as visible light. To block out the visible light, we use infrared filters cutting off at about 820 nm (see Fig. 2).

The infrared LEDs used for the beacons emit infrared light at 950 nm and have a radiation angle of about 80 degrees. Our system runs on a standard PC with a 300 MHz Pentium II processor. For video capturing tasks, we use ELTEC's PCEye2 framegrabber. This PCI-board has been developed for analog video cameras like the PULNIX TM-560. Besides acquiring the image, the PC also performs the image processing tasks described below. The two position values for head and hand, respectively, are transmitted to the computer running the VR software over standard LAN.

---

[2] For a short description of the resulting problem, see Chap. 5

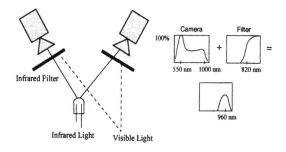

Fig. 2. Infrared LEDs combined with infrared filters

3.2   The Image Processing Pipeline

Our system consists of the following image processing pipeline which is shown in Fig. 3. A framegrabber acquires two images while the pipeline processes the last available image data. The following pipeline step, the beacon detection, is operating in two different modes. The first mode is a global search over the whole image data for a detection of all beacon positions. If the system knows the last two calculated positions, the second mode will do a local search because a prediction has restricted the area of interest. The next step is a 2-D transformation from distorted image coordinates to undistorted camera sensor coordinates. Afterwards, the epipolar constraint (see Chap. 4) will be used to get the correlated image points, and as a result out of this module, we obtain the 3-D locations.

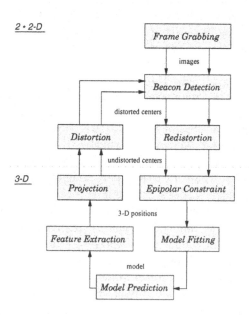

Fig. 3. The image processing pipeline

The next step has to fit the 3-D beacon positions into a model. In our scenario, our assumption is that the model has an initial position, i.e. the user's head is above the user's hand. Then, the output is a model with n degrees of freedom[3] which consists of the user's head and hand and is transferred to the render system for interaction purposes. Our image processing pipeline performs one further step in order to make the beacon detection faster. The beacon positions predicted in this step will be back-projected to both cameras' sensor plane and then converted to distorted image coordinates. The beacon detection will search in a local area close to the predicted positions.

3.3   Image Processing Tasks

To find the position of the user's hand (respectively that of the pointer carrying the infrared LED), the tracking system needs to perform a beacon detection after which the centre of gravity $(\bar{u}, \bar{v})$ of the beacon image is calculated (see (1) where $F(j, k)$ is the brightness of a pixel at the image plane with position (j, k)).

$$\bar{u} = \frac{\frac{1}{K}\sum_{j=1}^{J}\sum_{k=1}^{K} jF(j,k)}{\sum_{j=1}^{J}\sum_{k=1}^{K} F(j,k)} \quad \bar{v} = \frac{\frac{1}{J}\sum_{j=1}^{J}\sum_{k=1}^{K} kF(j,k)}{\sum_{j=1}^{J}\sum_{k=1}^{K} F(j,k)} \quad (1)$$

To make the task of finding the beacon in image $i+1$ easier (for performance reasons) after segmenting it in image i, we use a vector based prediction algorithm which makes a prediction on where the next position of the beacon in image $i+1$ will most probably be, based on the distance the beacon travelled between image $i-1$ and i. Using a Kalman filter (see [ZF92]) for the prediction would be too slow. The area where the beacon will likely be in image $i+1$ is enclosed in a so-called tracking window, in which the algorithm searches for the beacon first and only reverts to searching the whole image if the beacon cannot be found in the tracking window. The size of the tracking window is calculated to adapt to the size of the beacon image. In the future, the system will be enhanced such that velocity and acceleration will be taken into account. Reflections of the beacon on the projection area of the table are allowed for by using only the uppermost beacon image in the tracking window.

In the course of tracking the user, the two images of the beacons are moving around the image space. There are cases where an unambiguous establishment of the meaning of the beacon images is not possible because in one of the images one of the beacons is above the other, while it is below the other one in the second image. In these cases, the ambiguities can be resolved by using the epipolar constraint as described in [ZF92]. This works by extending a vector from the centre of projection (COP) through the centre of one of the beacon images into 3-D space in for example the left image. This ray is then projected on the right image plane (see Fig. 4). In case the system worked without errors, the projected

---

[3] Our currently used man model consists of 2*3-D positions, later we can extend it to a more complex one.

ray on the right image plane would intersect with the image of the respective beacon. As the two rays normally will not meet in space, the beacon image nearest the projected ray is assumed to be the corresponding one[4]. The position of the beacon in 3-D space is estimated by locating the middle of the minimal distance between the two rays.

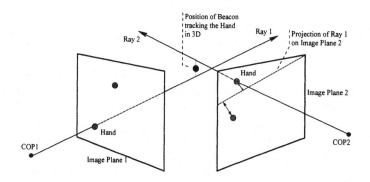

Fig. 4. Using the epipolar constraint

3.4   Simultaneous Head and Hand Tracking

As the beacons used for tracking the user do not have any special features to distinguish them from one another and as the tracking area captured by the two cameras has no preference for any direction, the tracking system needs a model of how to distinguish the different LEDs used to track the head and the hand of the user.

Under the precondition that both cameras are mounted in the same orientation (e.g. top of camera upwards) and that the tops of the CCD chips are facing upwards, the system may make three assumptions about the spatial position and the usage patterns of the infrared beacons by which it may determine which beacon tracks the head and which the hand of the user: Firstly, the beacon used to track the head is always working while the beacon used to track the hand is only active when the user interacts with objects in the scene. Secondly, the starting position of the head tracking beacon is normally above that for the hand tracking beacon and is beyond and above the volume used to display the objects on the projection table. Thirdly, the head tracking beacon is normally the first one working.

By using these assumptions, the system is able to assign the meaning of the beacons. After the initialisation, the user is able to move around freely and even put his hand over his head or move his head down into the image space (e.g.

---

[4] This is not always correct, but with only two beacons in the image with no known distances between them, a calculation of the correct beacon is not possible.

to have a closer look at some virtual objects) where the hand tracking beacon normally is, while the correct assignment of beacons is retained. Using the first assumption, the system is even able to correctly differentiate head and hand tracking beacons when the head tracking beacon is in object space while the hand tracking beacon goes off and on again when the user grabs and subsequently releases virtual objects.

4   Camera Calibration

Current calibration techniques typically need special known calibration objects. Those techniques usually rely on high precision measurements. Thus, as a practical matter, such calibration steps of computer vision systems are unpopular, cumbersome and time-consuming processes. But for bringing 3-D computer vision systems out of the laboratory and into practical use, it becomes increasingly crucial that camera systems are easy to calibrate.

All in all we have three coordinate systems, two for the cameras and one coordinate system located on the projection table. These systems are left-handed. For each camera the Z-axis is going out of the image plane and the image points are located at $Z = 0$. For a simplified calibration, the system works as follows:

1. To get an estimation of internal camera parameters, each camera is precalibrated for which we use a technique introduced by Tsai [Tsa86]. His method is aimed at determining the external position and orientation relative to the object reference frame as well as the effective focal length, radial lens distortion and image scanning parameters. We applied this technique to obtain the internal parameters only. The parameters we are using for the initialisation described later are the effective focal length f, the lens distortion coefficient κ_1, the origin in the image plane (C_x, C_y), the uncertainty scale factor s_x and the horizontal and vertical pixel size in frame buffer d'_x, d'_y. For more details see [Tsa86]. This calibration step is time-consuming and needs to be performed accurately, thus the internal camera calibration is done only once at the time the cameras are fitted with their lenses, as the configuration of the cameras remains the same afterwards.

2. The second calibration step is very easy to perform because we use an adaptive calibration method[5] which was first developed by Azarbayejani and Pentland [AP95a, AP95b]. Thus, our system can adaptively calibrate a stereo rig by tracking a single moving point acquired from each of two cameras. As a result, the calibration data may be entered by just waving a flashlight around. The internal parameters from calibration step 1 are needed as initial values. The result is a calibrated camera system where 3-D points are given in the right camera frame. A detailed description of this technique is given below.

---

[5] Adaptive means here that camera parameters are altered to get better estimated ones which requires no knowledge on the user's side.

3. Finally, the user has to move the infrared beacon to three predefined corners of the projection table. Applying two cross product operations to the two input vectors and, at last, a normalisation yields the coordinate system for the table. Our rendering system knows about this system definition and is able to calculate the asymmetric viewing frustum and the position of the hand in virtual world coordinates.

This adaptive calibration is based on the Iterated Extended Kalman Filter (IEKF). To apply this filter, the state vector is defined in (2) and consists of the relative orientation, the inverse focal lengths and the structure parameters described later.

$$x = \left(T, \mathcal{R}^{L \to R}, \beta^{(L)}, \beta^{(R)}, \alpha_1^{(L)}, \ldots, \alpha_N^{(L)}\right) \tag{2}$$

The conversion between the left and right camera coordinate systems is given by extrinsic camera parameters T and $\mathcal{R}^{L \to R}$ for translation and rotation. Currently, we are using the inverse folcal lengths $\beta^{(L)}, \beta^{(R)}$ only as intrinsic camera parameters, but forthcoming research will extend this state vector with a correction of the pre-estimated lens distortion. The structure parameters $\alpha_i^{(L)}$, designate the distance of the points to the left camera's image plane and are used to reconstruct the 3-D structure of the curve the user produced by waving around an infrared beacon. In order to get a good initial state vector x_0, the intrinsic parameters are set accordingly to the output of the first calibration step. The extrinsic parameters and the structure parameters are roughly estimated.

The computational approach of this adaptive calibration is shown in Fig. 5. First, all measured image points are transformed to their supposed undistorted locations according to Tsai's method. Then, a 2-D image point is back-projected to a 3-D point using $\alpha_i^{(L)}$ and the pre-calculated focal length as the internal orientation. Second, a transformation into the other camera frame is applied to the 3-D point using the relative orientation and translation. Finally, the 3-D point is projected into the second camera image plane using the internal orientation of the corresponding camera. The perspective projection can be mathematically described as (3), where the centre of projection has the coordinates $(0, 0, -\frac{1}{\beta})$ in the camera reference frame, (X, Y, Z) describes a point in the camera coordinate system, $\beta = \frac{1}{f}$ is the inverse focal length and (u_u, v_u) is the projected undistorted point localised at the image plane.

$$\begin{pmatrix} u_u \\ v_u \end{pmatrix} = \begin{pmatrix} X \\ Y \end{pmatrix} \frac{1}{1 + \beta Z} \tag{3}$$

With regard to this camera model, the above mentioned computational approach shown in Fig. 5 can be mathematically described. Firstly, the inverse projection is given by (4), where $(u_{u,i}^{(L)}, v_{u,i}^{(L)} [i = 1, ..., n])$ is an undistorted image point corresponding to a 3-D point $(X_i^{(L)}, Y_i^{(L)}, Z_i^{(L)})$ in the left camera reference frame. The distance information is given by $\alpha_i^{(L)}$. Later, we will show that the value of $\alpha_i^{(L)}$ is altered to get the mean correct undistorted position $(X_i^{(L)}, Y_i^{(L)}, Z_i^{(L)})$.

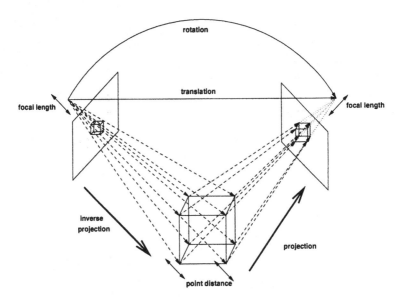

Fig. 5. The calibration idea

That is the reason why we use a different designation of $\alpha_i^{(L)}$ and $Z_i^{(L)}$.

$$
\begin{pmatrix} X_i^{(L)} \\ Y_i^{(L)} \\ Z_i^{(L)} \end{pmatrix} = \begin{pmatrix} u_{u,i}^{(L)} \\ v_{u,i}^{(L)} \\ 0 \end{pmatrix} + \alpha_i^{(L)} \begin{pmatrix} \beta^{(L)} u_{u,i}^{(L)} \\ \beta^{(L)} v_{u,i}^{(L)} \\ 1 \end{pmatrix} \tag{4}
$$

Secondly, the 3-D point transformation from the left to the right camera frame is given by (5), where $P^{(L)}$ is a 3-D point in the left camera frame, $\mathcal{R}^{L \to R}$ and T is the relative orientation and translation of the right camera frame with respect to the left camera. $P^{(R)} = (X^{(R)}, Y^{(R)}, Z^{(R)})$ is the obtained point located in the right camera frame.

$$
P^{(R)} = T + \mathcal{R}^{L \to R} P^{(L)} \tag{5}
$$

Finally, the perspective transformation for the right camera is given in Eq. 6:

$$
\begin{pmatrix} X^{(R)} \\ Y^{(R)} \\ 1 + \beta^{(R)} Z^{(R)} \end{pmatrix} = \begin{pmatrix} 1 & 0 & 0 \\ 0 & 1 & 0 \\ 0 & 0 & \beta^{(R)} \end{pmatrix} P^{(R)} + \begin{pmatrix} 0 \\ 0 \\ 1 \end{pmatrix} \tag{6}
$$

To obtain the undistorted position in the right image plane, the first and second components of the resulting vector are divided by the third (see (3)). Our calibration step works according to Fig. 6. After initialising the state vector x of our calibration system, we collect a data set of 100 image points. With access to the state vector, it is possible to transform the image point measurements of the left camera to the right camera image plane. A comparison of the transformed and the measured image points can be used for altering the state vector x with the IEKF until convergence is achieved. Afterwards, the system contains an arbitrary scale factor. However, after the third calibration step the corners of the projection table are well known and the scaling factors can be computed.

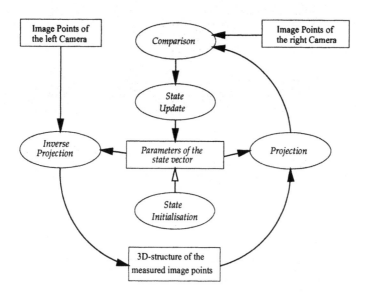

Fig. 6. The calibration working cycle

At the top of Fig. 7, the images of both video cameras are shown, including the last 100 points captured by each camera. In the middle of this figure, one can see the iterative calibration. The first image shows the left measurements again. In the next image, the samples taken by the right camera and the initialisation step with the projection to the camera's image plane are displayed. Then, the iteration will bring the calculated measured points closer to the real measured points by altering the state vector x. At the bottom of this figure, the state correction over 40 iterations is shown.

5   Experimental Results

With the system described in Sect. 3, we reach a frame rate of more than 23 frames/sec. Regarding accuracy, we calculated the error of 128 points measured and reconstructed with our system from a volume of $70cm * 70cm * 20cm$ aligned to the lower left corner of the projection table from the user's view. In this volume, we have a disparity in absolute positions of less than two 2 cm. This error is probably caused by an extreme lens distortion which is not completely corrected as well as the fact that we have to separate the image data which is stored interlaced in the computer's main memory and therefore only use a quarter of the image information due to processing time restrictions.

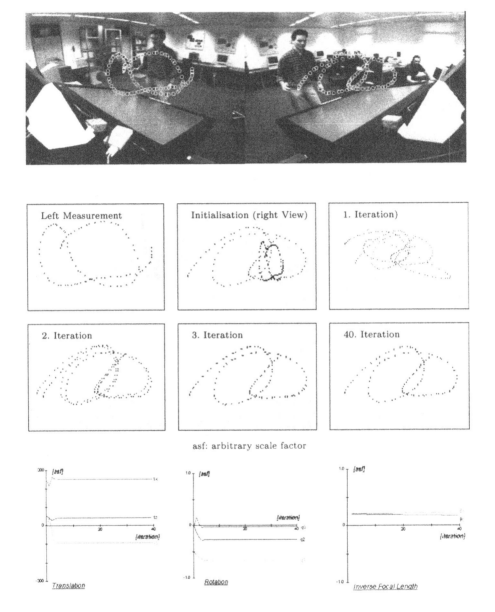

Fig. 7. The iterative calibration

6 Application Areas and Examples

An optical tracking system like the one described here may be used in any setup from the user sitting in front of a standard computer monitor (small volume of space), over tracking user actions over a projection table or in front of a projection screen (medium volume), to using it in a CAVE setup (large volume, see [CNSDF93]). While all of the set-ups mentioned are possible, optical tracking systems show their greatest benefits in applications where medium volumes of space have to be tracked (e.g. in front of a projection screen, over a desk) and where the conditions described in Sect. 3 are fulfilled.

Using a tracking system fixed on the user's hand enables the user to directly interact with objects, either by relying on the optical feedback of the infrared pointer alone or by attaching a virtual cursor to the tip of the pointer. Using the direct interaction metaphor, one may categorise different types of interactions:

1. Simple tasks like grabbing objects and moving them around.
2. Tasks where additional manipulators (helper geometry like e.g. a 3-D scale box) are needed to enable the interaction and to give the user feedback about the effect of the interaction.
3. Control tasks where the user interacts with user interface elements like buttons, menus, sliders etc.
4. Multi-modal interaction, e.g. using video tracking and speech at the same time

An optical tracking system like the one described here may be used for all of the categories described above. Category one works by pointing to the object and then turning on the infrared pointer. This attaches the object to the tip of the pointer. To release the object again, the infrared pointer is turned off. Categories two and three are variations of the first method. In category two, the user interacts with the helper geometry in order to be able to scale, shear, and rotate objects. Features of the helper geometry are grabbed (for example a resize box in the corner of the bounding box of an object) and is subsequently moved around. Finally, in the third category, the user uses the pointer to either trigger the user interface elements or to grab the controls of user interface elements like analogue valuators (one-, two-, and three-dimensional valuators are possible).

Generally, applications supporting this viewing and interaction model are applications where the user is accustomed to work with objects present on a table or a drawing board, like architecture, medicine, engineering etc. (see [WH97]).

7 Future Work

Future work will extend our system to six degrees of freedom each for the user's hand and head. Furthermore, we are interested in getting more information about the user's position such as the elbow and shoulder positions for building up a human kinematic model. For this task, it will be better to use passive markers. With regard to have a plug and play system, recursively updating the relative transformation for each measurement when it is obtained on-the fly (blunder detection after taking each measurement) is useful for an integrated calibration. Forthcoming research will segment the human hand in 3-D and will use a deformable model with kinematic properties, using a glove with markers (see Fig. 8) and an infrared source lighting the scene. Further in the future, tracking a whole body fitted with markers and animating a 3-D kinematic model of the human body with that data will allow even more sophisticated tasks to be performed like controlling a human model in an assembly simulation similar to the one shown in Fig. 9.

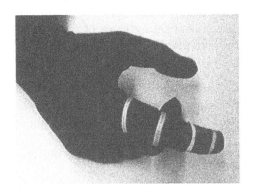

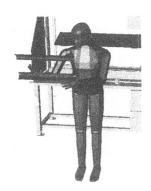

Fig. 8. A marked glove   Fig. 9. The RobCad man

8 Conclusions

In this paper, we have presented a real-time optical tracking system for virtual reality applications. The hardware setup of our system has been described as well as the software which has been developed to run the system and the environment our system operates in.

Our system uses a robust and fast algorithm to track the hand as well as the head of a user in a setting using a projection table to display the virtual environment. At the moment, our system is not sufficiently accurate to be used for interacting with the virtual environment as well as for controlling the perspective distortion needed to render the correct images for the user's viewpoint. The calibration procedure which has been described is easy to apply but needs to be extended to include a lens distortion correction.

Our research has shown that our system is at least as accurate as conventional magnetic tracking systems and is a robust means for interacting with virtual environments, also avoiding distortion problems inherent to magnetic tracking systems. One drawback opposed to magnetic tracking systems which our system has at its present development stage is that it only supports position tracking. Orientation tracking is not possible with the present setup, but will be added shortly by either using more LEDs as the tracking object or with reflective markers which can then be segmented from the grabbed pictures.

Acknowledgments

Portions of this work were done in cooperation with BMW, Munich, Germany. Thanks are due to all at BMW for their help and support, especially to R. Grandl. We would like to thank Prof. J. Encarnação for providing us with the research environment in which this work was carried out. Furthermore, we would like to thank all of our department, especially Dr.-Ing. A. Hildebrand, for their feedback and suggestions with which they came up in many discussions. Finally, thanks to the anonymous reviewers. Especially one gave us extremely useful comments.

References

[AP95a]   A. Azarbayejani and A. P. Pentland *Recursive Estimation of Motion, Structure, and FocalLength*, IEEE PAMI 17(6), June 1995

[AP95b]   A. Azarbayejani and A. P. Pentland *Camera Self-Calibration from One Point Correspondence*, Media Lab Technical Report 341, 1995

[AP96]   A. Azarbayejani and A. Pentland *Real-time Self-calibrating Stereo Person Tracking using 3-D Shape Estimation from Blob Features*, IEEE International Conference on Pattern Recognition, 1996

[CNSDF93]   Carolina Cruz-Neira, Daniel J. Sandin, and Thomas A. DeFanti *Surround-Screen Projection-Based Virtual Reality: The Design and Implementation of the CAVE*, Proceedings of the ACM SIGGRAPH 93 conference, Anaheim, August 1993

[HH96]   T. Heap and D. Hogg *Towards 3-D Hand Tracking using a Deformable Model*, 2nd International Face and Gesture Recognition Conference, 1996

[RK93]   J. Rehg and T. Kanade *Digiteyes: Vision-based Human Hand Tracking*, Technical Report CMU-CS-TR-93-220, Carnegie Mellon University, 1993

[RK94]   J. Rehg and T. Kanade *Visual Tracking of Self-occluding Articulated Objects*, Technical Report CMU-CS-94-224, Carnegie Mellon University, 1994

[MG96]   F.Madritsch and M. Gervautz. *CCD-Camera Based Optical Beacon Tracking for Virtual and Augmented Reality*, Eurographics 15(3), 1996

[Tsa86]   R. T. Tsai *An Efficient and Accurate Camera Calibration Technique for 3-D Machine Vision* , Proccedings of the IEEE Conference on Computer Vision and Pattern Recognition, 1986

[WADP96]   Christopher Wren, Ali Azarbayejani, Trevor Darrell and Alex Pentland. *Pfinder: Real-time Tracking of the Human Body*, Integration Issues in Large Commercial Media Delivery Systems. A. G. Tescher and V. M. Bove, 1996

[WH97]   H. Wirth, A. Hildebrand et al. *VIP Progress and Management Report No. 5*, Report for EC ESPRIT Project No. 20640 (VIP), June 1997

[Zach97]   G. Zachmann *Distortion Correction of Magnetic Fields for Position Tracking*, Proc. Computer Graphics International (CGI'97), 1997

[ZF92]   Z. Zhang and O. Faugeras *3-D Dynamic Scene Analysis*, Springer Series in Information Sciences, Springer-Verlag, Berlin 1992

A Graphics Compiler for a 3-Dimensional Captured Image Database and Captured Image Reusability

Tosiyasu L. Kunii[1,2,3], *Fellow, IEEE*, Yoshifuru Saito[1], *Member, IEEE*, and Motoyoshi Shiine[1]

[1] Department of Electronics and Electrical Engineering, Graduate School of Engineering, Hosei University, 3-7-2 Kajino-cho, Koganei City, Tokyo 184-8584 Japan
kunii@k.hosei.ac.jp ; ysaitoh@ysaitoh.k.hosei.ac.jp; shiine@ysaitoh.k.hosei.ac.jp
[2] Monolith Co., Ltd., 1-7-3 Azabu-Juban, Minato-ku, Tokyo 106-0045 Japan
tlk@mbp.com
[3] Institute of Digital Art and Science (IDAS), 1-25-21-602 Hongo, Bunkyo-ku, Tokyo 113-0033 Japan
tosi@kunii.com

Abstract. We present a new research direction named a graphics compiler for capturing and dynamic recovering of the shapes of 3-dimensional graphics targets. The graphics compiler is based on graphics parsing precedence rules. It interactively parses a 3-dimensional graphics shape data into a set of the basic geometrical and topological constructs of cellular spatial structures. It enables us to recover the target object shapes as seen from any viewpoints. An object-centered motion capture method is developed, as opposed to a camera-centered motion capture method. After capturing a graphics target images dynamically, a set of captured image data is compiled interactively and then the complied objects are stored in a graphics database. A sequence of images of the target objects captured at different time instances makes it possible to produce a set of compiled shape information of the objects containing a complete 3-dimensional geometrical shape information that inherits topological properties. Thus, the captured shapes are turned into reusable components to build new graphics contents on demand by assembling them.

1   Introduction

Most of the conventional image capturing is oriented to immediately store the snap shots of graphics image data as they are. Thereby, conventional image capturing methodology greatly depends on the development of hardware. With the develop-ment of the software and hardware technologies, the demand of high quality and high speed image capturing is explosively increasing for various industrial applications, e.g. product inspecting processes, security systems and so on. However, the simple

Nadia Magnenat-Thalmann, Daniel Thalmann (Eds.): CAPTECH'98, LNAI 1537, pp. 128-139, 1998.

increasing of the number of captured images as well as pixels ends up with an enormous data storage capacity.

In the present paper, we propose a new methodology named the graphics compiler. Fundamental difference between the conventional and proposed methodologies is in the conceptual aspects of image capturing techniques as well as applications. Graphics compiler translates the original image data into a set of basic geometrical objects. Each of the captured data is compiled into the basic geometrical objects deleting the duplicated object information. The compilation proceeds very often interactively as usual due to visual occlusion, and also the ambiguity and incompleteness of captured data.

As a matter of fact, the compilation consists of two separate phases. The first is the conversion of the image to a graph theoretical representation that is the only phase often requires human interaction. The second phase is for the repeated reuse of such compiled data obtained in the first phase and stored in the graphics database. This phase is completely automated and that is the phase to generate object images in the *scope of interest*. The scope of interest is given as a 3-dimensional range, in our case is a boxel that contains the graphics object of our interest.   Since the graphics object in the graphics database is already compiled in the first phase into a graph theoretical representation, we can automate the compilation based on the graphics parsing precedence rules, as explained in this paper.

After obtaining a set of complete geometrical objects by the graphics compiler, the target image in the scope of interest can be recovered in a 3-dimensional manner and projected onto a 2-dimensional screen. This makes it possible to show the target image in a static and dynamic manner. Also it serves to save the storage capacity by making all the objects and their components in the images reusable. The compiled reusable resources are stored in a database. Thus, the *graphics compiler* is an innovative methodology. It translates the captured image data into a set of basic geometrical objects containing the complete graphics information. Hence, original target object can be visualized in whatever ways we like to present it.

The kernel of the graphics compiler is based on the hierarchical space indexing method [1] and cellular spatial structures [8-10]. The hierarchical space indexing method is one of the methodologies for indexing a 3-dimensional space. When we employ a regular decomposition of the 3-dimensional space, this leads us to a tree structure and to store the geometrical objects in table forms. Thereby, quick access to an interest point can be carried out by means of a leaf node as an index.

This paper outlines the design strategy of graphics compiler and basic properties of the hierarchical space indexing method, and presents a prototype implementation example.

2   A Graphic Compiler

2.1   Basic Structure

The graphics compiler is composed of four major units. One is an image-capturing unit. This unit is similar to those of conventional one. The second is a compiling unit that translates the captured image data into hierarchical space indexed table objects. The third is a database unit, and the last is an image-recovering unit that displays a target image onto a computer screen according to the instructions given by an observer. **Figure 1** shows a schematic diagram of the graphics compiler.

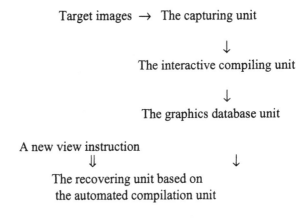

Target images → The capturing unit

↓

The interactive compiling unit

↓

The graphics database unit

A new view instruction
⇓   ↓
The recovering unit based on
the automated compilation unit

Fig. 1. A schematic diagram of the graphics compiler

2.2   Space Indexing

In order to work out the graphics compiler, the space-indexing method is of paramount importance. This is because the graphics compiler translates the captured image data into a set of primitive geometrical objects. One of the ways to carry out this translation is to employ a *space indexing method*, which constitutes a tree structure.

Indexing methods generally have been studied for the context searching problems. In such cases, quick access to the data to be selected from a large amount of data is of extremely importance. In database oriented management, efficient access and retrieval of stored data have been widely studied. In dealing with a large amount of data, it is effective to classify the search spaces into subspaces, recursively. This makes it possible to skip the data not containing interest items. A binary tree data structure is a typical one [2].

The key idea of the *hierarchical space indexing method* is to apply the indexing strategy to a 3-dimensional object for capturing and processing image data. The strategy is based on the precedence rules of parsing the topology of objects represented in a cellular spatial structure. Graphics objects are algebraic topologically modeled very simply as cellular design. We take *cellular spatial structures* as the foundation of the modeling. As a cell, we take an n-dimensional topological ball called an n-cell in terms of algebraic topology. For example, a 0-cell is a vertex, a 1-cell is an edge, and a 2-cell is a surface. When a surface is closed, it becomes a 3-cell that is a topological ball. Each hole is a 2-cell. Any cells are attached through a *cell-attaching map*. In a cellular structured space, the space thus obtained by attaching cells are called an *attaching space*, an *adjunction space* or an *adjoining space* [8-10].

The object shapes topologically defined have to be visualized and made into physically realizable forms. A three level hierarchical architecture for shape modeling is an excellent architecture: 1 the topological layer, 2 the geometrical layer and 3 the visualization layer. Defining shapes actually is carried out interactively through this architecture. It starts from the topological layer to define topological shapes, and visualizes the shapes in the visualization layer after giving temporary geometrical shapes to the objects in the geometrical layer. It goes back to the topological layer to change the topological definition as needed. In the geometrical layer, a 1-cell, that is an edge in the topological layer, can be a line or a curve; a 2-cell can be a plane or a curved surface, and a 3-cell a curved body.

A limited case of cellular spatial structure representations is a class of *boundary representations* usually abbreviated as *B-reps*. Generally, any object can be identified in terms of four geometrical entities in B-reps: a vertex, an edge, a surface and a body [3]. A body is the part inside an object enclosed by surfaces. A surface is a plane enclosed by its boundaries. An edge is composed of two vertices as its two end points. We have to impose a restriction that no object should be self-intersecting and inconsistency should be detected. Further, we have to hold the following conditions:

1. *Any two surfaces are either disjoint, meet at a common vertex or along with a common edge.*
2. *Any two edges are either disjoint or meet at one of their end vertices.*
3. *Any edge and surface are either disjoint, meet at a common vertex, or the edge is part of the surface boundary.*

In order to introduce a tree structure for indexing, a cube called the *entire universe* U should be defined. An arbitrary object to be represented must be in this entire universe U corresponding to the root of the tree. The entire universe U is subdivided into eight subspaces called *octants* corresponding to eight children in the tree. Each of the octants is recursively subdivided into eight octants. This means that every non-terminal node has eight children. Thus, an octal tree structure is usually referred to an *oct-tree* [3-7]. As opposed to pure oct-tree where subdivision recurs until either an octant becomes completely inside the object or completely outside the object within available resolution, we halt the subdivision when an octant becomes simple enough. The following definitions concerning with the index tree give the *precedence rules of parsing the topology of a graph- theoretically represented object shape*:

TYPE 1 Boundary -- An octant includes the boundary of the object. This type is denoted as P (partial).

TYPE 2 Non-boundary -- An octant does not include the boundary. This type is either completely inside the object denoted as 1 (full), or completely outside the object denoted as 0 (empty). This type never requires any more subdivision.

Each boundary octant P is further classified into two sub-types:

TYPE 1-1 Dividing -- The space in the octant is still dividable and requires further subdivision. The octant is denoted as T representing an oct-tuple (o, o, o, o, o, o, o, o), where the order o refers to the position of the octant.

TYPE 1-2 Non-dividing -- The space is simple enough to represent the cubical subset of the world and no more subdivision is necessary. This octant is denoted as L.

Three kinds of the non-dividing spaces are:

1. An octant includes one vertex. This octant neither includes the edge not having the vertex as its endpoint nor the face not having the vertex as its boundary point. Such an octant is called a *vertex space* and denoted as V. Corresponding node to this space in the tree is called a *vertex node*.
2. An octant does not include the vertex but one edge fraction, which is a part of an edge. This octant does not include the face not having the edge as its boundary. Such an octant is called an *edge space* and denoted as E. The corresponding node to this space in the tree is called an *edge node*.
3. An octant does not include any vertex as well as edge but includes one edge fraction, which is a part of an edge. Also, this octant does not include the face not having the edge as its boundary. Such an octant is called a *surface space* and denoted as S. The corresponding node to this space in the tree is called a *surface node* and denoted as S. **Figure 2** shows the typical examples of the above-defined spaces.

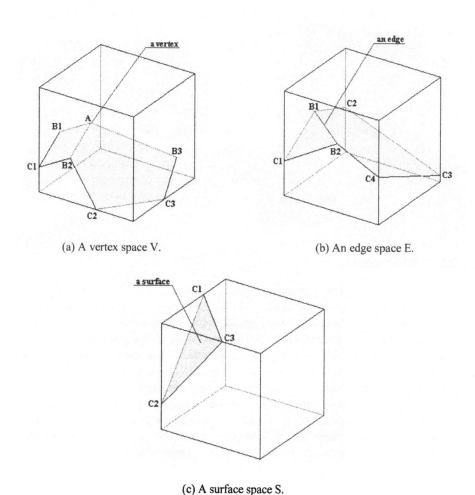

(a) A vertex space V.

(b) An edge space E.

(c) A surface space S.

Fig. 2. The octant spaces V, E and S as the intermediate meta-codes

Each geometrical object consists of a node that is a point (a 0-cell e^0), an edge that is a line (a 1-cell e^1), a surface (a 2-cell e^2) or a body (a 3-cell e^3). All cells are open. Further, they are hierarchically organized. As explained earlier, this hierarchically organized structure serves exactly as the basis of the *hierarchical space indexing method*. In a cellular spatial structure,

$$X^0 \subseteq X^1 \subseteq X^2 \subseteq X^3,$$

where X^i ($i = 1, 2, 3$) is a discrete space whose element is e^i. X^i is constructed from X^{i-1} by attaching a disjoint union of e^i to X^{i-1} via a continuous and surjective map called *an attaching map*

$$f_i \colon \partial e^i \to X^{i-1}$$

such that

$$X^i = X^{i-1} + \cap_k e^i_k / \sim \; = X^{i-1} \cap_{f_i} \cap_k e^i_k / (x \sim f_i(x) \mid x \in \partial e^i),$$

where ∂e^i is the topological boundary of e^i, and k is a natural number [10]. This method of constructing a cellular structured space is generally called *cell composition*. The reverse is *cell decomposition*. Basically, the graphics compiler performs cell decomposition. The type of graphics compiler presented in this paper is a special case based on the space index method. It produces a *intermediate meta-code set* that consists of 0-, 1- and P- octants. Each P-octant is a T- or L- octant, and the T-octant is further decomposed until the result become L-octants. Each L-octant is a V-, E- or S- space. + denotes a disjoint union and often a + symbol is used instead (sometimes it is called "exclusive or"). ~ is an equivalence relation. An *equivalence relation* is simply a relation that is reflexive, symmetric and transitive. It can be a set theoretical equivalence relation, a homotopic equivalence relation, a topological equivalence relation or a geometric equivalence relation. The transitivity divides the space into a disjoint union of subspaces called *equivalence classes*.

2.3 Implementation

Practical implementation requires a series of following steps. At first, each of the captured graphics data is compiled into the object cells by the hierarchical space indexing method. The data captured at the different viewpoints of the same target are similarly compiled and continued until the object cells do not grow up. This means that the stored object cells contain a set of complete 3-dimensional information of the target object. Using the stored object cell data, the 3-dimensional target object can be projected onto the 2-dimensional screen from any arbitrary viewpoints. Thus, application of the graphics compiler to the captured graphics data makes it possible to identify the 3-dimensional object in the indexing table but also makes it possible to reproduce the target object as seen from any viewpoints. When the hardware chips realize this graphics compiler, it leads us to a new graphics technology.

3   An Example

In this example, we employ an object-centered motion capturing method. It differs from the traditional camera-centered motion capturing method.

The first is the introduction of our image-capturing concept. Most of the computer image data capturing methodology is based on the idea such that captured images are memorized in a computer data storage system and presents the processed images onto a computer screen according to human instructions. That is basically the digitized photograph concept. However, when we look into the way a human captures images, a human captures the images conceptually as objects not as images *per se*.

Let us consider a simple example: a set of cups on a table. A human recognizes this image as a combination of a cup and a table. Further, the cup is identified by its characteristic shape, and the table is identified by its four leg structure as the shape characteristics. Furthermore, the cup and the table are regarded as a set of geometrical objects. Thus, human image capturing ability converts the image data into these object data and classifies them in a hierarchical manner. By means of the memorized object data and experience information, human is able to imagine the backside of the table shape and the other details. It is difficult to realize this human capturing ability by computers exactly. However, when we can derive 3-dimensional object data from captured static and dynamic target images, it is possible to recover the target objects viewed from any points by computers. This is our basic image capturing objective.

Secondly, we outline a simple and practical implementation of our image capturing technique. The image projected onto each of the human eyes is 2-dimensional. A human recognizes the target 3-dimensionally. This is because a human is equipped with the two eyes with the characteristic fixed distance. This obviously means that two cameras placed at a given distance can recognize 3-dimensional targets. However, computers initially lack memorized object data, experience information and the standard measure for estimating the relative target sizes. Thereby, in order to capture complete 3-dimensional object data, computers require 3 frames of images viewed from 3 distinct positions.

Let an arbitrary vertex point in an *i-th* 2-dimensional image data be denoted by $(p_i \Delta x, p_i \Delta y)$, then we project a unit vector $(1, 1, 1)$ in a 3-dimensional space onto the 2-dimensional *i*-th plane coordinate, where the origin $(0, 0, 0)$ in the 3-dimensional coordinate should coincide with the 2-dimensional origin $(0, 0)$. Considering a relationship between the 3- and 2- dimensional coordinate systems in **Figure 3**, we have a relationship:

$$(1, 0, 0) \rightarrow (U_x x_i, U_x y_i),$$

where $U_x x_i$ and $U_x y_i$ are the referred unit lengths on the X_i- and Y_i- 2-dimensional coordinate axes, respectively. Similarly, for the vertices $(0,1,0)$ and $(0,0,1)$ in 3-dimensions, we have the following relationships:

$$(0, 1, 0) \rightarrow (U_y x_i, U_y y_i)$$

and

$$(0, 0, 1) \rightarrow (U_z x_i, U_z y_i).$$

In these relationships, $U_x x_i, U_y y_i, U_z x_i$ and $U_z y_i$ are the referred unit lengths on the X_i- and Y_i- 2-dimensional coordinate axes, respectively. Further, the subscripts x, y and z denote the 3-dimensional x-, y- and z- axes, respectively. By means of these relationships, it is possible to derive a set of system equations for the 3 distinct images.

Thus, for the 3 distinct images, a following set of system equations holds:

$$
\begin{bmatrix} p_1\Delta x \\ p_1\Delta y \\ p_2\Delta x \\ p_2\Delta y \\ p_3\Delta x \\ p_3\Delta y \end{bmatrix} =
\begin{bmatrix}
U_x x_1 & U_y x_1 & U_z x_1 \\
U_x y_1 & U_y y_1 & U_z y_1 \\
U_x x_2 & U_y x_2 & U_z x_2 \\
U_x y_2 & U_y y_2 & U_z y_2 \\
U_x x_3 & U_y x_3 & U_z x_3 \\
U_x y_3 & U_y y_3 & U_z y_3
\end{bmatrix}
\begin{bmatrix} X \\ Y \\ Z \end{bmatrix}
\quad (1)
$$

$$\text{or}$$

$$\mathbf{P} = \mathbf{CQ} \qquad (2)$$

where the elements X, Y and Z are the exact 3-dimensional coordinate values to be evaluated. In order to obtain the unique X, Y and Z from Eq.(1), we have to impose the following constraint:

$$
\begin{aligned}
1 &= \sqrt{\left(U_x x_i\right)^2 + \left(U_x y_i\right)^2}, \\
1 &= \sqrt{\left(U_y x_i\right)^2 + \left(U_y y_i\right)^2}, \text{ and} \\
1 &= \sqrt{\left(U_z x_i\right)^2 + \left(U_z y_i\right)^2},
\end{aligned}
\qquad (3)
$$

$$\text{where } i = 1, 2, 3.$$

Using the constraint (3), it is possible to evaluate the vertex coordinate values X, Y and Z in the 3-dimensional coordinate. Thus, we can obtain the most fundamental indexing term of the target.

Figure 4 shows the examples of a series of the captured images. The target object in this example is a simple electronic calculator and our purpose is to get a set of compiled object data of this calculator in terms of vertices, edges, surfaces and bodies. The small dots on the captured images in **Figure 4** refer to the selected vertices in order to obtain the compiled object data. Also, a set of orthogonal lines denotes an attached 3-dimensional coordinate system. These 3-dimensional rectangular coordinate axes are fixed to the particular target position. Also, an A4 size curved paper sheet is included in the **Figures 4(a)** and **4(c)** as an extra rough reference of the target physical dimensions.

(a) The 1ˢᵗ captured image.   (b) The 2ⁿᵈ captured image.

(c) The 3ʳᵈ captured image.

Fig 4. An example of a series of captured images

Using these captured images and the relationships (1)-(3), we calculated and compiled the graphics data. After obtaining the graphic object data, we recovered the electronic calculator image. **Figure 5** shows one of the recovered calculator images. As shown in **Figure 5**, the shape of target electronic calculator is roughly reproduced. This roughness reflects the fuzzy nature of human pattern recognition and the ambiguity in the course of interactive generation of vertex points via graphics compilation. We can refine it by utilizing the selected object-centered information such as object shape information and image analysis information such as wavelet analysis information in generating the vertex points. By semi-transparently overlaying the reproduced images on the original images, they are further interactively refined to any extent as required. *Refinement by interactive semi-transparent overlay* is being pursued as another research theme.

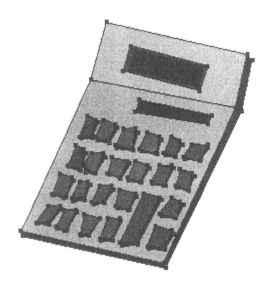

Fig 5. An example of a reproduced image

Thus, we have worked out a prototype graphics compiler and have made a basic verification of our methodology proposed here. The selected target object is relatively simple and is only to illustrate our image capturing and reproducing method at the most primitive level up to 3-cells as we have discussed so far.

4   Conclusion

We have developed a new methodology named a graphics compiler. An engine of the graphics compiler based on the space indexing approach has been described. After obtaining a set of complete geometrical object cells by the graphics compiler, the target object shapes are recovered in a 3-dimensional manner and projected onto a 2-dimensional screen.

The graphics compiler is an innovative methodology that translates the captured image data into a set of reusable basic geometrical objects containing the complete 3-dimensional graphics information. Hence, the original target object can be visualized on demand as seen from any sides.

To be more specific, after capturing a graphics target images dynamically, a series of captured image data is compiled and then the complied objects are stored in a graphics database. A sequence of images of the target objects captured at different time instances makes it possible to produce a set of compiled shape information of the objects containing a complete 3-dimensional geometrical shape information that also inherits topological properties in cellular structured spaces. Thus, the captured shapes are turned into reusable components to build new graphics contents freely by assembling them.

When a hardware chip realizes this graphics compiler as a system-on-chip, it leads us to a new graphics technology.

This paper has outlined the designing strategy of the graphics compiler and the basic properties of the hierarchical space indexing method. A simple example has shown our new methodology for image data capturing. Another example to illustrate the reusability of the compiled object data is under preparation. Further research is in progress for wide applications including sporting motion capturing and dynamic scene capturing.

References

1. K. Fujimura and T. L. Kunii, "A hierarchical space indexing method," *Proceedings of Computer Graphics Tokyo '85*, edited by T. L. Kunii (Springer-Verlag 1985) pp.21-33.
2. J. L. Bentley, "Multi-dimensional binary search tree used for associative searching," *CACM* Vol.18, No.9 (1975) pp.509-517.
3. K. Yamaguchi, T. L. Kunii, K. Fujimura and H. Toriya, "Octree related data structure and algorithms," *IEEE CG & A*, Vol.3 (1983).
4. K. Fujimura, H. Toriya, K. Yamaguchi and T. L. Kunii, "An enhanced Oct-tree data structure and operations for solid modeling," *Proceedings of NASA Computer-Aided Geometry Modeling*, Hampton, Virginia, April 20-22 (1983) pp.279-287.
5. L .J. Doctor and J. D. Torborg, "Display techniques for octtree encoded object," *IEEE CG & A*, Vol.1, No.1 (1981) pp.29-38.
6. C. L. Jacking and S. L. Tanimoto, "Oct-trees and their use in representing 3-dimensional objects", *Computer Graphics and Image Processing*, Vol.14, No.3 (1980) pp. 249-270.
7. D. Meagher, "Geometric modeling using oct-tree encoding", *Computer Graphics and Image Processing*, Vol.19, No.2 (1982) pp.129-147.
8. T. L. Kunii, "The 3rd Industrial Revolution through integrated intelligent processing systems", *Proceedings of IEEE First International Conference on Intelligent Processing Systems*, October 28-31, 1997, Beijing, China (ICIPS '97), pp. 1-6, The Institute of Electrical and Electronics Engineers, New York, NY, U.S. A.
9. T. L Kunii and T. Wachi,, "Topological dress making as fashion media modeling", *Proceedings of MultiMedia Modeling Conference (MMM'98)*, October 12-15, 1998, Lausanne, Switzerland, in press, IEEE Computer Society Press, Los Alamitos, California, U.S. A.
10. T. L. Kunii, "Graphics with shape property inheritance", *Proceedings of Pacific Graphics '98*, (October 26-29, 1998, Singapore), in press, IEEE Computer Society Press, Los Alamitos, California, U.S. A.

VideoVR: A Real-Time System for Automatically Constructing Panoramic Images from Video Clips

Ding-Yun Chen, Murphy Chien-Chang Ho, Ming Ouhyoung

Communications and Multimedia Lab.
Dept. of Computer Science and Information Engineering
National Taiwan University, Taipei, Taiwan, 106, R.O.C.

Abstract. An authoring system is proposed to construct panoramic images of real-world scenes from video clips automatically. Instead of using special hardware such as fish-eye lens, our method is less hardware-intensive and more flexible to capture real-world scenes without loss of efficiency. Unlike current panoramic stitching methods, where users need to select a set of images before constructing a panoramic image, our system will choose essential frames and stitch them together automatically in 16 seconds on a Pentium-II PC. In addition to popular image-based VR data formats, we also output the panoramic images in VRML97 format.

1 Introduction

In recent years, panoramic images have been widely used to build virtual environments from real-world scenes[1,2,8,10,11,12]. Hybrid geometry- and image-based approach for the rendering of architectures is also propose [13]. Besides using special hardware to capture panoramic images of real-world scenes[5,6,9], a number of techniques based on "stitching" have been developed[10,11,12]. However, most of the techniques of this class are of high computational complexity, need multiple steps to build a single panoramic image, and users are required to adjust parameters interactively.

In this paper, we introduce a real-time system to capture panoramic images of real-world scenes automatically[3] by simply panning a hand-held camcorder. Our implementation of constructing a panoramic image from 6 seconds long CIF format video clip takes 16 seconds on a Pentium II-233 PC.

2 System Overview

Video clips provide more information about recorded scenes than that of photos. Due to the characteristic of high similarity and low difference between successive video frames, correctness rate of stitching is higher. In general, for a 320x240 true-color video clip, the uncompressed data rate is about 6.6 Megabytes per second. To efficiently construct panoramic images, we use the folowing multi-stage approach:

Stage1: Capture and choose necessary frames
Stage2: Calculate accurate translation of selected frames, and stitch them together
Stage3: Cylindrical stitching
Stage4: Output in VRML97 format or other formats

Nadia Magnenat-Thalmann, Daniel Thalmann (Eds.): CAPTECH'98, LNAI 1537, pp. 140-143, 1998.

In general, stitching and constructing a 360° panoramic image needs 15 to 30 images in average. It is unnecessary to use all frames in video clips to construct a single panoramic image. So, capturing and choosing necessary frames in entire video clips is done at the first stage. Then, the next stage is to stitch together selected frames. The algorithm to capture and stitch frames is described in section 3.

After the completion of stitching all selected frames, seeking and stitching the beginning and the ending parts is needed to construct a 360° panoramic image. Section 4 describes this algorithm.

3. Capturing and Stitching Frames

The method we use to stitch two frames together is by minimizing the gradient error between two frames, and uses the following equation,

$$E(\Delta x, \Delta y) = \sum_{x,y} [G_1(x'+\Delta x, y'+\Delta y) - G_0(x,y)]^2 \qquad (1)$$

where G is gradient operator, (Δx, Δy) is the translation which is the same for all pixels, ($x'+\Delta x, y'+\Delta y$) and (x,y) are corresponding points in two images, and E is error term.

In the first stage, choosing a frame depends on the distance of the translation between previously selected frames. If the distance is smaller than a threshold (we use one-sixteenth of frame size), the frame is dropped until there are enough distance between previously selected frames. In this stage, all we want to know is the approximate distance to decide whether to choose a frame or not. Therefore, we use decimated image of the full frame to calculate the translation efficiently using equation (1). For example, we first sub-sample an 64x48 image from 320x240 image. Next, prediction is used to decrease the search space, which allows this algorithm to be more efficient. In our implementation, this stage could process the input video clips in real-time.

To accurately stitch together selected frames, the error that happens during calculating the translation can not be ignored. So, we make a local search to find the minimal gradient error in stage 2. After obtaining accurate translation, the selected frames are painted on a canvas according to their translation. To reduce

Fig. 1. Capturing and stitching frames: (a) six frames in video clips; (b) stitched frame in a panoramic image

discontinuities in intensity and color between frames, we weight the pixels in each frame proportionally to their distance away from its border. Fig 1 shows the selected frames from video clips and the stitched image.

4. Cylindrical Stitching

To construct a 360° panoramic image, seeking and stitching the beginning and the end of a canvas which is constructed in stage2 (Fig 2a, 3a) is needed. The way to seek is also depending on equation (1). We get a block from the right side of the canvas, and match it in the left region. Once the correct location is found, the redundant region will be clipped out. However, due to accumulated errors during stitching frames, the vertical location of the beginning of the canvas can be different from the vertical location of the end. To solve this problem, the canvas (Fig 2a, 3a) is sheared smoothly to compensate for vertical difference (Fig 2b, 3b).

Fig. 2. Indoor scene (a) capturing and stitching frames; (b) cylindrical stitching

Fig. 3. Outdoor scene (a) capturing and stitching frames; (b) cylindrical stitching

5. Conclusion

In this paper, we have developed a real-time system to capture panoramic images of real-world scenes automatically from video clips. We take advantage of using video clips because it provides a lot of information. We also avoid redundant video frames by choosing essential frames and then stitching them together. There is a fundamental assumption that focal length and aperture change slowly between successive frames and do not change in tilting or rotation. Therefore, instead of warping the input frames and estimating the focal length [1, 11] to stitch frames in cylindrical coordinate, input frames were stitched together directly to construct panoramic images. In short, this is not intended for challenging cases of forward motion and of zoom, but for quick construction in "rotation" only cases. Experiment results are given in Table 1. After the panoramic image is constructed, it can be converted to other formats and we can use some image-based browsers such as LivePicture[8] and PhotoVR[14] to navigate it in Web pages. In our implementation, we can also output the panoramic images in VRML97 format. This allows us to use standard VRML browsers to navigate. For further information, such as executable programs and demos, please refer to http://www.cmlab.csie.ntu.edu.tw/cml-/g/VideoVR.

References

[1] R. Szeliski and H.Y. Shum, "Creating Full View Panoramic Image Mosaics and Environment Maps". Proc. of ACM SIGGRAPH'97 (Los Angeles), pp.251-258, August 1997.

[2] S. E. Chen, "QuickTime VR – an Image-based Approach to Virtual Environment Navigation". Proc. of ACM SIGGRAPH'95, pp. 29-38, August 1995.

[3] Video Brush, http://www.videobrush.com

[4] QuickTime VR, http://qtvr.quicktime.apple.com

[5] IPIX, http://www.ipix.com

[6] Be Here, http://www.behere.com

[7] Smooth Movie, http://www.smoothmove.com

[8] Live Picture, http://www.livepicture.com

[9] OmniCam,http://www.cs.columbia.edu/CAVE/ omnicam

[10] R. Szeliski, "Video Mosaics for Virtual Environments", IEEE Computer Graphics and Applications , pp. 22-30, March 1996.

[11] B. Rousso, S. Peleg, I. Finci and A. Rav-Acha, "Universal Mosaicing Using Pipe Projection", International Conference on Computer Vision , pp. 945-952, 1998.

[12] S. Peleg and J. Herman, "Panoramic Mosaics with VideoBrush". In IUW-97, New Orleans, Louisiana, May 1997. Morgan Kaufmann, pp. 261-264.

[13] P. E. Debzvec, C. J.Taylor, J. Malik, "Modeling and Rendering Architecture from Photographs: A Hybrid Geometry and Image-based Approach", pp.11-20, Proc. of ACM SIGGRAPH'96, New Orleans, USA, 1996.

[14] J.J. Su, Z.Y. Zhuang, S.D. Lee, J.R. Wu, and M. Ouhyoung, "Photo VR: An Image-Based Panoramic View Environment Walk-Through System", Proc. of IEEE International Conference on Consumer Electronic (ICCE'97), pp. 224-225, Chicago, USA 1997.

The Video Yardstick*

Tomáš Brodský, Cornelia Fermüller, and Yiannis Aloimonos

Computer Vision Laboratory, Center for Automation Research,
University of Maryland, College Park, MD 20742-3275, USA,
{brodsky, fer, yiannis}@cfar.umd.edu

Abstract. Given uncalibrated video sequences, how can we recover rich
descriptions of the scene content, beyond two-dimensional (2D) measurements such as color/texture or motion fields – descriptions of shape and
three-dimensional (3D) motion? This is the well known structure from
motion (SFM) problem. Up to now, SFM algorithms proceeded in two
well defined steps, where the first and most important step is recovering the rigid transformation between two views, and the subsequent step
is using this transformation to compute the structure of the scene in
view. This paper introduces a novel approach to structure from motion
in which both steps are accomplished in a synergistic manner. It deals
with the classical structure from motion problem considering a calibrated
camera as well as the extension to an uncalibrated optical device. Existing approaches to estimation of the viewing geometry are mostly based on
the use of optic flow, which, however, poses a problem at the locations
of depth discontinuities. If we knew where depth discontinuities were,
we could (using a multitude of approaches based on smoothness constraints) accurately estimate flow values for image patches corresponding
to smooth scene patches; but to know the discontinuities requires solving
the structure from motion problem first. In the past this dilemma has
been addressed by improving the estimation of flow through sophisticated optimization techniques, whose performance often depends on the
scene in view. In this paper we follow a different approach. We directly
utilize the image derivatives and employ constraints which involve the
3D motion and shape of the scene, leading to a geometric and statistical
estimation problem. The main idea is based on the interaction between
3D motion and shape which allows us to estimate the 3D motion while
at the same time segmenting the scene. If we use a wrong 3D motion
estimate to compute depth, we obtain a distorted version of the depth
function. The distortion, however, is such that the worse the motion estimate, the more likely we are to obtain depth estimates that are locally
unsmooth, i.e., they vary more than the correct ones. Since local variability of depth is due either to the existence of a discontinuity or to
a wrong 3D motion estimate, being able to differentiate between these
two cases provides the correct motion, which yields the "smoothest" estimated depth as well as the image locations of scene discontinuities.
We analyze the new constraints introduced by our approach and show
their relationship to the minimization of the epipolar constraint, which

---

* Patent pending.

Nadia Magnenat-Thalmann, Daniel Thalmann (Eds.): CAPTECH'98, LNAI 1537, pp. 144–158, 1998.
© Springer-Verlag Berlin Heidelberg 1998

becomes a special case of our theory. Finally, we present a number of experimental results with real image sequences indicating the robustness of our method and the improvement over traditional methods. The resulting system is a video yardstick that can be applied to any video sequence to recover first the calibration parameters of the camera that captured the video and, subsequently, the structure of the scene.

1   Introduction and Motivation

In this paper, instead of attempting to estimate flow at all costs before proceeding with structure from motion, we ask a different question: Is it possible to utilize local image motion information, such as normal flow for example, in order to obtain knowledge about scene discontinuities which would allow better estimation of 3D motion? Or, equivalently, is it possible to devise a procedure that estimates scene discontinuities while at the same time estimating 3D motion? We show here that this is the case and we present a novel algorithm for 3D motion estimation.

The idea behind our approach is based on the interaction between 3D motion and scene structure, which only recently has been formalized [3]. If we have a 3D motion estimate which is wrong and we use it to estimate depth, we obtain a distorted version of the depth function. Not only do incorrect estimates of motion parameters lead to incorrect depth estimates, but the distortion is such that the worse the motion estimate, the more likely we are to obtain depth estimates that locally vary much more than the correct ones. The correct motion then yields the "smoothest" estimated depth and we can define a measure whose minimization yields the correct egomotion parameters. The measure can be computed from normal flow only, so the computation of optical flow is not needed by the algorithm.

Intuitively, the proposed algorithm proceeds as follows: first, the image is divided into small patches and a search for the 3D motion – which, as explained in Sect. 3, takes place in the 2D space of translations – is performed. For each candidate 3D motion, using the local normal flow measurements in each patch, the scene depth corresponding to the patch is computed. If the variation of depth for all patches is small, then the candidate 3D motion is close to the correct one. If, however, there is a significant variation of depth in a patch, this is either because the candidate 3D motion is inaccurate or because there is a discontinuity in the patch. The second situation is differentiated from the first if the distribution of the depth values inside the patch is bimodal with the two classes of values spatially separated. In such a case the patch is subdivided into two new ones and the process is repeated. When the depth values computed in each patch are smooth functions, the corresponding motion is the correct one and the procedure has at the same time given rise to the locations of some discontinuities.

The organization of the paper is as follows: Sect. 2 defines the imaging model and describes the equations of the motion field induced by rigid motion; it also makes explicit the relationship between distortion of depth and errors in 3D motion. Sect. 3 is devoted to an outline of the approach taken here and the description of the algorithm. It also analyzes the introduced constraints and formalizes the relationship of the approach to algorithms utilizing the epipolar constraint. Sect. 4 generalizes the algorithm to the case of uncalibrated imaging systems and Sect. 5 describes a number of experimental results with real image sequences.

2   Preliminaries

The camera is a standard calibrated pinhole with focal length f and the coordinate system $OXYZ$ is attached to the camera, with Z being the optical axis. Image points are represented as vectors $\mathbf{r} = [x, y, f]^\mathrm{T}$, where x and y are the image coordinates of the point and f is the focal length in pixels. A scene point $\mathbf{R}$ is projected onto the image point

$$\mathbf{r} = f \frac{\mathbf{R}}{\mathbf{R} \cdot \hat{\mathbf{z}}} \tag{1}$$

where $\hat{\mathbf{z}}$ is the unit vector in the direction of the Z axis. Let the camera move in a static environment with instantaneous translation $\mathbf{t}$ and instantaneous rotation $\boldsymbol{\omega}$ (measured in the coordinate system $OXYZ$). Then a scene point $\mathbf{R}$ moves with velocity (relative to the camera)

$$\dot{\mathbf{R}} = -\mathbf{t} - \boldsymbol{\omega} \times \mathbf{R} \tag{2}$$

The image motion field is then the usual:

$$\dot{\mathbf{r}} = -\frac{1}{(\mathbf{R} \cdot \hat{\mathbf{z}})}(\hat{\mathbf{z}} \times (\mathbf{t} \times \mathbf{r})) + \frac{1}{f}\hat{\mathbf{z}} \times (\mathbf{r} \times (\boldsymbol{\omega} \times \mathbf{r})) = \frac{1}{Z}\mathbf{u}_\mathrm{tr}(\mathbf{t}) + \mathbf{u}_\mathrm{rot}(\boldsymbol{\omega}) \tag{3}$$

where Z is used to denote the scene depth $(\mathbf{R} \cdot \hat{\mathbf{z}})$, and $\mathbf{u}_\mathrm{tr}, \mathbf{u}_\mathrm{rot}$ the direction of the translational and the rotational flow respectively. Due to the scaling ambiguity, only the direction of translation (focus of expansion – FOE, or focus of contraction – FOC, depending on whether the observer approaches or moves away from the scene) and the three rotational parameters can be estimated from monocular image sequences.

The structure of the scene, i.e., the computed depth, can be expressed as a function of the estimated translation $\hat{\mathbf{t}}$ and the estimated rotation $\hat{\boldsymbol{\omega}}$. At an image point $\mathbf{r}$ where the normal flow direction is $\mathbf{n}$, the inverse scene depth $\hat{Z}$ can be estimated from (3) as

$$\frac{1}{\hat{Z}} = \frac{\dot{\mathbf{r}} \cdot \mathbf{n} - \mathbf{u}_\mathrm{rot}(\hat{\boldsymbol{\omega}}) \cdot \mathbf{n}}{\mathbf{u}_\mathrm{tr}(\hat{\mathbf{t}}) \cdot \mathbf{n}} \tag{4}$$

where $\mathbf{u}_\mathrm{rot}(\hat{\boldsymbol{\omega}}), \mathbf{u}_\mathrm{tr}(\hat{\mathbf{t}})$ refer to the estimated rotational and translational flow respectively.

Substituting into (4) from (3), we obtain

$$\frac{1}{\hat{Z}} = \frac{1}{Z} \frac{\mathbf{u}_{tr}(\mathbf{t}) \cdot \mathbf{n} - Z\mathbf{u}_{rot}(\delta\omega) \cdot \mathbf{n}}{\mathbf{u}_{tr}(\hat{\mathbf{t}}) \cdot \mathbf{n}}$$

where $\mathbf{u}_{rot}(\delta\omega)$ is the rotational flow due to the rotational error $\delta\omega = (\hat{\omega} - \omega)$. To make clear the relationship between actual and estimated depth we write

$$\hat{Z} = Z \cdot D \tag{5}$$

with

$$D = \frac{\mathbf{u}_{tr}(\hat{\mathbf{t}}) \cdot \mathbf{n}}{(\mathbf{u}_{tr}(\mathbf{t}) - Z\mathbf{u}_{rot}(\delta\omega)) \cdot \mathbf{n}}$$

hereafter termed the distortion factor. Equation (5) shows how wrong depth estimates are produced due to inaccurate 3D motion values. The distortion factor for any direction $\mathbf{n}$ corresponds to the ratio of the projections of the two vectors $\mathbf{u}_{tr}(\hat{\mathbf{t}})$ and $\mathbf{u}_{tr}(\mathbf{t}) - Z\mathbf{u}_{rot}(\delta\omega)$ on $\mathbf{n}$. The larger the angle between these two vectors, the more the distortion will be spread out over the different directions. Thus, considering a patch of a smooth surface in space and assuming that normal flow measurements are taken along many directions, a rugged (i.e., unsmooth) surface will be computed on the basis of wrong 3D motion estimates.

To give an example, we show the estimated depth for a sequence taken with a hand-held camera in our lab, which we will refer to throughout the paper as "the lab sequence" (one frame is shown in Fig. 1a). For two different translations we estimate the rotation from the vectors perpendicular to the respective translational vectors, as explained in Sect. 3.1, and plot the estimated values of (4). Notice the reasonably smooth depth estimates for the correct FOE in Fig. 1b, and compare the sharp changes in the depth map (neighboring black and white regions) in Fig. 1c.

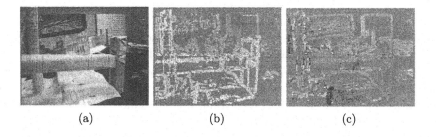

(a)   (b)   (c)

Fig. 1. (a) One input frame of the lab sequence. (b) Inverse depth estimated for the correct FOE ($(397, -115)$ pixels from the image center). (c) Inverse depth for an incorrect FOE ($(-80, 115)$ pixels from image center). The grey-level value represents inverse estimated depth with mid-level grey shown in places where no information was available; white represents positive $1/\hat{Z}$ and black represents negative $1/\hat{Z}$

3   Estimating 3D Motion and Structure

There exists a lot of structure in the world and almost any scene can be thought of as a collection of smooth surface patches separated by abrupt discontinuities. Here the term "smoothness" is not used to mean differentiability, but rather to describe small depth changes within the individual surface patches.

Many previous approaches have used the assumption of locally smooth (constant, linear, or smoothly varying) scene depth. Without the detection of depth discontinuities, however, such approaches are based on an assumption which is not valid everywhere in the image. Explicit consideration of the depth discontinuities brings about one fundamental difference. If (and only if) we are able to detect the depth boundaries between surface patches, we no longer need to make smoothness *assumptions*; we are merely utilizing a property of the world which in the sequel we call the "patch smoothness constraint."

The significance of incorporating the discontinuities has long been understood, and in the past various efforts have been made to estimate smooth flow fields while at the same time detecting discontinuities. (See, for example, Heitz and Bouthemy [5].) Previous work, however, is based on 2D image information only. Here, we attempt to bring in information about the 3D world, in particular the 3D motion and the depth of the scene, and to utilize it together with image measurements for segmentation.

In classical approaches the process of optic flow estimation, which involves smoothing, is separated from the process of 3D motion estimation and structure computation. After optic flow has been fitted to the image data, that is the normal flow, the information about the goodness of the fit is discarded and not considered in the later processes. By combining the processes of smoothing, 3D motion and structure estimation, we utilize this information in all the processes. The estimation of structure and motion thus becomes a geometrical and statistical problem. The challenge lies in understanding how the statistics of the input relate to the geometry of the image information and how to combine the constraints in an efficient way in the development of algorithms.

Due to the large number of unknowns, it is not possible to carry out the computations in a strict bottom-up fashion; they have to be performed in a feedback loop. In the proposed algorithm, first preliminary candidate motion estimates are obtained which are used to segment the scene. On the basis of the segmentation, the 3D motion is recomputed. The basic approach of the algorithm is quite simple. For a given candidate translation, we perform the following steps: estimate the rotation, perform depth segmentation, and finally evaluate a measure of depth smoothness taking into account the segmentation. A search in the space of translations for a minimum of the smoothness measure then yields the best 3D motion. Next we describe a fast technique to estimate the rotation, which is used only to narrow the space of possible 3D motion estimates.

3.1   Projections of Motion Fields and Estimation of Rotation

The search for candidate 3D motions is achieved by searching for the translational component, i.e., the FOE. Given a candidate FOE, we need to estimate the rotation that best fits the image data together with that translation. One possibility is to examine normal flow vectors, in particular, directions. Of particular interest are the *copoint* projections [4], where the flow vectors are projected onto directions perpendicular to a certain translational flow field. Let point $\hat{\mathbf{t}}$ be the FOE in the image plane of this translational field and consider the vectors emanating from $\hat{\mathbf{t}}$. Vectors perpendicular to such vectors are $\mathbf{v}_{cp}(\mathbf{r}) = \hat{\mathbf{z}} \times \mathbf{u}_{tr}(\hat{\mathbf{t}}) = \hat{\mathbf{z}} \times (\hat{\mathbf{z}} \times (\hat{\mathbf{t}} \times \mathbf{r}))$.

Let the camera motion be $(\mathbf{t}, \boldsymbol{\omega})$. The projection of the flow (3) onto $\mathbf{v}_{cp}$ is

$$\dot{\mathbf{r}} \cdot \frac{\mathbf{v}_{cp}}{\|\mathbf{v}_{cp}\|} = \frac{1}{\|\mathbf{v}_{cp}\|} \left(\frac{1}{Z} f\,(\mathbf{t} \times \hat{\mathbf{t}}) \cdot \mathbf{r} + (\boldsymbol{\omega} \times \mathbf{r}) \cdot (\hat{\mathbf{t}} \times \mathbf{r}) \right) \qquad (6)$$

In particular, if we let $\hat{\mathbf{t}} = \mathbf{t}$, the translational component of the copoint projection becomes zero and (6) simplifies into

$$\dot{\mathbf{r}} \cdot \frac{\mathbf{v}_{cp}}{\|\mathbf{v}_{cp}\|} = \frac{1}{\|\mathbf{v}_{cp}\|} (\boldsymbol{\omega} \times \mathbf{r}) \cdot (\hat{\mathbf{t}} \times \mathbf{r}) \qquad (7)$$

Equation (7) can serve as a basis for estimating the rotation. Assume that the translation $\mathbf{t}$ is known. As long as there are some normal flow measurements in the direction of the appropriate copoint vectors, we can set up a linear least squares minimization to estimate $\boldsymbol{\omega}$. Thus, theoretically the 3D motion can be estimated by fitting the best rotation for every candidate translation and checking the size of the residual of the fit. It is easy to compute rotation from copoint vectors, but the dependence on the existence of suitable image measurements is crucial in practice, since such measurements may not be available. As the goodness of the rotational fit doesn't change smoothly between neighboring FOE candidates, it becomes difficult to speed up the search for the correct 3D motion with gradient descent methods. Nevertheless, the residual of the least squares estimate (scaled to account for the varying number of measurements) is usually sufficient to approximately locate the region of interest that most probably contains the correct translation. We thus use this measure first to narrow the space of solutions and then apply the more sophisticated criterion explained in the next section.

3.2   The Criterion

Consider a small image region $\mathcal{R}$ that contains a set of measurements $\dot{\mathbf{r}}_i$ with directions $\mathbf{n}_i$. Given candidate motion parameters, we can estimate the inverse depth from (4) up to the overall scale ambiguity. To treat different patches equally, we normalize the estimated translation $\mathbf{u}_{tr}(\hat{\mathbf{t}})$ to be a unit vector in the middle of the region.

One possible measure of depth variation is the variance of the depth values, or, rather, the sum of squared differences of the depth values from a mean $1/\bar{Z}$:

$$\sum_i \left(\frac{\dot{\mathbf{r}}_i \cdot \mathbf{n}_i - \mathbf{u}_{rot}(\hat{\boldsymbol{\omega}}) \cdot \mathbf{n}_i}{\mathbf{u}_{tr}(\hat{\mathbf{t}}) \cdot \mathbf{n}_i} - \frac{1}{\bar{Z}} \right)^2 \tag{8}$$

Approaches that directly evaluate variations of estimated depth (or inverse depth) include [1][6]. However, depth estimates may present a numerical problem, since for many measurements the depth estimate is unreliable (due to division by a small $\mathbf{u}_{tr} \cdot \mathbf{n}$). Thus we can either ignore many measurements where the depth estimate is unreliable, making comparisons between different translations difficult, or, alternatively, we have to deal with numerical instabilities. We choose a third possibility, defining a whole family of depth smoothness measures that includes the variance of estimated depth as well as many other measures.

In region $\mathcal{R}$ we compute

$$\Theta_0(\hat{\mathbf{t}}, \hat{\boldsymbol{\omega}}, \mathcal{R}) = \sum_i W_i \left(\dot{\mathbf{r}}_i \cdot \mathbf{n}_i - \mathbf{u}_{rot}(\hat{\boldsymbol{\omega}}) \cdot \mathbf{n}_i - (1/\hat{Z})(\mathbf{u}_{tr}(\hat{\mathbf{t}}) \cdot \mathbf{n}_i) \right)^2 \tag{9}$$

where $1/\hat{Z}$ is the depth estimate minimizing the measure, i.e., not necessarily the mean $1/\bar{Z}$.

By setting $W_i = 1/(\mathbf{u}_{tr}(\hat{\mathbf{t}}) \cdot \mathbf{n}_i)^2$ we obtain (8). Another natural choice is $W_i = 1$. Then Θ_0 becomes the sum of squared differences between the normal flow measurements and the corresponding projections of the best flow obtained from the motion parameters. This measure has been used in [7].

With different choices of W_i we can either emphasize the contributions from the copoint vectors (that is, the vectors perpendicular to the translational component), which are independent of depth, or the vectors parallel to the translation, which are most strongly influenced by depth. As long as we keep W_i bounded, criterion (9) nicely combines the contribution of the two perpendicular components. In our algorithm we use two sets of weights to achieve different numerical properties for the estimation of different parameters, as will be discussed later in the paper.

We first minimize Θ_0 with respect to $1/\hat{Z}$. The best inverse depth is

$$\frac{1}{\hat{Z}} = \frac{\sum_i W_i \left(\dot{\mathbf{r}}_i \cdot \mathbf{n}_i - \mathbf{u}_{rot}(\hat{\boldsymbol{\omega}}) \cdot \mathbf{n}_i \right) \left(\mathbf{u}_{tr}(\hat{\mathbf{t}}) \cdot \mathbf{n}_i \right)}{\sum_i W_i \left(\mathbf{u}_{tr}(\hat{\mathbf{t}}) \cdot \mathbf{n}_i \right)^2} \tag{10}$$

If more precision is required (in our experiments with small patches, the constant approximation worked quite well), we can model the scene patch by a general plane and use a linear approximation $1/\hat{Z} = \mathbf{z} \cdot \mathbf{r}$ (note that the third component of $\mathbf{r}$ is a constant f, so $\mathbf{z} \cdot \mathbf{r}$ is a general linear function of the image coordinates). Then we have

$$\frac{\partial \Theta_0(\hat{\mathbf{t}}, \hat{\boldsymbol{\omega}}, \mathcal{R})}{\partial \mathbf{z}} = \sum_i W_i (\mathbf{z} \cdot \mathbf{r}_i)(\mathbf{u}_{tr}(\hat{\mathbf{t}}) \cdot \mathbf{n}_i)^2 \mathbf{r}_i$$

$$- \sum_i W_i (\dot{\mathbf{r}}_i \cdot \mathbf{n} - \mathbf{u}_{rot}(\hat{\boldsymbol{\omega}}) \cdot \mathbf{n}_i)(\mathbf{u}_{tr}(\hat{\mathbf{t}}) \cdot \mathbf{n}_i) \mathbf{r}_i = 0 \tag{11}$$

a set of three linear equations for the three components of $\mathbf{z}$.

Substituting (10) (or the solution of (11)) into (9), we obtain $\Theta_1(\hat{\mathbf{t}}, \hat{\omega}, \mathcal{R})$, a second order function of $\hat{\omega}$. Notice that the computation can be performed symbolically even when $\hat{\omega}$ is not known. This allows us to use the same equations to obtain both the rotation and a measure of depth smoothness.

To estimate $\hat{\omega}$, we sum up all the local functions and obtain a global function:

$$\Theta_2(\hat{\mathbf{t}}, \hat{\omega}) = \sum_{\mathcal{R}} \Theta_1(\hat{\mathbf{t}}, \hat{\omega}, \mathcal{R}) \tag{12}$$

Finally, global minimization yields the best rotation $\hat{\omega}$ and also a measure of depth smoothness for the apparent translation $\hat{\mathbf{t}}$:

$$\Phi(\hat{\mathbf{t}}) = \min_{\hat{\omega}} \Theta_2(\hat{\mathbf{t}}, \hat{\omega}) \tag{13}$$

The computation of $\Phi(\hat{\mathbf{t}})$ involves two separate steps. First we estimate the best rotation $\hat{\omega}$ and in the second step we evaluate the global smoothness measure for the motion $(\hat{\mathbf{t}}, \hat{\omega})$. In the two steps of computing $\Phi(\hat{\mathbf{t}})$ we choose different weights W_i in function Θ_0.

To estimate the rotation, we use one set of weights W_i' defining Θ_0' and subsequently Θ_1', Θ_2'. The rotation is computed as

$$\hat{\omega}_0 = \operatorname*{argmin}_{\hat{\omega}} \Theta_2'(\hat{\mathbf{t}}, \hat{\omega})$$

We also define Θ_0 using a different set of weights W_i. Functions Θ_1 and Θ_2 are derived from Θ_0 and the global depth smoothness function $\Phi(\hat{\mathbf{t}})$ becomes

$$\Phi(\hat{\mathbf{t}}) = \Theta_2(\hat{\mathbf{t}}, \hat{\omega}_0) = \Theta_2(\hat{\mathbf{t}}, \operatorname*{argmin}_{\hat{\omega}} \Theta_2'(\hat{\mathbf{t}}, \hat{\omega})) \tag{14}$$

Now we need to describe our choices of the weights. Ideally, if we could guarantee the existence of a sufficient number of copoint measurements, we could estimate the rotation $\hat{\omega}$ from (7). Such measurements are independent of the scene depth; thus they are the best source of information about $\hat{\omega}$ and consequently should have more influence on Θ_0. Direct evaluation of the depth variance, however, means that in (8) the weighting factor for copoint vectors tends to infinity.

To prevent numerical instability, the weights W_i' should certainly be bounded. For the rotation estimation part, we use

$$W_i' = \frac{1}{\cos^2 \psi_i + \lambda} \tag{15}$$

where ψ_i is the angle between $\mathbf{u}_{\mathrm{tr}}(\hat{\mathbf{t}})$ and $\mathbf{n}_i$, λ is a small positive number.

After we use weights W_i' to obtain the best rotation from Θ_2', we need to evaluate a global depth smoothness function to obtain $\Phi(\hat{\mathbf{t}})$. As we need to compare $\Phi(\hat{\mathbf{t}})$ values for different directions of $\hat{\mathbf{t}}$, we choose constant weights

$$W_i = 1 \tag{16}$$

Then the contribution to $\Phi(\hat{\mathbf{t}})$ of a single normal flow measurement is $(\dot{r}_i \cdot \mathbf{n}_i - \mathbf{u}_{\mathrm{rot}}(\hat{\omega}) \cdot \mathbf{n}_i - (1/\hat{Z})(\mathbf{u}_{\mathrm{tr}}(\hat{\mathbf{t}}) \cdot \mathbf{n}_i))^2$ and has a clear geometrical meaning. It is the squared difference between the normal flow and the corresponding projection of the best flow obtained from the motion parameters. More importantly, such squared errors can be easily compared for different directions of $\hat{\mathbf{t}}$.

3.3 Algorithm Description

The translation is found by localizing the minimum of function $\Phi(\hat{\mathbf{t}})$ described in (14). To obtain $\Phi(\hat{\mathbf{t}})$:

1. Partition the image into small regions, in each region compute $\Theta_0'(\hat{\mathbf{t}}, \hat{\omega}, \mathcal{R})$ using (15), and perform local minimization of $\hat{Z}$ (the computation is symbolic in the unknown elements of $\hat{\omega}$). After substitution, the function becomes $\Theta_1'(\hat{\mathbf{t}}, \hat{\omega}, \mathcal{R})$. At the same time, compute Θ_0 and Θ_1 using (16).
2. Add all the local functions $\Theta_1'(\hat{\mathbf{t}}, \hat{\omega}, \mathcal{R})$ and minimize the resulting $\Theta_2'(\hat{\mathbf{t}}, \hat{\omega})$ to obtain $\hat{\omega}_0$. Also add $\Theta_1(\hat{\mathbf{t}}, \hat{\omega}, \mathcal{R})$ to obtain $\Theta_2(\hat{\mathbf{t}}, \hat{\omega})$.
3. Estimate depth using $\hat{\mathbf{t}}$, $\hat{\omega}_0$ and perform patch segmentation.
4. Taking the segmentation into account, update both Θ_2 and Θ_2', use Θ_2' to compute a better rotational estimate, and the updated Θ_2 then provides $\Phi(\hat{\mathbf{t}})$.

After the segmentation, we recompute the error measure by enforcing smoothness only within image regions that do not contain a depth discontinuity. However, it is not necessary to re-derive Θ_1 for all the image regions, as we need to compute the change of Θ_1 only for the regions that are segmented. To find the minimum of Φ and thus the apparent translation, we perform a hierarchical search over the two-dimensional space of epipole positions. In practice, the function Φ is quite smooth; that is, small changes in $\hat{\mathbf{t}}$ give rise to only small changes in Φ. One of the reasons for this is that for any $\hat{\mathbf{t}}$, the value of $\Phi(\hat{\mathbf{t}})$ is influenced by all the normal flow measurements and not only by a small subset. Furthermore, as explained before, $\Phi(\hat{\mathbf{t}})$ is only computed when the residual of fitting the copoint vectors (7) is small enough. The details of the segmentation process will not be discussed here due to lack of space. The interested reader is referred to [2].

3.4 Algorithm Analysis

Consider the function Θ_0 in a small image region $\mathcal{R}$. The vectors $\mathbf{u}_{\mathrm{tr}}(\hat{\mathbf{t}})$ and $\mathbf{u}_{\mathrm{rot}}(\hat{\omega})$ are polynomial functions of image position $\mathbf{r}$ and can usually be approximated by constants within the region. We use a local coordinate system where $\mathbf{u}_{\mathrm{tr}}(\hat{\mathbf{t}})$ is parallel to $[1, 0, 0]^{\mathrm{T}}$. Without loss of generality we can write (in that coordinate system)

$$\mathbf{u}_{\mathrm{tr}}(\hat{\mathbf{t}}) = [1, 0, 0]^{\mathrm{T}} \qquad \mathbf{u}_{\mathrm{rot}}(\hat{\omega}) = [u_{\mathrm{rx}}, u_{\mathrm{ry}}, 0]^{\mathrm{T}}$$
$$\mathbf{n}_i = [\cos\psi_i, \sin\psi_i, 0]^{\mathrm{T}} \qquad u_{\mathbf{n}_i} = \dot{r}_i \cdot \mathbf{n}_i \tag{17}$$

As the following analysis proves, the depth smoothness measure for a single image region can be decomposed into two components, one component which measures the deviation of the patch from a smooth scene patch (which is a fronto-parallel plane in the given analysis) and a second component which constitutes a multiple of the epipolar constraint. To show this, consider the problem of fitting the best constant optical flow (u_x, u_y) to the measurements in $\mathcal{R}$, using weights W_i, i.e., minimizing

$$\sum_i W_i \left(u_{n_i} - (u_x, u_y) \cdot \mathbf{n}_i\right)^2 \tag{18}$$

The vector (u_x, u_y) minimizing (18) is obtained by differentiating (18) and solving a linear system. We obtain

$$\begin{pmatrix} u_x \\ u_y \end{pmatrix} = \frac{1}{S_{cc}S_{ss} - S_{cs}^2} \begin{pmatrix} S_{ss} & -S_{cs} \\ -S_{cs} & S_{cc} \end{pmatrix} \begin{pmatrix} S_{uc} \\ S_{us} \end{pmatrix} \tag{19}$$

and the minimum error is

$$E_F = S_{uu} - \frac{1}{S_{cc}S_{ss} - S_{cs}^2}(S_{us}^2 S_{cc} + S_{uc}^2 S_{ss} - 2S_{uc}S_{us}S_{cs}) \tag{20}$$

with

$$\begin{aligned} S_{cc} &= \sum W_i \cos^2 \psi_i & S_{uc} &= \sum W_i \, u_{n_i} \cos \psi_i \\ S_{cs} &= \sum W_i \cos \psi_i \sin \psi_i & S_{us} &= \sum W_i \, u_{n_i} \sin \psi_i \\ S_{ss} &= \sum W_i \sin^2 \psi_i & S_{uu} &= \sum W_i \, u_{n_i}^2 \end{aligned} \tag{21}$$

Using the notation (17) we have

$$\Theta_0 = \sum_i W_i \left(u_{n_i} - u_{rx} \cos \psi_i - u_{ry} \sin \psi_i - \frac{1}{\hat{Z}} \cos \psi_i\right)^2 \tag{22}$$

It can be verified that u_{rx} only shifts the best $1/\hat{Z}$, but it does not influence the final measure. Thus we can set u_{rx} to zero without loss of generality and expand Θ_0 to $\Theta_0 = S_{uu} + u_{ry}^2 S_{ss} + (1/\hat{Z})^2 S_{cc} - 2u_{ry}S_{us} - 21/\hat{Z}S_{uc} + 21/\hat{Z}u_{ry}S_{cs}$. Minimization of Θ_0 yields $1/\hat{Z} = (S_{uc} - u_{ry}S_{cs})/(S_{cc})$. Let us denote $u_{ry} = u_y + \delta u_{ry}$. Measure Θ_1 is thus obtained by substituting the above equations into Θ_0. We obtain

$$\Theta_1 = \frac{S_{cc}S_{ss} - S_{cs}^2}{S_{cc}} \delta u_{ry}^2 + E_F \tag{23}$$

As we show in the next section, if the optical flow in the patch were estimated based on minimization of (18), δu_{ry} would represent the distance of the estimated flow from the epipolar line.

Thus the first component in (23) is related to the epipolar constraint and it depends on the 3D motion estimate, as well as the gradient distribution in the patch. The second component in (23), E_F, represents how well the scene is approximated by a plane and it is independent of the 3D motion estimate. In classic approaches, after optic flow is computed, the term E_F is not considered any further and the estimation of 3D motion parameters is based only on the distance from the epipolar line. Here we keep this term to utilize it for segmentation.

3.5   The Epipolar Constraint

The depth smoothness measure is closely related to the traditional epipolar constraint and we examine the relationship here. In the instantaneous form the epipolar constraint can be written as

$$(\hat{\mathbf{z}} \times \mathbf{u}_{tr}(\hat{\mathbf{t}})) \cdot (\dot{\mathbf{r}} - \mathbf{u}_{rot}(\hat{\boldsymbol{\omega}})) = 0 \tag{24}$$

Usually, the distance of the flow vector $\dot{\mathbf{r}}$ from the epipolar line (determined by $\mathbf{u}_{tr}(\hat{\mathbf{t}})$ and $\mathbf{u}_{rot}(\hat{\boldsymbol{\omega}})$) is computed, and the sum of the squared distances, i.e.,

$$\sum \left((\hat{\mathbf{z}} \times \mathbf{u}_{tr}(\hat{\mathbf{t}})) \cdot (\dot{\mathbf{r}} - \mathbf{u}_{rot}(\hat{\boldsymbol{\omega}})) \right)^2 \tag{25}$$

is minimized.

Methods based upon (25) suffer from bias, however, and a scaled epipolar constraint has been used to give an unbiased solution:

$$\sum \frac{\left((\hat{\mathbf{z}} \times \mathbf{u}_{tr}(\hat{\mathbf{t}})) \cdot (\dot{\mathbf{r}} - \mathbf{u}_{rot}(\hat{\boldsymbol{\omega}})) \right)^2}{\|\mathbf{u}_{tr}(\hat{\mathbf{t}})\|^2} \tag{26}$$

Again, we use the coordinate system and notation of (17). Suppose that the flow vector $\dot{\mathbf{r}}$ has been obtained by minimization of (18) and write it as (u_x, u_y). Substituting into (26) we obtain

$$\frac{\left((\hat{\mathbf{z}} \times \mathbf{u}_{tr}(\hat{\mathbf{t}})) \cdot (\dot{\mathbf{r}} - \mathbf{u}_{rot}(\hat{\boldsymbol{\omega}})) \right)^2}{\|\mathbf{u}_{tr}(\hat{\mathbf{t}})\|^2} = (u_y - u_{ry})^2 = \delta u_{ry}^2 \tag{27}$$

Equations (27) and (23) illustrate the relationship of the epipolar constraint (for the general case using non-standard weights to estimate flow) and the smoothness measure Θ_1.

4   Uncalibrated Camera and Self-Calibration

In the case of an uncalibrated camera the approach remains essentially the same, although technically more involved, and will not be described here. The interested reader is referred to [2]. In this case, the image motion field is

$$\dot{\mathbf{r}} = -\frac{1}{F(\mathbf{R} \cdot \hat{\mathbf{z}})} (\hat{\mathbf{z}} \times (\mathbf{K}\mathbf{t} \times \mathbf{r})) + \frac{1}{F} (\hat{\mathbf{z}} \times (\mathbf{r} \times (\mathbf{K}[\boldsymbol{\omega}]_\times \mathbf{K}^{-1}\mathbf{r})))$$

$$= \frac{1}{Z} \mathbf{u}_{tr}(\mathbf{K}\mathbf{t}) + \mathbf{u}'_{rot}(\mathbf{K}[\boldsymbol{\omega}]_\times \mathbf{K}^{-1}) \tag{28}$$

where Z is used to denote the scene depth $(\mathbf{R} \cdot \hat{\mathbf{z}})$ and

$$[\boldsymbol{\omega}]_\times = \begin{pmatrix} 0 & -\gamma & \beta \\ \gamma & 0 & -\alpha \\ -\beta & \alpha & 0 \end{pmatrix}, \quad \mathbf{K} = \begin{pmatrix} f_x & s & \Delta_x \\ 0 & f_y & \Delta_y \\ 0 & 0 & F \end{pmatrix}$$

the matrix of the calibration parameters in common notation F is a constant we can choose, also used as the third coordinate of image point vectors $[x, y, F]^\mathrm{T}$. The translational component of the field is identical to a calibrated translational field with translation $\mathbf{Kt}$. The rotational component $\mathbf{u}'_\mathrm{rot}$ is slightly more complicated in the uncalibrated case (compare (28) and (3)). The flow $\mathbf{u}'_\mathrm{rot}$ is determined by the matrix $\mathbf{A} = \mathbf{K}[\boldsymbol{\omega}]_\times \mathbf{K}^{-1}$ with seven degrees of freedom. As shown in [1], for a given translation $\tilde{\mathbf{t}}$, matrix $\mathbf{A}$ can be decomposed into $\mathbf{A} = \mathbf{A}_\mathrm{c} + \mathbf{A}_\mathrm{t} = \mathbf{A}_\mathrm{c} + F\tilde{\mathbf{t}}\mathbf{w}^\mathrm{T} + w_0\,\mathbf{I}$.

Matrix $\mathbf{A}_\mathrm{c}$ (also called a copoint matrix) depends on five independent parameters and is the component of $\mathbf{A}$ that can be estimated (together with the direction of $\mathbf{Kt}$) from a single flow field. The vector $\mathbf{w}$ determines the plane at infinity and it cannot be obtained from a single flow field. Finally, w_0 can be computed from the condition trace $\mathbf{A} = 0$. If $\hat{\mathbf{t}}$ is an estimate of $\mathbf{Kt}$ and $\hat{\mathbf{A}}_\mathrm{c}$ an estimate of the copoint matrix $\mathbf{A}_\mathrm{c}$, we use $\mathbf{u}'_\mathrm{rot}(\hat{\mathbf{A}}_\mathrm{c})$ instead of $\mathbf{u}_\mathrm{rot}(\hat{\boldsymbol{\omega}})$ in (9) to obtain

$$\Theta_0(\hat{\mathbf{t}}, \hat{\mathbf{A}}_\mathrm{c}, \mathcal{R}) = \sum_i W_i \left(\dot{\mathbf{r}}_i \cdot \mathbf{n}_i - \mathbf{u}'_\mathrm{rot}(\hat{\mathbf{A}}_\mathrm{c}) \cdot \mathbf{n}_i - (1/\hat{Z})(\mathbf{u}_\mathrm{tr}(\hat{\mathbf{t}}) \cdot \mathbf{n}_i) \right)^2 \qquad (29)$$

The solution proceeds as before, with one difference. In the calibrated case, the rotational component of $\dot{\mathbf{r}}$ can be compensated for completely by the correct $\hat{\boldsymbol{\omega}}$. Here, the unknown parameters in $\hat{\mathbf{A}}$ introduce a component of the image normal flow in the form $(\mathbf{w} \cdot \mathbf{r})\mathbf{u}_\mathrm{tr}(\hat{\mathbf{t}})$ that cannot be expressed as part of $\mathbf{u}'_\mathrm{rot}(\hat{\mathbf{A}}_\mathrm{c})$. We therefore have to use a linear fit to the scene inverse depth $1/\hat{Z} = (\mathbf{z} \cdot \mathbf{r})$, i.e., define Θ_1 using the solution of (11). Then $\mathbf{z}$ incorporates the unknown rotational parameters $\mathbf{w}$ and the resulting smoothness criterion is independent of the rotation.

5   Experimental Results

We present various experiments testing the different aspects of the introduced method. In particular, we demonstrate the ability of the technique to extract depth edges and provide a comparison between the smoothness measure and the epipolar constraint. The optical flow fields needed in the comparison were derived with the method of Lucas and Kanade. Throughout this section, two sequences are used, the lab sequence, as shown in Fig. 1a, and the well known Yosemite fly-through sequence.

Experiment 1. In this experiment we evaluated the accuracy in 3D motion estimation. In particular, we compared our method using a minimization based on the function $\Phi(\hat{\mathbf{t}})$ without segmentation, with segmentation, and a minimization based on the epipolar constraint.

For the Yosemite sequence, both our method and the epipolar minimization perform quite well. The known epipole location in the image plane was $(0, -100)$. The estimated epipole locations for the different methods are summarized in Table 1.

Experiment 2. The lab sequence contained several significant depth discontinuities and for the majority of frames our method performed better than the epipolar minimization. No ground truth was available, but we visually inspected the instantaneous scene depth recovered. Out of a 90-frame subsequence tested with both methods, the epipolar minimization yielded 25 frames with clearly incorrect depth (i.e., many negative depth estimates or reversed depth order for large parts of the scene). The performance of our method was significantly better, as only 7 frames yielded clearly incorrect depth. Some failures of the epipolar minimization are shown in Fig. 2. For some frames, the recovered depth was reversed, i.e., the background was closer than the foreground, as in Fig. 2b. In other frames, some parts of the scene had negative recovered depth, as in Fig. 2d, where the black regions correspond to negative depth.

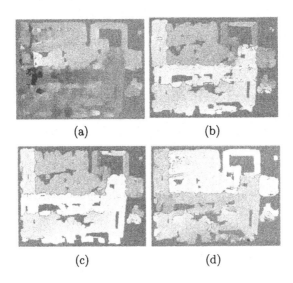

(a)   (b)

(c)   (d)

Fig. 2. Comparison of recovered inverse depth for the lab sequence using the epipole positions as estimated with the proposed algorithm and the epipolar minimization. (a, b) Frame 134. (a) Depth variation, epipole: $(377, -125)$, (b) Epipolar minimization, epipole: $(-612, 256)$. (c, d) Frame 142. (a) Depth variation, epipole: $(483, -123)$, (b) Epipolar minimization, epipole: $(-153, 18)$

Experiment 3. The lab sequence was taken by a hand-held Panasonic D5000 camera with a zoom setting of approximately 12mm. Unfortunately, the effective focal length of the pinhole camera model was also influenced by the focus setting and we thus knew the intrinsic parameters only approximately. The internal parameters were fixed and were approximately $f_x = f_y = 450$, $\Delta_x = \Delta_y = s = 0$. The focal lengths were slightly overestimated, but consistent for different frames of the sequence. The calibration results are summarized in Table 2.

Table 1. Estimated epipole locations for the Yosemite sequence.

method	epipole
ground truth	$(0.0, -100.0)$
epipolar minimization	$(10.5, -94.8)$
$\Phi(\hat{\mathbf{t}})$ (no segmentation)	$(2.4, -96.7)$
$\Phi(\hat{\mathbf{t}})$ (incl. segmentation)	$(0.0, -103.6)$

Table 2. Self-calibration results for the lab sequence.

frms.	f_x	f_y	Δ_x	Δ_y	s
001–300	536	522	16	26	3
001–100	541	543	−33	6	−25
101–200	544	475	26	−38	14
201–300	548	513	−11	8	6

Experiment 4. The self-calibration results can be used to build Euclidean models of the scene, but further research is needed to link the individual frames and reliably combine the partial depth estimates in order to create a volumetric model of the scene. Here we present a reconstruction that shows the depth values obtained from the Lab sequence during the motion estimation process.

Fig. 3. Two views of a 3D reconstruction of the recovered depth combined from 15 image frames

6 Conclusions

In classical approaches to visual motion analysis the processes of smoothing, 3D motion estimation, and structure estimation are separated from each other. Statistical information obtained from the raw data in early processes (image motion estimation) is not utilized any longer in later ones (3D motion and structure estimation). By combining the different processes one can utilize this information throughout. This gives us the potential ability to solve the problem of structure from motion without making assumptions regarding the scene structure throughout the computations. Such an approach was developed in this paper. We computed 3D motion and structure by minimizing function Θ_1 defined on the normal flow data. We showed that at an image patch $\Theta_1 = C\, \delta u_{\mathrm{ry}}^2 + E_{\mathrm{F}}$, with E_{F} the error of the least squares fit to the image measurements of an optical flow corresponding to a linear scene depth, δu_{ry} the deviation from the epipolar constraint and C a factor that depends only on the positions and directions of the normal flow measurements in the region. The larger the variation of the normal flow directions, the larger C is, thus giving more weight to regions where more information is available. In a smooth patch (i.e., an image patch corresponding to a smooth scene patch), $E_F = 0$, making the minimization of Θ_1 equivalent to weighted epipolar minimization. But for a non-smooth patch where the optic flow computation is unreliable, $E_F \neq 0$ and this statistical information was utilized for finding depth boundaries.

References

[1] Brodský, T., Fermüller, C., Aloimonos, Y.: Self-Calibration from Image Derivatives in: *Proc. International Conference on Computer Vision* 1998 83–89
[2] Brodský, T., Fermüller, C., Aloimonos, Y.: Simultaneous Estimation of Viewing Geometry and Structure Technical report Center for Automation Research University of Maryland (1998) To appear
[3] Cheong, L., Fermüller, C., Aloimonos, Y.: Effects of Errors in the Viewing Geometry on Shape Estimation Computer Vision and Image Understanding **71** (1998) 356–372
[4] Fermüller, C.: Navigational Preliminaries in: Aloimonos, Y. (ed.), *Active Perception* Lawrence Erlbaum Associates, Hillsdale, NJ Advances in Computer Vision 1993 103–150
[5] Heitz, F., Bouthemy, P.: Multimodal Estimation of Discontinuous Optical Flow Using Markov Random Fields IEEE Transactions on Pattern Analysis and Machine Intelligence **15** (1993) 1217–1232
[6] Horn, B. K. P., Weldon, E. J.: Direct methods for recovering motion International Journal of Computer Vision **2** (1988) 51–76
[7] Mendelsohn, J., Simoncelli, E., Bajcsy, R.: Discrete-Time Rigidity Constrained Optical Flow in: *Proc. 7th International Conference on Computer Analysis of Images and Patterns* Springer, Berlin 1997

Real-Time Inverse Kinematics through Constrained Dynamics

Wen Tang, Marc Cavazza, Dale Mountain & Rae Earnshaw

Department of Electronic Imaging and Media Communications, University of Bradford
Bradford, BD7 1DP, United Kingdom
E-mail:{W.Tang, M.Cavazza, D.L.Mountain, R.A.Earnshaw}@Bradford.ac.uk

Abstract. Motion capture is an essential technique for interactive systems, such as distributed virtual reality, video games, and entertainment. Inverse kinematics algorithms are often used to minimize the number of trackers required for motion capture systems. The solving of inverse kinematics problems can be computationally expensive. We introduce a real-time algorithm for inverse kinematics computation, originally from the field of molecular simulation, called SHAKE. We also describe the implementation of the algorithm in our motion capture system for avatar motion generation through constraint dynamics. We demonstrate that the algorithm has advantages over conventional methods with properties of fast convergence, energy stability, and constraint system consistency when adding additional constraints.

1. Introduction

Realistic animation of avatars in distributed virtual environments is best achieved through real-time motion capture for example electromagnetic and optical trackers. Inverse kinematics methods are often used to minimize the number of trackers required by solving the values of joint angles of the avatar using constraints such as geometric relationships of avatar components. However the algorithm needs to produce results within a time range compatible with the tracker's sampling frequency. Inverse kinematics algorithms are also used to generate smoothed motion of the avatar from the goal position through minimization of constraints such as energy [1].

One of the conventional methods to solve inverse kinematics problems is to find the inverse matrix to the Jacobian Matrix J. Equation (1) gives the relationship between joint velocities and the velocity of the end-effector [2].

$$x = J(q)q$$
$$J = \frac{\partial f}{\partial q} \qquad (1)$$

Nadia Magnenat-Thalmann, Daniel Thalmann (Eds.): CAPTECH'98, LNAI 1537, pp. 159-170, 1998.

In many cases, however, such as when J is not a square matrix, there is no unique inverse to J. This may result in multiple solutions to the same trajectory. Furthermore the formal method is to minimize the Moor-Penrose generalized inverse matrix [2].

$$\tilde{J} = J^T \cdot [J \cdot J^T]^{-1} \qquad (2)$$

Researchers have used the pseudo-inverse method for gait generation and control systems [3], [4].

The alternative approach to the above matrix inversion method is to use iterative optimization techniques to minimize the objective functions for the goal position approximation. These objective functions can be any arbitrary functions so long as they represent the characteristics of the system constraints [5], [1]. The global minimization is not guaranteed in this kind of approach [6]. Moreover adding extra constraints to the system is not always straightforward and may change the entire computational strategy.

For avatar motion generation, the skeleton of the avatar can be considered as a system of rigid bodies interconnected by joints with fixed inter-joint distances and subject to the interaction-forces acting on the constraints. In such a case, the methods for solving the inverse kinematics problem are to find the solutions of the constrained equations of motion, which can be expressed as differential equations as follows [7]:

$$\frac{d}{dt} q = M^{-1} p$$

$$\frac{d}{dt} p = -\nabla_q F(q) - g_q(q)^T \lambda \qquad (3)$$

$$0 = q(p)$$

Where $p, q \in \mathbf{R}^n$, M is a n x n regular (symmetric, positive definite) mass matrix, F(q) is the (empirical) potential energy function, and λ represents the n Lagrange multipliers or constraint force coupled to the system by the n x n constraint matrix $G := \partial q / \partial p$.

To solve these differential equations, several numerical integration algorithms can be applied. Iterative discretization schemes for numerical integration of constrained motion in a Lagrange framework such as the system described as equation (3) are very popular methods for solving inverse kinematics problems in computer animation and motion capture [6], [8]. This is because the schemes can provide relatively simple computational operations and avoid the complex matrix inversion step, which lacks generality and flexibility for the changes of the geometry and trajectory of the skeleton.

In this paper, we described the implementation of an alternative solving method for inverse kinematics computations, which is also an iterative algorithm. It is based on a numerical algorithm called SHAKE which was originally developed in the field of molecular dynamics [9], [10]. This algorithm has recently been applied to inverse kinematics problems in the field of robotics [2], and we hereby present a real-time implementation adapted to motion capture for avatar motion generation.

2. The SHAKE Algorithm

The SHAKE algorithm is essentially an iterative algorithm for numerical integration of constrained motion in a Lagrange framework. The primary purpose of introducing the algorithm is to reduce computation time by increasing the time step, since molecular dynamics simulation on large systems is computationally expensive. The algorithm is considered as a modification to the Verlet method [11] to solve constrained motions in molecular models in which all constraints can be represented by fixed distances (angle constraints can also be expressed in this way). In the following section, we give a brief overview of the method, which is based on [12], [13], [14], and [15].

2.1 The Constrained Chain Structure of the Avatar

The SHAKE algorithm has been initially described by Ryckaert et al to solve equations of motion for branched linear chains [9]. It is thus easily adapted to a skeletal model of an avatar such as the one illustrated in Figure 1, in which the skeleton has a similar set of constraints.

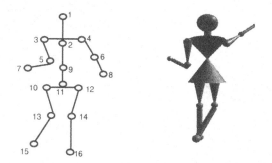

Fig. 1. Constrained chains of a skeletal model and an avatar

We designed a chain body structure for our initial implementation, which is a collection of constraint-joint masses with fixed inter-joint distances.   Sixteen constraint joints are used.   As the body system possesses a small number of constraints, the inverse kinematics of the system can be solved efficiently by the algorithm. The total convergence time of a constraints system is a function of the number of constraints and the constraint geometry topology. Some experimental work shows that the time complexity is approximately $O(n^2)$, where n is the number of constraints [12]. In [13], it stated that on a single processor, SHAKE typically takes 5 ~ 20 % of the total computation time for a molecular simulation. Adding additional constraints can be done without redesigning the existing system. Circular constraints can also be handled[1]

2.2 The Algorithm

Considering that all constraints in a linked dynamic system can be represented by fixed distances, a constraint on the distance between joints i and j can be expressed by the following geometric relation:

$$|r|^2 - l^2 = 0 \qquad (4)$$

Where r is the vector from joint i to j, and l is the distance from joint i to j.

A simple two-step discretization was used by Verlet [11] to solve unconstrained equations. In contrast, the SHAKE algorithm is a direct numerical integration scheme based on the Verlet method to solve the constrained equations of motion, as expressed in equation (3), using a set of appropriate Lagrange multipliers. In the case of inverse kinematics, there is no integration of the potential energy and only the constraint component has to be integrated.

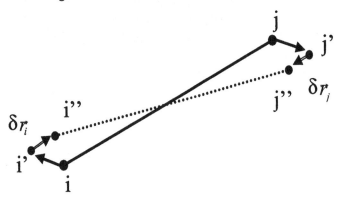

Fig. 2. The SHAKE algorithm: after i and j are allowed unconstrained displacements (i',j'), correcting steps are applied to enforce the constraint

The SHAKE algorithm consists of applying correcting vectors to the unconstrained displacements of the constraint vectors' vertices, as shown in Figure 2. The SHAKE algorithm involves a two step schemes. The original positions of vertices are firstly moved by a given small amount of movement, say i-to-i' and j-to-j'. In order to restore the constraint, a constraint force is then applied to enforce the vertices moving toward one another (i'-to-i" and j'-to-j") along the vector direction given at the previous time step $\mathbf{r}_{ij}$ by amounts that are inversely proportional to their respective

---

[1] Ko & Badler have described the closed-loop problem in their system for animating human locomotion with inverse dynamics [19].

masses. The iterations are carried out until the absolute values of all constraints are within the given tolerance.

Where the correcting step can be derived from a Lagrange-type constraint force acting to enforce the previously defined constraints [9]:

$$\vec{r}'' = \vec{r}' + \delta \vec{r} \qquad (5)$$

The constraint force can be expressed with following equation:

$$c_i(t) = -\lambda \vec{\nabla}_i \sigma(t) = 2\lambda \ \vec{r}(t) \qquad (6)$$

From which it can be shown that the correcting vectors take the form:

$$\delta \vec{r} = \gamma \frac{(\Delta t)^2}{m_i} \vec{r} \qquad (7)$$

The corresponding Lagrange multipliers can be computed from the requirement that the constraint (of length l) should be enforced after applying the correcting step:

$$(\vec{r}' + \delta \ \vec{r})^2 - l^2 = 0 \qquad (8)$$

Which yields a simple quadratic equation [10]:

$$M^2 \gamma^2 \vec{r} \cdot \vec{r} + 2M\gamma \ \vec{r} \cdot \vec{r}' + \vec{r}' \cdot \vec{r}' - l^2 = 0$$

$$M = \frac{1}{m_i} + \frac{1}{m_j} \qquad (9)$$

Where m_i and m_j are the masses of the particles linked by the constraint.

For sufficiently small time steps (or in our case sufficiently high sampling frequencies) the quadratic term can be ignored. This gives the following formula for γ:

$$\gamma = \frac{l^2 - \vec{r}' \cdot \vec{r}'}{2M\vec{r} \cdot \vec{r}'} \qquad (10)$$

As shown in Figure 2, the displacements are parallel to the direction of the original vector. In this perspective SHAKE essentially consists of applying correcting steps to those vertices that have moved. As enforcing a constraint might disrupt another constraint in which the same joint was participating, the SHAKE procedure is iterated over all the constraints until they are all within a given tolerance. Despite this popular and "trivial" interpretation, it should not be overlooked that SHAKE belongs to a family of classical integration approaches and is still "matrix integration in disguise"

[14]. More specifically, SHAKE is derived from a leapfrog/Verlet approach[2], which was introduced as an alternative to multi-step schemes and Runge-Kutta methods [14]. It has also been shown that SHAKE is equivalent to a 1-step non-linear Gauss-Siedel-Newton iteration [15][3]. In theory the convergence of SHAKE was not guaranteed, and it was sometimes referred to as "unreasonably efficient", however, it has recently been revisited by Leimkuhler and Skeel [14]. They demonstrate a mathematical proof for its convergence. Local convergence of SHAKE is guaranteed precisely when standard Gauss-Seidel iteration converges for the linear system as long as the unconstrained approximations such as the first displacements to the system are sufficiently small.

3. Experimental Results

We adapted the SHAKE algorithm to our motion capture system to solve the inverse kinematics problem for the avatar motion generation and motion control. Experiments have been carried out to test the feasibility of SHAKE for avatar motion generation and to confirm SHAKE's properties in terms of fast convergence and long term energy stability ("no drift" integration). These two properties are particularly useful for real-time motion capture applications and computer animation. In these experiments, each time step corresponds to an unconstrained movement followed by an application of SHAKE until convergence. Bearing in mind that in the case of inverse kinematics the positions of the trackers are accurate, we associate extremely large masses to the joints associated with the trackers to keep them stationery when resolving the skeletal system using SHAKE e.g. Kastenmeier & Vesely [2] use an infinite mass.

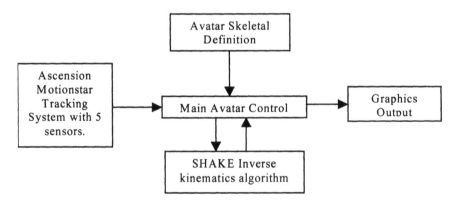

Fig. 3. Overview of the system architecture

---

[2] Which explains that SHAKE is sometimes referred to as "constrained Verlet" [10]. Derivation of SHAKE from the Verlet algorithm is demonstrated in [14].

[3] This method arises from iterative solutions based on a Moore-Penrose pseudoinverse matrix [16] A formulation in terms of the Moore-penrose pseudoinverse matrix is also given by Kastenmeier &Vesely [2].

Figure 3 shows the overview of the system architecture. The motion tracking system exports the values of positional translation and angular rotation of each sensor to our gesture generation system via TCP/IP protocol. The information of sensors is mapped onto the avatar skeletal definition. The SHAKE algorithm acts as a "black box" which is provided with tracker data representing new positions of selected joints and outputs the resolved avatar for graphics display.

We have developed a body model based on a small set of constraints as shown in Figure 1. This can support various kinds of avatar and virtual humans' representations. It is designed for use with 5 electromagnetic trackers (see, e.g. [17], [18]).

Experiments were carried out with two sensors to define the characteristics of the applications that we can simulate. Considering the fast convergence property of the SHAKE algorithm we show it to be compatible with the tracker speed for a range of actions for general theatre rehearsal. We use the MotionStar electromagnetic tracker system from Ascension Technology Co.[4]. We have completed several computer simulations where movements are defined as 3D trajectories with time steps derived from normal speed movements and sampling frequencies (which depend on the particular set of trackers used, and are typically in the 50-150Hz range). We have taken as a realistic set of parameters a sampling frequency of 144 Hz and a maximum movement speed of 2 ~ 4 m/s, which should account for most current gestures in theatre applications.

Gesture	Average Speed (m/s)	Maximum Speed (m/s)	Average Initial Displacement (%)	Maximum Initial Displacement (%)
Punch	2.39	10.8	12.9	69.1
Throw	1.63	13.0	8.84	62.2
Bow	0.89	3.5	3.71	22.6
Raise Arm	0.89	3.6	4.81	7.9
Pickup Object	0.64	2.0	3.46	9.8
Stretch	0.56	1.8	3.02	15.4

Table 1. Speed mesurements of typical actions

We measured the speed and initial displacements of several typical actions, which is the percentage of tracker movement over the length of the constraint. In our example, the tracker is attached to the wrist and the constraint is the forearm. Shown in Table 1, the average speed for general smooth motions are in the range of 0.6 m/s ~ 1.0 m/s with the maximum speed in the range of 1 m/s ~ 4 m/s. We consider a time step to correspond to a single sample, so the unconstrained maximum deformation would be approximately 10% of a limb segment length and this can be increased to 30% for

---

[4] http://www.ascension-tech.com

simple geometrical distortions. This might seem a large variation, however, as described in above section, SHAKE has been specifically developed to allow larger time steps than other integration methods. We can see by the above table that the maximum displacements of actions typically used within the theatre environment such as bowing, stretching, raising an arm and picking up objects are well within this limit. Faster actions that may be used in other simulations such as virtual sports have maximum displacements above the 30% limit and more research into SHAKE is needed to confidently handle such actions.

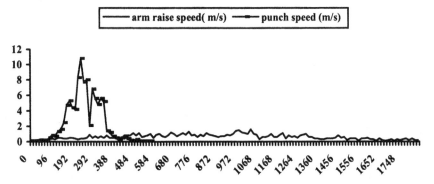

Fig. 4. Motions of arm raise actions and punch action

Figure 4 illustrates the motions of an arm raising action and a punching action. The arm raise action is generally smooth with an average speed of 0.89 m/s, whereas the punch action has large accelerations during the course of the motion.

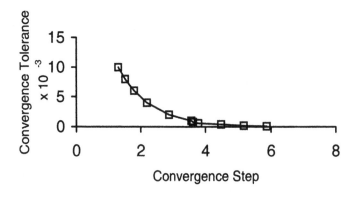

Fig. 5. An example of convergence of SHAKE (steps)

During the iteration process, each individual constraint is assigned a local tolerance. A global tolerance, which is the sum of all local tolerances, is used for global convergence of the system. We tested the number of iterations against different criteria for the global convergence tolerance between 10^{-3} - 10^{-4}, where the local tolerance is 10 times higher than that of global tolerance. Figure 5 illustrated an example data of convergence steps against the different global tolerance from 10^{-3} ~ 10^{-4} for the movement of 25 cm. The convergence takes place between 1 ~ 6 iterations and each convergence step takes approximately less than 1 ms for our skeletal model on 175MHz R10000 processor, which can be considered as real-time.

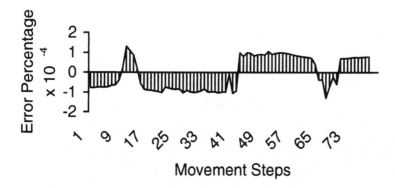

Fig. 6. Residual errors after convergence.

These experiments confirm the fast convergence of the SHAKE algorithm for real-time motion capture and animation applications. The results are of course due to the small number of constraints that define the body model as shown in Figure 1 (<20). However SHAKE is known to converge within 4 ~ 40 steps for a typical molecular simulation system [13].

The SHAKE algorithm can be used without any drift correction, unlike other algorithms for motion integration [13]. There is no accumulation of errors throughout the various steps of motion when using the SHAKE algorithm to enforce constraints. We tested the residual of the total constraints in a number of convergences. Figure 6 illustrates the plot of residual errors against the convergence steps forming the movement of the avatar. The experimental data explains that errors occurring in former time steps are corrected in the successive steps, thus the overall error percentage is small and can be considered no accumulation of residual errors through time.

4. Posture Generation

We have used a set of simulated tracker data to generate a number of simple avatar postures. The SHAKE algorithm is used to solve the values of joint angles of the model based on the geometric constraints imposed by the skeleton chain structure (Figure 1). The postures of the model are generated based on the hierarchical structure of the model. The walking movement of the model, for instance, is controlled by a set of simulated walking data on the movement of the feet and which determine the overall position and orientation of the whole body. The postures of the upper body are derived from the data given for pelvis and chest. The data of the pelvis gives the basis of the spine and the data of the chest gives the goal position, hence simple bending or twisting movement of the spine can be generated using the SHAKE algorithm.

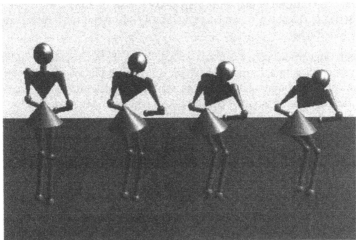

Fig. 7. Simple postures of the model

Figure 7 shows a number of simple postures generated by our virtual actor system. We also introduced group logical constraints to determine the vector directions of initial unconstraint disruption in some situations, for instance, the standing posture when the legs are perpendicular to the floor. As defined in the SHAKE algorithm, the unconstraint displacement is along the vector direction of the previous time step. The movement of feet would not automatically generate the correct position for the knee joint, since the initial vector direction of foot to knee and knee to hip are also perpendicular to the floor. Additional constraints such as logical constraints are required to enforce the initial unconstraint displacements to be taken along the logical direction, in this case, the knee should be outward along the walking direction rather than inward.

5. Conclusion and Future Work

The SHAKE algorithm has been very popular in molecular simulations, since it has properties of fast convergence speed and is able to work with a large number of constraints. The advantages of the method are particularly useful to computer graphics applications such as motion capture and real time animation. Our experimental results demonstrate that the SHAKE algorithm can be used for various kinds of gestures found in theatre rehearsals. The realism and complexity of the gesture can be achieved by imposing additional constraints to the body system without having to redesign the entire constraint structure. As stated in section 3, the convergence of the inverse kinematics algorithm takes place after only a few iteration steps for most average movements in terms of the maximum disruption and speed of the movement. The interactive frame rate of the motion generation is guaranteed provided that reasonable tolerance criteria are chosen according to the specific body system designed.

Currently our constraint system is still under specified. It does not taking into account angular constraints. Additional constraints to accurately represent human joints are needed to resolve complex body deformations. We are working on coupling our avatar model to a realistic human model and incorporating it into a distributed virtual environment for interactive applications.

Acknowledgments

This research is part of the programme of Digital VCE, the Virtual Centre of Excellence for Digital Broadcasting and Multimedia Technology Ltd[5].

References

1.   Zhao, J. & Badler, N. I. 1989. Real-time inverse kinematics with joint limits and spatial constraints. Technical Report MS-CIS-89-09, Computer and Information Science, University of Pennsylvania, Philadelphia, PA.

---

[5] http://www.digital-vce.com

2. Kastenmeier, T. & Vesely, F.J., 1996. Numerical Robot Kinematics Based on Stochastic and Molecular Simulation Methods, Robotica, Vol. 14, part 3, pp 329-337.
3. Girard, M and Maciejewski, A. Computational modeling for the computer animation of legged figures. Computers Graphics, 19(3): 263-270, July 1985.
4. Sims, K and Zeltzer, D. A figure editor and gait controller for task level animation. In SIGGRAPH Course Notes: Synthetic Actors: The Impact of Artificial Intelligence and Robotics on Animation, 1988.
5. Badler, N, Phillips, C. and Zhao, J. Interavtive real-time articulated figure manipulation using multiple kinematic constraints. In Proceedings, 1990 Symposium on Interactive 3D Graphics, 245-250, 1990.
6. Welman, C., 1993. Inverse Kinematics and Geometric Constraints for Articulated Figure Manipulation. MSc Thesis (Computing Science), Simon Fraser University.
7. Hildebrand, F.B., Methods of Applied Mathematics, 2nd Ed., Prentice-Hall, 1965.
8. Baraff, D., 1996. Linear-Time Dynamics using Lagrange Multipliers. Computer Graphics proceedings, Annual Conference Series, 1996, ACM SIGGRAPH, pp. 137-146.
9. Ryckaert, J.P., Ciccotti, G. & Berendsen, H.J.C., 1977. Numerical integration of the cartesian equations of motion of a system with constraints: molecular dynamics of n-alkanes, Journal of Computational Physics, 23:327-341.
10. McCammon & Harvey, 1987. Dynamics of Proteins and Nucleic Acids. Cambridge University Press.
11. Verlet, L. 1967. Computer "experiments" on classical fluids. I. Thermodynamical properties of Lennard-Jones molecules, Physical Review, 159, 98.
12. Cavazza, M., 1986. Etudes d'algorithmes utilisables en graphisme moléculaire. Rapport de DEA de l'Universite Paris 6 (unpublished, in French).
13. Bekker, H. Molecular Dynamics simulation Methods Revised. Ph. D. Thesis, University of Groningen, ISBN 90-367-0604-1.
14. Leimkuhler, B. & Skeel, R.D., 1994. Symplectic Numerical integrators in Constrained Hamiltonian Systems, Journal of Computational Physics, Vol. 16, No. 10, pp. 1192-1209.
15. Barth, E., Kuczera, K, Leimkuhler, B. & Skeel, R.D., 1995. Algorithms for Constrained Molecular Dynamics. Journal of Computational Chemistry.
16. Fuhrer, C., and Leimkuhler, B., 1991. Numerical Solution of Differential-Algebraic Equations for Constrained Mechanical Motion, Numerische Mathematik, 59: 55-69.
17. Badler, N.I., Hollick, M.J. & Granieri, J.P., 1993. Real-Time Control of a Virtual Human Using Minimal Sensors. Presence, 2:1, pp. 82-86.
18. Hirose, M., Deffaux, G. & Nakagaki, Y., 1996. A study on Data input of Natural Human Motion for Virtual Reality Systems. Proceedings of Interface to Real & Virtual Worlds'96, pp. 195-204.
19. Ko, Hyeongseok & Badler, Norman I. Animating Human Locomotion with Inverse Dynamics. IEEE Computer Graphics and Applications, Vol. 16, No.2 pp. 51-59, March 1996.

Goal-Directed Navigation for Animated Characters Using Real-Time Path Planning and Control

James J. Kuffner, Jr

Computer Science Robotics Lab, Stanford University
Stanford, CA 94305-9010, USA,
kuffner@stanford.edu,
http://robotics.stanford.edu/~kuffner/

Abstract. This paper presents a new technique for computing collision-free navigation motions from task-level commands for animated human characters in interactive virtual environments. The algorithm implementation utilizes the hardware rendering pipeline commonly found on graphics accelerator cards to perform fast 2D motion planning. Given a 3D geometric description of an animated character and a level-terrain environment, collision-free navigation paths can be computed between initial and goal locations at interactive rates. Speed is gained by leveraging the graphics hardware to quickly project the obstacle geometry into a 2D bitmap for planning. The bitmap may be searched by any number of standard dynamic programming techniques to produce a final path. Cyclic motion capture data is used along with a simple proportional derivative controller to animate the character as it follows the computed path. The technique has been implemented on an SGI Indigo2 workstation and runs at interactive rates. It allows for real-time modification of the goal locations and obstacle positions for multiple characters in complex environments composed of more than 15,000 triangles.

1 Introduction

Advances in computing hardware, software, and network technology have enabled a new class of interactive applications involving 3D animated characters to become increasingly feasible. Many such applications require algorithms that enable animated characters to move naturally and realistically in response to task-level commands. This paper addresses the problem of quickly synthesizing from navigation goals the collision-free motions for animated human figures in changing virtual environments. The method presented here combines a path planner, a path-following controller, and cyclic motion capture data. The resulting animation can be generated at interactive rates and looks fairly realistic. This work is part of a larger project to build autonomous animated characters equipped with motion planning capabilities and simulated sensing[1]. The ultimate goal of this research is to create animated agents able to respond to task-level commands and behave naturally within changing virtual environments.

Nadia Magnenat-Thalmann, Daniel Thalmann (Eds.): CAPTECH'98, LNAI 1537, pp. 171–186, 1998.
© Springer-Verlag Berlin Heidelberg 1998

A prolific area of research in the robotics literature has been the design and implementation of task-level motion planning algorithms for real-world robotic systems[2]. The inspiration for the fundamental ideas in this paper arises from this research. Section 2 provides a background and motivation for task-level control in the context of animation. Related work in building autonomous agents for the purposes of graphic animation is summarized in Section 3. Section 4 describes an approach for computing goal-directed navigation motions for animated human figures. Section 5 gives an overview of the algorithm, while Section 6 and Section 7 describe in greater detail the path planning and path following phases of the approach respectively. In Section 8 the current implementation and performance results are presented. Section 9 concludes with a discussion of the limitations and possible extensions to the ideas presented here.

2   Motivation

The primary motivation for task-level control in animation stems from the time and labor required to specify motion trajectories for complex multi-jointed characters, such as human figures. Traditional keyframe animation techniques are extremely labor-intensive and often yield motion that looks unrealistic or is physically invalid. Motion capture techniques offer a simple alternative for obtaining realistic-looking motion. Unfortunately, both keyframed-motion and motion capture data alone are inflexible in the sense that the motion is often only valid for a limited set of situations. Frequently, such motions must be redesigned if the locations of other objects or starting conditions change even slightly. Motion warping or blending algorithms[3, 4] offer some added flexibility, but usually can only be applied to a limited set of situations involving minor changes to the environment or starting conditions. Significant changes typically result in unrealistic motions.

Dynamic simulation and physically-based modeling techniques nicely handle the problems of physical validity and applicability to arbitrary situations. Given initial positions, velocities, forces, and dynamic properties, an object's motion is simulated according to natural physical laws[5, 6]. However, aside from specifying initial conditions, the user has no control over both the resulting motion and the final resting position of the object. Spacetime constraints provide a more general mathematical framework for addressing this problem of control [7, 8, 9]. Constraint equations imposed by the initial and final conditions, obstacle boundaries, and other desired properties of the motion are solved numerically. Unfortunately, the large number of constraints imposed by complex obstacle-cluttered environments can severely degrade the performance of such methods.

New approaches and algorithms are needed to compute natural, collision-free motions quickly in changing virtual environments. The method described in this paper combines a fast 2D path planner along with a proportional derivative (PD) controller to compute natural-looking motions for navigation tasks. The controller is used to synthesize cyclic motion capture data for an animated character as it follows a computed path towards a goal location. The goal location can be can be user-specified or defined by a behavior script. The implemented planner executes in roughly one-tenth of one second on average, thus allowing real-time modification of the goal location or obstacle positions.

3   Related Work

Previous work in motion synthesis for animated characters has traditionally been divided between real-time applications and off-line animation production. However, as processor speeds continue to increase, algorithms originally intended for off-line animations will gradually become feasible in real-time virtual environments.

Much research effort in robotics has been focused on designing control architectures for autonomous agents that operate in the real world[10, 11]. Using rasterizing computer graphics hardware to assist robot motion planning algorithms was previously investigated by Lengyel, et al[12]. Recently, motion planning tools and algorithms have been applied to character animation. Koga et al. combined motion planning and human arm inverse kinematics algorithms for automatically generating animation for human arm manipulation tasks[13]. Hsu and Cohen combined path planning with motion capture data to animate a human figure navigating on uneven terrain [14]. Researchers at the University of Pennsylvania have been exploring the use of motion planning to achieve postural goals using their Jack human character model[15, 16], incorporating body dynamics[17], and high-level scripting[18].

Research in designing fully-autonomous, interactive, artificial agents has also been on the rise. Tu and Terzopoulos implemented a realistic simulation of autonomous artificial fishes, complete with integrated simple behaviors, physically-based motion generation, and simulated perception[19]. Noser, et al. proposed a navigation system for animated characters based on synthetic vision, memory and learning[20]. Other systems include Perlin and Goldberg's Improv software for interactive agents[21, 22], the ALIVE project at MIT[23, 24], Johnson's WavesWorld, and perhaps one of the earliest attempts at creating an agent architecture for the purposes of graphic animation: the Oz project at CMU[25]. The goals of the Oz project were to create agents with "broad" but "shallow" capabilities, rather than "deep" capabilities in a narrow area. Researchers at Georgia Tech have combined physically-based simulation with group behaviors for simulating human athletics[26]. They have also designed a controller for human running in 3D[27]. Despite these achievements, building autonomous agents that respond intelligently to task-level commands remains an elusive goal, particularly in real-time applications.

4   Goal-Directed Navigation

Consider the case of an animated human character given the task of moving from one location to another in a flat-terrain virtual environment. One would like to produce a reasonable set of motions to accomplish the task while avoiding obstacles and other characters in the environment. Our strategy will be to divide the computation into two phases: *path planning* and *path following*. The planning phase computes a collision-free path to the goal location using the graphics hardware for speed, while the path following phase uses a proportional derivative (PD) controller to guide the character's motion along the path. The path planning phase should run very quickly, since the locations of other characters or objects in the environment may change without warning. Such changes may invalidate the collision-free nature of the current path being followed, and necessitate re-planning. The controller should be fast and flexible enough to allow the current path being followed to be replaced without warning, and still generate smooth motions.

5   Algorithm Overview

Initialization: A general 3D description of the environment and characters suitable for rendering is provided, along with a goal location. Motion capture data for a single cycle of a locomotion gait along a straight line is pre-processed as described in Section 7.2.

Projection: The planning phase begins by performing an off-screen projection of the environment geometry into a 2D bitmap. An orthographic camera is positioned above the environment, pointing down along the negative normal direction of the walking surface. The *near* clipping plane of the camera is set to correspond to the maximum vertical extent of the character's geometry, and the *far* clipping plane is set to be slightly above the walking surface. All geometry within the given height range is projected (rendered) to either the back buffer or an offscreen bitmap via the graphics hardware.

Path Search: The bitmap from the previous step is searched directly for a collision-free path using any standard dynamic programming technique. Examples include Dijkstra's algorithm, or A* with some appropriate heuristic function. If planning is successful, the complete path is sent to the path following phase. Otherwise, the controller is notified that no path exists.

Path Following: Cyclic motion capture data along with a PD controller on the position and velocity is used to generate the final motion for the character as it tracks the computed path. If no path exists, an appropriate stopping motion or waiting behavior is performed.

6   Path Planning

The theory and analysis of motion planning algorithms is fairly well-developed in the robotics literature, and is not discussed in detail here. For a broad background in motion planning, readers are referred to [2]. For any motion planning, it is important to minimize the number of degrees of freedom (DOFs), since the time complexity of known algorithms grows exponentially with the number of

DOFs[28]. For character navigation on level-terrain, the important DOFs are the position and orientation (x, y, θ) of the base of the character on the walking surface. As detailed in Section 7, the orientation (forward-facing direction) of the character is computed by the controller during the path following phase. Thus, we need only to consider the position (x, y) of the base of the character during the planning phase. Bounding the character's geometry by a cylinder allows motion planning for level-terrain navigation to be reduced to planning collision-free trajectories for a circular disk in 2D. Figure 1 shows one of the characters used in our experiments along with the computed bounding cylinder.

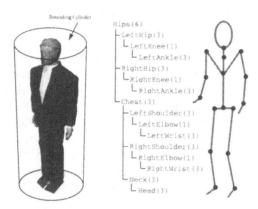

Fig. 1. The character's geometry is bounded by an appropriate cylinder. This effectively reduces the navigation problem to one involving motion planning for a circular disc among obstacles in 2D. The character's joint hierarchy is shown, along with the number of DOF for each joint.

The path planning approach adopted in this paper is one instance of an *approximate cell decomposition* method[2]. The search space (in this case, the walking surface) is discretized into a fine regular grid of cells. All obstacles are projected onto the grid and "grown" as detailed in Section 6.1. Hence, the grid approximately captures the free regions of the search space at the given grid resolution, and can ultimately be used for fast collision checking.

6.1 Obstacle Projection

All obstacle geometry within the character's height range $[z_{min}, z_{max}]$ is projected orthographically onto the grid. The height range limitation assures that only obstacle geometry that truly impedes the motion of the character is projected. Cells in the grid are marked as either *FREE* or *NOT-FREE*, depending upon whether or not the cell contains any obstacle geometry. The resulting 2D bitmap $\mathcal{B}$ now represents an occupancy grid of all obstacles within the character's height range projected at their current locations onto the walking surface.

Cells in $\mathcal{B}$ marked as *NOT-FREE* are "grown" by R, the radius of a cylinder that conservatively bounds the character's geometry. This is done by marking all neighboring cells within a circle of radius R from each original *NOT-FREE* cell as *NOT-FREE*. In effect, this operation computes the Minkowski difference of the projected obstacles and the character's bounding cylinder, thus reducing the problem of planning for a circular disc, into planning for a point object. To check whether or not a disc whose center is located at (x, y) intersects any obstacles, we can simply test whether $\mathcal{B}(x, y)$, the cell in $\mathcal{B}$ containing the point (x, y) is marked *FREE*.

For increased speed, the obstacle projection operation is performed using rendering hardware. Here, the rendering pipeline enables us to quickly generate the bitmap needed for fast point collision checking. An orthographic camera is positioned above the scene pointing down along the negative normal direction of the walking surface with the clipping planes set to the vertical extents of the character's geometry. The other dimensions of the orthographic view volume are set to enclose the furthest extents of the walking surface as depicted in Figure 2. All geometry within the view volume is projected (rendered) into either the back buffer or an offscreen bitmap via the graphics hardware. Since we are only concerned with whether or not any obstacle geometry maps to each pixel location, we can effectively ignore the pixel color and depth value. Thus, we can turn off all lighting effects and depth comparisons, and simply render in wireframe all obstacle geometry in a uniform color against a default background color. Under most reasonable graphics hardware systems, this will significantly speed up rendering. Furthermore, if the graphics hardware supports variable line-widths and point-sizes, we can perform the obstacle growth at no additional computational cost! We simply set the line-width and point-size rendering style to correspond to the projected pixel length of R, the radius of the character's bounding cylinder. In this way, we can efficiently perform both obstacle projection and growth simultaneously.

6.2   Path Search

The bitmap $\mathcal{B}$ is essentially an approximate map of the occupied and free regions in the environment. Assume that the goal location $\mathcal{G} = (g_x, g_y)$ and the starting location $\mathcal{S} = (s_x, s_y)$ in the bitmap are both *FREE*. Let us consider $\mathcal{B}$ as an embedded graph of cells, each connected to its neighboring cells. By searching $\mathcal{B}$, we can conservatively determine whether or not a collision-free path exists from the start location to the goal location at the current grid resolution. Moreover, if we assign a cost to each arc between cells, we can search for a path that connects $\mathcal{S}$ and $\mathcal{G}$ while minimizing our cost function. Here, we use a relative measure of the Euclidean distance between adjacent cells as our cost. Arcs between directly adjacent cells are assigned a cost of 1, while diagonally-adjacent cells are assigned a relative cost of 1.4. Our task has been effectively reduced to that of searching for a path between two nodes in a weighted graph.

Any number of standard dynamic programming techniques may be used to search $\mathcal{B}$. For simplicity, Dijkstra's algorithm is used in the implementation

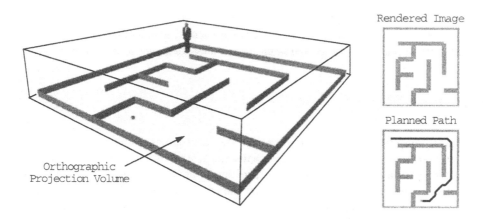

Fig. 2. The view volume resulting from an overhead orthographic camera is outlined. The near and far clipping planes of the camera are defined according to the vertical extents of the character geometry. All obstacle geometry contained within the view volume is projected to 2D via an off-screen renderer. The resulting bitmap is searched directly for a collision-free path connecting the character's starting position to the goal.

described here. This search strategy will always return a path containing a list of *FREE* cells between S and G if one exists at the given grid resolution. Moreover, since a relative measure of the Euclidean distance is used as the single-step cost between cells during the search, the returned path will be of minimal length (for the given grid resolution).[1] From the list of free cells connecting S to G , a final path P is constructed by linking in sequence the line segments connecting the centers of adjacent cells along the path.

6.3   Complexity Analysis

If planning is successful, the complete path is sent to the path following controller. Otherwise, the controller is notified that no path exists. The planner is *resolution-complete*, meaning that it is guaranteed to find a collision-free path from S to G if one exists at the current grid resolution, and otherwise report failure[2].

The running time of the obstacle projection step is proportional to the number and geometric complexity of the obstacles. Searching for a path in the bitmap using Dijkstra's algorithm runs in quadratic time with respect to the number of free cells in the grid. Extracting the path (if one exists) runs in time proportional to the length of the path. Overall, this planning strategy can be implemented very efficiently and robustly even for complex environments. It is interesting to

---

[1] In this implementation, fixed-point math is used for the distance and cost computations, resulting in a planner that runs almost entirely using fast integer arithmetic.

note that paradoxically, the search phase of the planner may run *faster* for complex, obstacle-cluttered environments, since such environments result in fewer free cells to search. Detailed performance results are given in Section 8.

7   Path Following

Simply computing a collision free path in the environment is not enough to produce realistic animation. The implementation described here uses cyclic motion capture data applied to the joints of the character, plus a simple low-level proportional derivative controller to follow the computed path. The quality of the final motion arises primarily from the motion capture data, but there are other alternatives that could be used for path following. So-called "footstep"-driven animation systems could be applied to place the feet at points nearby the computed path, along with real-time inverse kinematics (IK) to hold them in place. As computer processing power increases, physically-based models of the character dynamics along with complex controllers such as the one presented in [27] could also potentially be used to simulate locomotion gaits along the path. For the purposes of these experiments, applying cyclic motion capture data proved to be a fast and simple method of obtaining satisfactory motion.

Although the path planning and following concept generally applies to many types of characters and motions, we will concentrate on generating walking or running motions for a human-like biped. We would like the character's motion to be smooth and continuous, natural-looking, and follow the computed path as closely as possible. Though many kinds of path following techniques could potentially be used, the one described here was chosen for its simplicity and efficiency.

7.1   Mathematical Model

Human figure walking or running is essentially a quasi-nonholonomic system, since the typical turning radius is usually subject to some minimum radius depending upon the velocity. Of course, a person can turn in place, but typically, this will only happen at the beginning or end of a path following procedure, not in the middle of a path. Humans tend to only walk forward, not backward or sideways (no direction reversals during path following).

With this in mind, the path following phase is modeled as one involving an oriented disc smoothly tracking a geometric path in the plane. The disc center corresponds to the projected point at the base of the character's geometry, and the orientation of the disc corresponds to the character's forward-facing direction as illustrated in Figure 3. The linear velocity of the disc is constrained to always lie along the forward-facing direction. This corresponds to the character's ability to walk or run forward. Turning is modeled by considering the disc's rotational velocity about its center.

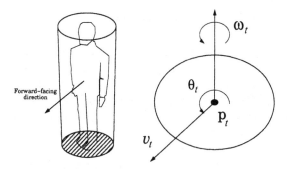

Fig. 3. The controller model considers the character's motion as that of an oriented disc in the plane. The center of the disc corresponds to the projection of the origin of the root joint of the figure onto the walking surface.

A discrete time simulation of the following state variables is used:

$\mathbf{p}_t$ position (x_t, y_t) if the disc center
θ_t orientation (forward-facing direction)
v_t linear speed along the direction of θ_t
ω_t angular speed about $\mathbf{p}_t$

The tuple $(\mathbf{p}_t, \theta_t, v_t, \omega_t)$ represents the simulated state of the character at time t. At each time step, any combination of the following two controls may be applied:

a_t linear acceleration along the direction of θ_t
α_t angular acceleration about $\mathbf{p}_t$

These controls model the four basic controls for our character: (*speed up, slow down, turn left, turn right*). Speeding up and slowing down are represented by positive and negative values of a_t respectively. Similarly, positive values of α_t correspond to left turns, while negative values correspond to right turns. Section 7.3 explains how these controls are calculated at each time step.

Once the controls a_t and α_t have been specified, the state variables are integrated forward discretely by the time step Δt. In these experiments, simple fixed-step Euler integration was used, but more sophisticated integration methods may be used if desired. For Euler integration, the state propagation equations are as follows:

$$x_{t+\Delta t} = x_t + (v_t \cos \theta_t) \Delta t$$
$$y_{t+\Delta t} = y_t + (v_t \sin \theta_t) \Delta t$$
$$\theta_{t+\Delta t} = \theta_t + \omega_t \Delta t$$
$$v_{t+\Delta t} = v_t + a_t \Delta t$$
$$\omega_{t+\Delta t} = \omega_t + \alpha_t \Delta t$$

The simulation proceeds in this fashion iteratively. As long as the values of the controls are reasonable relative to the size of the time step Δt , the motion will be smooth and continuous.

7.2   Preparing the Motion Capture Data

As a one-time pre-processing step, the motion capture data to be applied to the path is prepared for the path following phase. Here we assume that the original motion capture data is cyclic, and roughly follows a straight line. To begin, the transformation of the root joint (for example, the *Hip* joint) for each data frame is factored into two parts: the transformation of a *base point* (the point of projection of the origin of the root joint to the walking surface) moving in a straight line at a constant speed throughout the duration of the cycle, and the relative transformation of the root joint with respect to the moving base point.

The reason for performing this decomposition is to allow us to apply the motion capture data to an arbitrary curve much more easily. Traditionally, motion capture data comes in a format that specifies the transformation of the root joint relative to some fixed global frame. Instead of trying to control the root joint directly to follow a computed path, we can control the base point, which by construction travels in a straight line and at a constant speed throughout the duration of the motion cycle.

The trajectory of the base point is computed by first projecting the origin of the root joint onto the walking surface for both the first frame and the last frame of the motion cycle. The base point should move in the direction corresponding to the translational difference between these two projected points. The total distance traveled by the base point should be the length of this translational difference. The velocity of the base point is simply this distance divided by the time elapsed during playback of the motion cycle. The base point is the point to which we will map the center of our oriented disc model for path following. The direction of motion of the base point corresponds to the forward-facing direction of the disc model.

The velocity of the base point is the *canonical average velocity* V of the root joint over the duration of the motion. If the base point is made to move along a straight line at this velocity, the motion capture data will appear as it does in its raw form. Since we will be controlling the base point for path following, it will move along curved paths, and at differing velocities. In order to improve the appearance of the motion for velocities other than the average velocity, we can incorporate other motion capture data sets taken at different walking or running speeds. An alternative to this, is to pre-compute a table of interpolation factors for the joint rotations, indexed by velocity. Smaller base point velocities will result in smaller joint rotations. For example, for a basic walk cycle, the interpolation factors can be pre-selected for each base point velocity such that sliding of the character's feet along the walking surface is minimized. This simple interpolation method is used in the implementation described here, and results in fairly reasonable motions for transitioning between a standing position to a full-speed walk, and in coming to a stop at the end of a path. A more sophisticated method might utilize IK to enforce "no-sliding" constraints on the feet of the character.

7.3   Calculating the Controls

In this section, we describe a simple method for computing the two control variables, a_t and α_t for our character during each time step of the simulation. The method is based on proportional derivative (PD) control. Given the current state of the system $(\mathbf{p}_t, \theta_t, v_t, \omega_t)$, a *desired* state $(\hat{\mathbf{p}}_t, \hat{\theta}_t, \hat{v}_t, \hat{\omega}_t)$ is calculated. The controls a_t and α_t are then computed to move the system towards the desired state.

The computation proceeds as follows: Given a path $\mathcal{P}$ computed by the planning phase, a desired position along the path $\hat{\mathbf{p}}_t$ is calculated relative to the current position $\mathbf{p}_t$. The desired position is typically set to be slightly ahead of the current position along the path, as this tends to smooth out any sharp corners on the path. Next, the desired orientation $\hat{\theta}_t$ is computed so as to face the character towards the desired position $\hat{\mathbf{p}}_t$. The desired angular speed $\hat{\omega}_t$ is set proportional to the difference (error) between the current orientation θ_t and the desired orientation $\hat{\theta}_t$. The desired linear speed $\hat{v}_t$ has three alternatives. If the error in orientation is *small*, $\hat{v}_t$ is simply set to be the canonical average velocity V of the motion capture cycle. Otherwise, if the error in orientation is *large*, the character is facing the wrong direction, so the speed is set to be some small non-zero value to force the character to slow down and turn around. Lastly, if the character is nearing the end of the path (the goal location), $\hat{v}_t$ is calculated proportional to the difference between the current position and the goal location. After $\hat{v}_t$ is obtained, the controls a_t and α_t are calculated. The linear acceleration a_t is set proportional to the difference between the current and desired linear speed, while the angular acceleration α_t is set proportional to the difference between the current and desired angular speed. The state of the system is integrated forward by a discrete time step Δt, and the entire process is repeated for the next time step.

All of the calculations involving proportional derivative terms above require the following gains[2] to be specified:

k_p position gain	k_θ orientation gain
k_v linear speed gain	k_ω angular speed gain

As long as the gains are set to reasonable values relative to the size of the time step Δt, the resulting motion will be smooth and continuous.

To summarize, all of the control calculations are listed below. First, we calculate the desired state $(\hat{\mathbf{p}}_t, \hat{\theta}_t, \hat{v}_t, \hat{\omega}_t)$, and then compute the controls needed to move towards the desired state.

---

[2] The gains represent how quickly errors (differences between the current and the desired) are resolved. Since a discrete time step is being used, some care must be taken when setting the gains. Gains set too high will cause oscillations (an *underdamped* system), while gains set too low will fail to correct errors (an *overdamped* system). Setting the gains properly will result in a *critically-damped* system, that asymptotically corrects errors without overshoot. The reader is referred to any textbook on feedback control for more detailed information.

$$\hat{\mathbf{p}}_t = (\hat{x}_t, \hat{y}_t) \text{ from path } \mathcal{P}$$
$$\hat{\theta}_t = \text{atan2}(\hat{y}_t - y_t, \hat{x}_t - x_t)$$
$$\hat{\omega}_t = k_\theta(\hat{\theta}_t - \theta_t)$$
$$\hat{v}_t = \begin{cases} \text{canonical speed } V \text{ if } |\hat{\theta}_t - \theta_t| \le \theta_{turn} \\ \text{small speed } \epsilon \quad\;\; \text{if } |\hat{\theta}_t - \theta_t| > \theta_{turn} \\ k_p(|\hat{\mathbf{p}}_t - \mathbf{p}_t|) \quad \text{if near the goal} \end{cases}$$
$$a_t = k_v(\hat{v}_t - v_t)$$
$$\alpha_t = k_\omega(\hat{\omega}_t - \omega_t)$$

In the computation of $\hat{\theta}_t$, atan2(y, x) is the standard two-argument arctangent function.

After all controls are calculated, the state is integrated forward discretely by the time step Δt , as described in Section 7.1. The subsequent state becomes the new location and orientation for the base point of the character. To animate the remaining joints, the current velocity v_t is used to index into the motion interpolation table as described in Section 7.2.

8   Experimental Results

The algorithm described here has been implemented on a 200MHz SGI Indigo2 running Irix 6.2 with 128MB of RAM and an SGI EXTREME graphics accelerator card. Good performance has been achieved, even on complex scenes with multiple characters and environments composed of more than 15,000 triangle primitives. During an interactive session, the user can click and drag on the goal location or obstacles, and the path planner will calculate an updated, minimal-length, collision-free path (if one exists) in approximately one-tenth of one second on average. The path is then sent directly to the controller, and the character will immediately begin following the new path. The precise timing results are summarized in Section 8.1.

The generation of the projection bitmap for path planning was accomplished by rendering all obstacles to the back buffer using standard OpenGL calls. The rendering style optimizations for fast obstacle growth were implemented as described in Section 6.1. The resulting pixel values were subsequently read directly from the framebuffer. The Dijkstra's algorithm implementation uses fixed-point math, resulting in a planner that runs almost exclusively using fast integer arithmetic.

For the purposes of path following, the simple PD controller described in Section 7 was implemented for a human-like character with 17 joints. Two sets of motion capture data were used in the experiments: a walk cycle and a jog cycle. As expected, the slower canonical speed of the walk cycle facilitated much better tracking performance along the path compared with the jogging motion. The values of the gains used for the controller were as follows: ($k_p= 1.0$, $k_\theta= 5.0$, $k_v= 5.0$, $k_\omega= 10.0$). These gain values are compatible with standard units of meters, radians, and seconds, which were used throughout the experiments. The value of the time step was $\Delta t = 0.0333$ seconds (1/30 sec). Although these gain values were obtained via trial and error, research is underway to automatically compute the optimal gains for path following.[1] Sample output is illustrated in Figure 4. Multiple characters were run simultaneously, each planning around the other characters as they followed their own computed paths.

Fig. 4. Screen shots of interactive animation sessions. The left image shows multiple characters navigating in an office environment. The image on the right shows a single character in more detail.

8.1 Timing Results

The average projection, search, and total *elapsed* execution times during repeated invocations of the planner during an interactive session were tabulated. The timing results are summarized in Table 8.1. All values listed in the table are in units of milliseconds, and were averaged from N = 100 independent trials with varying goal locations and obstacle positions. Different grid resolutions were tested ranging between 45 and 150 cells on a side. The total number of triangle primitives in the Maze scene and the Office scene were 2,780 and 15,320 respectively.

9   Discussion and Future Work

Graphic Animation by computer lies at the boundary of modeling and simulating the real world, and shares much in common with the design and control of robotic systems. In this paper, a fast path planner along with a simple path following controller is used to quickly synthesize collision-free motions for level-terrain navigation goals for human-like animated characters. Navigation goals are specified at the task level, and the resulting animation is derived from underlying

Table 1. Average Total Execution Time for Path Planning.

Scene (grid size)	Project	Search	Total (msec)
Maze (50 x 50)	9.5	7.2	16.7
Maze (100 x 100)	34.5	37.4	72.0
Maze (150 x 150)	82.9	79.8	163.0
Office (45 x 45)	47.7	13.9	61.7
Office (90 x 90)	62.7	27.4	90.2
Office (135 x 135)	139.2	56.8	196.0

motion capture data driven by a simple proportional derivative controller. The speed of the planning algorithm enables it to be used effectively in environments where obstacles and other characters move unpredictably.

Although useful in its present form, the algorithm could be improved in a number of important ways. The most severe limitation of the planner is the level-terrain requirement. Extending the algorithm to handle uneven-terrain is possible, but it would involve redesigning the geometry clipping and projection operations. Perhaps the approach taken by Hsu and Cohen would be more appropriate in this situation [14]. Possible extensions to the basic algorithm, include incorporating into the planning process the ability to step over low obstacles, or duck under overhangs. One idea might be to utilize the depth information information that is generated, but is currently being ignored during the projection process. The hardware Z-buffer stores a relative measure of the depth, yielding a simple height field of the environment, which might be useful for deciding a navigation strategy. The same basic idea could perhaps be applied to even more aggressive means of circumventing obstacles, such as utilizing stairs/elevators, climbing, jumping, or crawling. Another limitation of the current approach is the approximate nature of the grid, which may fail to find a free path when one exists, especially when it involves navigating through narrow passages. Perhaps a multi-resolution strategy would be appropriate.

The path following controller as described here is overly-simplistic, and ignores such subtleties of human motion as turning in-place, or side-stepping between narrow openings. Incorporating more motion capture data sets at different velocities, or along curved paths would also likely improve the final appearance of the animation. In addition, the ability to automatically compute the optimal values for the controller gains based on the simulation constants and the canonical speed of the motion capture data would be a very useful improvement. Knowing these optimal gains might also facilitate the calculation of conservative error-bounds on the performance of the path following controller.

Efforts to incorporate active perception based on simulated vision into the planning process are currently underway[1]. In addition, some simple velocity prediction to take into account the estimated motion of other characters and obstacles during planning is also being investigated. Clearly, many challenging research issues must be faced before more interesting motions and intelligent behaviors for autonomous animated characters can be realized.

Acknowledgments

Much gratitude is extended to David Hsu for his thoughtful insights and helpful suggestions, and to Diego Ruspini for reviewing the initial manuscript in detail. Thanks also to Yotto Koga, Craig Becker, Michael Svihura, David Lin, Jing Xiao, and Jean-Claude Latombe, who through informal conversations helped to formulate the ideas presented here. This research is supported in part by a National Science Foundation Graduate Fellowship in Engineering.

References

[1] J. J. Kuffner Jr., *An Architecture for the Design of Intelligent Animated Characters*, Ph.D. thesis, Stanford University *(in preparation)*.

[2] J. C. Latombe, *Robot Motion Planning*, Kluwer Academic Publishers, Boston, MA, 1991.

[3] A. Witkin and Z. Popovic, "Motion warping," in *Proc. SIGGRAPH '95*, 1995.

[4] A. Bruderlin and L. Williams, "Motion signal processing," in *Proc. SIGGRAPH '95*, Robert Cook, Ed. ACM SIGGRAPH, Aug. 1995, Annual Conference Series, pp. 97–104, Addison Wesley, held in Los Angeles, California, 06-11 August 1995.

[5] D. Baraff, "Analytical methods for dynamic simulation of non-penetrating rigid bodies," in *Proc. SIGGRAPH '89*, 1989, pp. 223–231.

[6] B. Mirtich, *Impulse-Based Dynamic Simulation of Rigid Body Systems*, Ph.D. thesis, University of California, Berkeley, CA, 1996.

[7] A. Witkin and Kass M., "Spacetime constraints," in *Proc. SIGGRAPH '88*, 1988, pp. 159–168.

[8] J. T. Ngo and J. Marks, "Spacetime constraints revisited," in *Proc. SIGGRAPH '93*, 1993, pp. 343–350.

[9] Z. Liu, S. J. Gortler, and F. C. Cohen, "Hierachical spacetime control," in *Proc. SIGGRAPH '94*, 1994, pp. 35–42.

[10] R. A. Brooks, "A layered intelligent control system for a mobile robot," in *Robotics Research The Third International Symposium*. 1985, pp. 365–372, MIT Press, Cambridge, MA.

[11] R. C. Arkin, "Cooperation without communication: Multiagent schema based robot navigation," *Journal of Robotic Systems*, pp. 351–364, 1992.

[12] J. Lengyel, M. Reichert, B. R. Donald, and D. P. Greenberg, "Real-time robot motion planning using rasterizing computer graphics hardware," in *Proc. SIGGRAPH '90*, 1990.

[13] Y. Koga, K. Kondo, J. Kuffner, and J.-C. Latombe, "Planning motions with intentions," in *Proc. SIGGRAPH '94*, 1994, pp. 395–408.

[14] D. Hsu and M. Cohen, "Task-level motion control for human figure animation," Unpublished Manuscript, 1997.

[15] M. R. Jung, N. Badler, and T. Noma, "Animated human agents with motion planning capability for 3D-space postural goals," *The Journal of Visualization and Computer Animation*, vol. 5, no. 4, pp. 225–246, October 1994.

[16] J. P. Granieri, W. Becket, B. D. Reich, J. Crabtree, and N. L. Badler, "Behavioral control for real-time simulated human agents," in *1995 Symposium on Interactive 3D Graphics*, Pat Hanrahan and Jim Winget, Eds. ACM SIGGRAPH, Apr. 1995, pp. 173–180, ISBN 0-89791-736-7.

[17] E. Kokkevis, D. Metaxas, and N. I. Badler, "Autonomous animation and control of four-legged animals," in *Graphics Interface '95*, Wayne A. Davis and Przemyslaw Prusinkiewicz, Eds. Canadian Information Processing Society, May 1995, pp. 10–17, Canadian Human-Computer Communications Society, ISBN 0-9695338-4-5.

[18] N. Badler, "Real-time virtual humans," *Pacific Graphics*, 1997.

[19] X. Tu and D. Terzopoulos, "Artificial fishes: Physics, locomotion, perception, behavior," in *Proc. SIGGRAPH '94*, Andrew Glassner, Ed. ACM SIGGRAPH, July 1994, Computer Graphics Proceedings, Annual Conference Series, pp. 43–50, ACM Press, ISBN 0-89791-667-0.

[20] H. Noser, O. Renault, D. Thalmann, and N. Magnenat Thalmann, "Navigation for digital actors based on synthetic vision, memory and learning," *Comput. Graphics*, vol. 19, pp. 7–19, 1995.

[21] K. Perlin and A. Goldberg, "IMPROV: A system for scripting interactive actors in virtual worlds," in *Proc. SIGGRAPH '96*, Holly Rushmeier, Ed. ACM SIGGRAPH, 1996, Annual Conference Series, pp. 205–216, Addison Wesley.

[22] K. Perlin, "Real time responsive animation with personality," *IEEE Transactions on Visualization and Computer Graphics*, vol. 1, no. 1, pp. 5–15, March 1995, ISSN 1077-2626.

[23] B. M. Blumberg and T. A. Galyean, "Multi-level direction of autonomous creatures for real-time virtual environments," in *Proc. SIGGRAPH '95*, Robert Cook, Ed. ACM SIGGRAPH, Aug. 1995, Annual Conference Series, pp. 47–54, Addison Wesley, held in Los Angeles, California, 06-11 August 1995.

[24] P. Maes, D. Trevor, B. Blumberg, and A. Pentland, "The ALIVE system full-body interaction with autonomous agents," in *Computer Animation '95*, Apr. 1995.

[25] J. Bates, A. B. Loyall, and W. S. Reilly, "An architecture for action, emotion, and social behavior," in *Artificial Social Systems : Proc of 4th European Wkshp on Modeling Autonomous Agents in a Multi-Agent World*. 1994, Springer-Verlag.

[26] D. C. Brogan and J. K. Hodgins, "Group behaviors with significant dynamics," in *Proc. IEEE/RSJ International Conference on Intelligent Robots and Systems*, 1995.

[27] J. K. Hodgins, "Three-dimensional human running," in *Proc. IEEE Int. Conf. on Robotics and Automation*, 1996.

[28] J. H. Reif, "Complexity of the mover's problem and generalizations," in *Proc. 20th IEEE Symp. on Foundations of Computer Science (FOCS)*, 1979, pp. 421–427.

Real-Time Requirements for the Implementation of Speech-Controlled Artificial Actors

Marc Cavazza, Ian Palmer, and Steve Parnell

Electronic Imaging and Media Communications Department, University of Bradford
Bradford, West Yorkshire, BD7 1DP, United Kingdom
{M.Cavazza, I.J.Palmer, S.Parnell}@Bradford.ac.uk

Abstract. Avatars and Artificial Actors in Virtual Environments can be controlled by speech, as an alternative to motion capture techniques. In this paper, we discuss some specific requirements for the successful implementation of speech-based control of guided actors. We describe our sublanguage approach to speech-based control and its associated parsing techniques, based on lexicalised grammars. After an introduction to the REALISM animation software, we report work in progress in the real-time processing of spoken commands based on the integration of speech processing in the REALISM control loop. We conclude by discussing the possible impact of voice-controlled artificial actors in interactive systems.

1 Introduction

Artificial actors can be controlled through various interface paradigms: i) classical input devices such as keyboard (+ mouse or joystick) or keypads, ii) real-time motion capture techniques and iii) language technologies [1]. Control through keyboard or keypad is the current standard for video games. Motion capture is certainly the most natural interface, but can only reflect real users' movements, which can be a limitation, e.g. for controlling games. In this paper, we explore the use of speech and language technologies to control guided actors or avatars as an alternative to motion capture techniques. We will specifically restrict our study to guided actors with no autonomous behaviour, for which speech input is in direct control of motion parameters, hence competing with traditional motion capture techniques.

There are numerous advantages to the use of language technologies in the control of guided actors. While speech input is recognised as a user-friendly interface, it can also bring new dimensions to the control of artificial actors or avatars. The use of speech control enables the user to concentrate on the visual scene rather than on the I/O devices. In the case of computer games, it brings increased realism and can reinforce the relation between the player and the controlled character. Speech can also convey more abstract information or higher-level commands. The latter does not really apply to guided actors, which do not implement high-level behaviours or intentional representations as an entry point for such high-level descriptions. However, on

Nadia Magnenat-Thalmann, Daniel Thalmann (Eds.): CAPTECH'98, LNAI 1537, pp. 187-198, 1998.
© Springer-Verlag Berlin Heidelberg 1998

the user's side, abstract information can express artistic and emotional judgements that can be translated into movements' parameters. Hence, there can be a mapping between natural language semantics and the specific parameters of the guided actor's motion.

Our target applications are mainly in the field of computer animation and video games. In the case of video games, the speech interface is meant to free the player from traditional interfaces, like keyboard or keypad. It then enhances the tactical aspects of the game over the physical control of the character. In order for the game to retain its original nature, it should be assumed that the character does not have a too high level of autonomous behaviour (in which case we would no longer be in the field of motion capture).

2   Previous and Related Work

Several authors have reported the animation of artificial characters responding to speech or language input. Beardon & Ye [2] have developed a simple Natural Language Processing (NLP) interface to a set of behavioural rules controlling animation. The PERSONA project at Microsoft Research [3] addresses the speech-based animation of an autonomous interface agent. However, the most specific project in language-based animation to date remains the AnimNL project at the University of Pennsylvania [1]. AnimNL is developing a Natural Language (NL) interface to the Jack™ character. It is more specifically dedicated to the unsupervised animation of the Jack™ character from natural language instructions, such as those encountered in maintenance manuals. The automatic processing of these instructions, together with the autonomous behaviour of the Jack™ character, would make possible Human Factors simulations, experimenting the validity of these instructions in a given environment. NL instructions, such as "go into the kitchen and get the coffee urn" are to be executed by the agent without any further human intervention. This assumes that the agent can tune its high-level behaviours using data from its environment. These high-level behaviours are implemented through planning techniques, while the interface between plans and natural language semantics is based on a theory of intentions and expectations [1]. The work of Chapman analysing bystanders' advice to video games players [4] should obviously also be mentioned for its high descriptive value, though some of his conclusions cannot be directly applied to the control of guided actors.

Unlike the AnimNL project, our work is currently addressing the direct control of a guided actor by a human operator. Such an actor does not implement high-level behaviours, though its is desirable that it can still react to its environment. Hence the granularity of commands is bound to be finer. In the next section, we will discuss the requirements of speech understanding in that context.

3   How to Address a Guided Actor

The Speech recognition component can implement various paradigms, bearing in mind that high-performance unconstrained speech recognition is still beyond state-of-the-art. Some kind of sublanguage approach seems the most appropriate choice. It is also consistent with the fact that speech recognition can be made accurate enough only through the definition of a recognition grammar. This grammar, together with the corresponding vocabulary implicitly defines the application sublanguage. Even moderately complex sublanguages can allow a large range of spoken commands that will cope with most of the configurations encountered. A related concept is the notion of habitability [5], which consists in mapping a constrained syntax to a set of alternative formulations of the same utterance. It is generally implemented by encoding a significant number of alternative expressions when defining the sublanguage grammar and vocabulary.

One of the first steps in the design of a speech interface is to specify the application sublanguage. It seems difficult to carry a "Wizard of Oz" experiment for such a real-time interactive system. Besides, it is not clear whether in that case such an experiment would be appropriate for the design of a sublanguage, as we are not dealing with a conversational interface. In our case, spoken instructions are likely to be 5-15 words in length, and we would expect them to be relatively free from hesitations [6]. Also, in the context of video games and unlike other user interfaces, we would expect a significant level of adaptation from the user. Our hypothesis is thus that adaptation to the specific task, together with the fact that short commands do not include repair situations, would make speech recognition easier than in generic consumer applications.

We will assume that the speech recognition system outputs a single string corresponding to the recognised sentence. We won't consider multiple recognition hypotheses, like e.g. n-best analysis. Nor will we deal at this stage with speech recognition errors, substitutions, deletions, etc. Also, we describe the use of our speech recognition system in an offline mode, in which the recognition process starts after completion of the utterance. An alternative mode would consist in a "real-time" recognition, where words are output as they are recognised. Taking advantage of such a recognition mode would however call for different NLP techniques, like e.g. deterministic parsing, that we should not discuss here.

The NLP module takes as input the string produced by the speech recognition system and converts it into an appropriate system command to the guided actor. The use of optional words in the recognition grammar can accommodate for some deviations from normal use. The sublanguage grammar can also be easily designed to account for some syntactic variants. In the next section, we will describe our NLP approach, which is based on a simplified variant of Tree-Adjoining Grammars (TAG). The reason why we do not use the speech recognition grammar (based on a Context-Free Grammar) is essentially to be able to develop an integrated parser for syntax and semantics. As we should see, this is much easier to achieve in a TAG variant and syntax-semantics integration is a key condition for real-time speech understanding.

The requirements on the Natural Language Processing step can be stated as follows:

- it should be carried in minimal time to keep global reaction time as short as possible and generally below one second
- it should produce a self-contained semantic representation that can be directly used by the animation system (through an appropriate API or other communication channel)

In order to specify the kind of linguistic phenomena that are likely to constitute the NLP module's requirements, we have looked for a representative corpus. We have found the so-called "video games spoilers" to constitute a good approximation for such a corpus. These texts describe on a step-by-step basis the traversal of a game level, including the optimal paths and the various actions to be taken. We thus carried a preliminary analysis of an on-line DOOM™ spoiler corpus[1]. Each of these actions is often described as a specific instruction, such as "enter the door with the skull on it", "backup and wait for the door to close", "go back to the stairs", "shoot the Cyberdemon with a chaingun". What this analysis confirmed at the syntactic level was the high frequency of prepositional phrases corresponding to spatial expressions and nominal or definite descriptions. These are known to generate syntactic ambiguities and require semantic feedback to the parser. At the semantic level, the distinction to be made is between commands that can be executed by a guided actor and commands that require extensive interpretation. Examples of the latter, which cannot be processed by a guided actor, are *doctrine* statements and *purpose* statements (following Webber's terminology in [1]). Doctrine statements express general rules with no direct connection with the situation at hand, such as "shoot first, ask questions later"or "just battle away with rockets, chaingun, etc.". Purpose clauses describe actions that cannot be determined from the given instruction alone. One example in our corpus is "shoot a barrel to get rid of most of the pink demons". Proper processing of that command can only be achieved through plan generation, generating complex preconditions for action, such as the determination of demons and barrels' relative positions, etc. Underspecified commands can lead to similar problems. Webber discusses Chapman's example on the "use the knife" command in the context of video games, where the knife can have several uses (as a tool or a weapon) [1]. If semantic interpretation is to restrict itself to those commands with a direct procedural meaning, it is however desirable to give the guided actor some capabilities to react to its immediate environment. These minimal capabilities can for instance correspond to obstacle avoidance or path generation towards a given target ("go to the door"). In the case of fixed targets, the path can be computed with the A* algorithm [7]. In the case of moving targets, with Korf's LRTA* [8]. These interpretations should be allowed only insofar as they can be carried autonomously as a compiled plan, on the basis that they react purely to the environment without any decision making process.

---

[1] DOOM is a trademark of Id Software. Many spoilers are available on-line through the various DOOM-related web sites. The one we have been using has been compiled by Ian Mapleson.

4 The NLP Layer: Interpreting Spoken Instructions

Our NLP technology is based on the Tree Furcating Grammars (TFG) formalism, and integrates syntactic and semantic processing, performing both syntactic disambiguation and the construction of a semantic representation for the sentence parsed [9]. Tree Furcating Grammar is a variant of the Tree-Adjoining Grammar (TAG) formalism, in which adjunction is replaced by the *furcation* operation [10] that adds an additional branch to the target node in the initial tree, instead of copying the auxiliary tree under it. Though some syntactic phenomena are not properly handled by furcation [11], the fact that it introduces modifiers without embedding them into the tree structure is a definite advantage for syntax-semantics integration, and was the rationale for choosing it. Successive tree combinations do not increase tree depth and complexity, producing derived trees that retain some properties of dependency trees. These can support the integrated construction of a semantic representation, based on the appropriate association of semantic functions to the tree structures. Besides, as the limitations of TFG mainly deal with discontinuous components and long-distance dependencies they do not affect the description of sublanguages. The lexicon representation includes a syntactic tree for which the word is an anchor, a set of semantic features used in selectional restrictions and a semantic representation that corresponds to the word "meaning". These semantic contents will be aggregated through the syntactic links to produce a final representation to be mapped to the behaviours implemented in the REALISM animation system [12].

Due to the interleaving of syntactic and semantic processing in our system, we have opted for an ad hoc parsing strategy, which eventually resulted quite similar to the one described by Nasr [13] for its dependency syntax. The main idea is to make the syntactic part of the algorithm as simple as possible and to avoid "hidden" integration of syntax and semantics through contextual constraints on syntactic operations. This also offers more space for the integration of semantic processing. The first step, which corresponds to a lexical filtering of the grammar, consists in generating all the possible set of trees (often termed forests) compatible with the input string. This step is very similar to the construction of a pushdown stack for trees as described in [13]. The parsing algorithm consists in scanning the forest left-to-right and determining possible tree fusions from the explicit typing of the trees considered. Adjacent trees in a forest are considered for a possible fusion on a pairwise basis. From their explicit categories, the corresponding operation is given by a compatibility table. This table specifies the nature of the operation (substitution, furcation, or nil) as a function of the types of the adjacent trees. Left (resp. right) auxiliary trees are combined through right (resp. left) furcation. initial trees and substituable trees are combined through substitution. The process is iterated until the forest is reduced to a single tree or no further operations are possible [9]. All the forests not reduced to a single tree are discarded as unsuccessful parses. Though the processing is syntax driven, its main object is to produce the corresponding semantic representation, which constitutes the final output of the parser. The syntactic roles are converted into appropriate semantic relations which can be attributed an interpretation in terms of behaviours to be passed to the REALISM system.

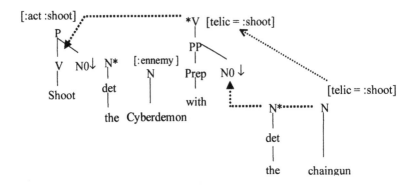

Fig. 1. Parsing a spoken command.

It should be noted that PP-attachments are a major requirement for the processing of definite descriptions, spatial expressions and instrumental actions, which constitute a significant fraction of the requirements for speech-based multimedia applications. Throughout parsing, there is a full integration of semantic processing , which consists both in semantic features propagation, selectional restriction on PP-attachments and attribution of semantic/functional links. Figure 1. shows the processing of the sentence "Shoot the Cyberdemon with the chaingun" from the DOOM™ spoilers' corpus. The syntactic ambiguity due to the PP-attachment of "with" is solved through semantic feature compatibility between "shoot" and "chaingun". The resulting semantic interpretation in that case is a complete action with its relevant parameters.

The parser is implemented in Common LISP and runs on a SGI O2™ workstation with an R10000 processor at 150 MHz. Processing of a single forest corresponding to a 10-15 word sentence is regularly carried in 10-20 ms CPU time. The important point is that, even when parsing several forests for a sentence, the user time remains below 200 ms. Though this was measured with small vocabularies (typically less than 300 words), it is expected to remain roughly unchanged for sublanguages up to 500 words in size, which should be sufficient for the control of an artificial character. The reason is that global response times depend on the number of forests to parse, which is a function of the trees/word ratio. This ratio tends to remain stable within small sublanguages and is certainly much smaller than the generic ratio of 7 mentioned in [14].

5   Integration with the REALISM System

The REALISM animation system [12] normally operates in a non-interactive way. In this mode (Figure 2), the animation is defined by a predefined script (using the AScript language which is then preprocessed to produce an executable) or a C++ program via the REALISM API. The animation can be viewed in real-time via OpenInventor™ or frame description files can be generated for use with non-real time rendering packages (e.g. raytracing software such as Rayshade™). As such the system can produce animated sequences in the same way as many other animation packages. The script or C++ program specifies the precise movements of the objects involved, such a translation, rotation, etc. At each animation frame, this information is used to "step" each object by the required amount. This allows simple animations to be produced quickly, and provides the top-level of control and interaction for the scene. The number of simulation frames per second can be set, and this is implemented when the system runs in interactive mode by using a SoTimeSensor element within the main OpenInventor™ loop.

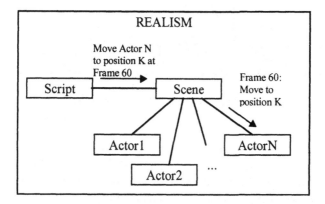

Fig. 2. The non-interactive mode of the REALISM System.

A second level of control is offered by using the object behaviour model. This provides a mechanism by which objects may be in control of their own progress throughout the animation, and as such may override the scene script (Figure 3). For example, a script may contain a key-frame sequence for an object but the object's behaviour may constrain it from movement in a particular way resulting in a different motion from that defined in the script. A simple real example would be a door that the script held key frame information the made it open, whilst its behaviour may specify that it is in fact locked and so will not open. When the object receives a "step" command from the script the current state of the object is passed to the list of behaviours for processing and the new state returned to the object. This allows complex behaviours to be built into the objects without need for specification in the top-level script. An example would be the walking motion of a human character. The top-level script may require the character to move to a new location and this could be simply specified in a similar way to a key frame sequence. However, when the human character receives the command to move to a new location, it passes this information to its behaviour list which results in the joint angles of the character being modified to give a walking action during the translation, thus giving a realistic motion.

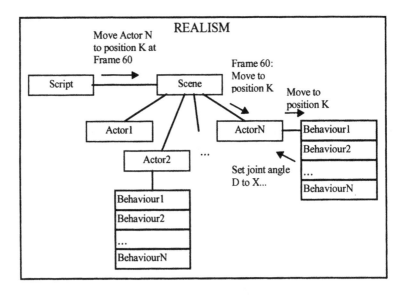

Fig. 3. The object behaviour model.

The complex behaviour of the object is shielded from the user and is in fact broken down into a number of behaviours that control different parts of the character. This distinction between high-level and low-level behaviours in animation has been advocated by several authors, including in the context of speech-driven animation. In the PERSONA project [3] there is a distinct representation for high-level and low-level behaviours. While the former are under control of the main interaction loop (based on speech understanding), the latter can be directly triggered by the animation context.

The final level of control is that added by the work described in this paper. This accepts commands from an external process (Figure 4), in this case from the NLP engine. These could be used to control the system using a sample or interrupt driven scheme. The current implementation samples the socket for commands at an interval defined by a variable in the system. This approach was chosen for the following reasons:

- The REALISM system already uses a sampling system for the other control elements.
- By careful choice of the sample interval in relation to the frame rate and the time taken to process the spoken commands a guaranteed real time performance can be achieved.
- The flexibility given by this allows different processing vs. animation load balances to be tried.

The command interface allows messages to be passed to either the scene for global queries or commands, or more usually to individual actors or objects for applications like avatar control. In this latter case, the commands are processed when they sampled effectively overriding the script for that period of time (the precise timing of this operation is described later in the paper). This means that animation will progress under the control of the script and object behaviours until the command sampling process captures a command. This is then processed and implemented and the animation then continues from this new state.

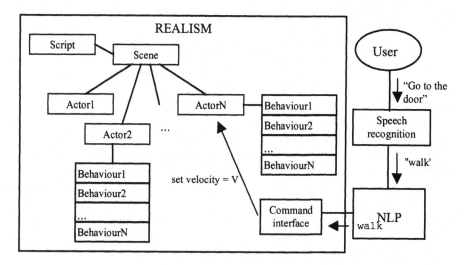

Fig. 4. Modifying behaviours from spoken commands.

The system hardware architecture consists of three main components that correspond to the functional units of the system. Figure 5 shows this in block diagram form. The user input to the system is via the speech recognition system running on a Windows NT™ PC. The recognised command tokens are then passed to the NLP process running on an SGI O2™ over an Ethernet socket connection. The final commands are then passed on through another socket connection to the REALISM running either on the same O2 or on another workstation (as in Figure 5).

The animation loop within REALISM operates at 50 fps. Using the SoTimerSensor, the graphics system effectively 'samples' the REALISM animation process every 0.02 seconds. To accomodate the new command interface, and additional sample period has been introduced. In the current system, this samples a socket connection through which the commands are passed every 0.1 seconds. To ensure that a command is not missed the system waits for data to become available on the socket for 10ms. This is shown in Figure 6. This also shows the worst case for processing a command. This particular diagram ignores the network delays due to the Ethernet connections between machines. This is because this has been found to be negligible at less than 5 ms, and even taking this into account the system response time is less than 1 second.

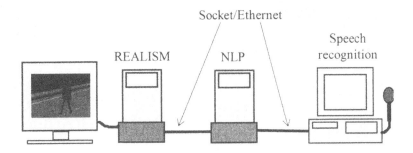

Fig. 5. System Architecture.

The overall time for the system is therefore as follows:

- The speech recognition process on the NT PC takes approximately 500 ms to complete. The recognised sentence is sent to the NLP engine on the O2 workstation.
- The NLP is completed within 100-200 ms. The result of this is a number of control tokens that are passed to the REALISM command interface either running on the same O2 or another workstation.
- The worst case scenario is now that the command token arrives just after the command sample period, and so the system must wait until the next command sample period to detect the command. This adds another 90 ms to the processing time (100ms cycle time – 10 ms wait time).
- Once the next sample occurs, the command is immediately processed (as it is already in the queue). In the worst case this can take up to 50 ms for the REALISM system to respond to the command. In practice, most of the commands are fairly simple to process, for example a command that translates into a 'WALK' action (e.g., to instruct a voice controlled character to start moving) merely involves setting the character's velocity to a non-zero value, which happens virtually instantaneously.
- The change in state is then implemented at worst 30 ms later.

This therefore gives a maximum command to action delay of 870 ms. It also has the effect that the animation frame rate drops. The command sample period of 10 ms on a 100 ms cycle time results in a loss of 10% of the frames from the REALISM system when no commands are being issued (although the OpenInventor™ display will provide a better display rate than this the underlying simulation rate is what interests us here). When a command is issued their is a further loss in animation time due to the 50 ms command processing, resulting in this case of 50% of the frames being dropped. However, this is the worst case processing time and this poor frame rate only occurs during a single 100 ms period, once the command has been processed the loss of frame returns to the 10% level. If the user issues commands every second (an unlikely if not impossible situation), the overall frame rate will drop by 14%.

If the delay between command issue and implementation is too long, the only option to improve this using the current hardware & software is to increase the command sampling rate within the REALISM system. For example, decreasing the command sample interval to 20 ms would result in a worst case delay of 790 ms, but would give frame rate drop of 50% during command-free periods, rising to 52% during command intensive periods. Whilst this is a high percentage, the frame rate of 50 fps is relatively high, giving an effective frame at in this situation of 25 fps which is still acceptable for interactive animation. Although this is acceptable, this is a relatively high price to pay for such a modest improvement if command delay.

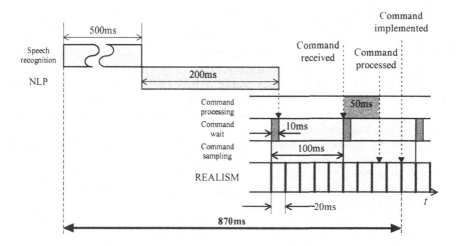

Fig. 6. Response times and sampling in the integrated system.

6 Conclusion

Due to recent advances in speech recognition and NLP, it now appears possible to control guided actors through speech, as an alternative to traditional I/O devices and motion capture techniques. The implementation of speech understanding in the context of computer animation or video games is however faced with stringent requirements in terms of response time, that cannot currently be met on low-end hardware platform. There appears to be a complex relation between speech-based control and the level of autonomous behaviour implemented for artificial actors. While intelligent actors with highly autonomous behaviour can make the best use of speech input, many interactive systems are not designed to accommodate autonomous actors. This is why have so far restricted ourselves to the case of guided actors, implementing only simple behaviours in reaction to their immediate environment.

References

1. Webber, B., Badler, N., Di Eugenio, B., Geib, C., Levison, L., Moore, M.: Instructions, Intentions and Expectations. IRCS Report 94-01, Institute for Research In Cognitive Science, University of Pennsylvania (1994).

2. Beardon, C., Ye, V.: Using Behavioral Rules in Animation. Computer Graphics: Developments in Virtual Environments, Academic Press, San Diego (1995) 217-234

3. Kurlander, D., Ling, D.T.: Planning-Based Control of Interface Animation. Proceedings of CHI'95 Conference, ACM Press, New York (1995) 472-479.

4. Chapman, D.: Vision, Instruction and Action. MIT Press, Cambridge (1991)

5. Trost, H., Heinz, W., Matiasek, J., Buchberger, E.: Datenbank-DIALOG and the Relevance of Habitability, Proceedings of the Third Conference on Applied Natural Language Processing, ACL Press, (1992)

6. Oviatt, S.: User-centered Modeling for Spoken Language and Multimodal Interfaces, IEEE Multimedia, 3 (1996) 26-35

7. Bandhi, S., Thalmann, D.: Space Discretization for Efficient Human Navigation, Proceedings of EUROGRAPHICS Annual Conference, (1998)

8. Ishida, T., Korf, R.E.: Moving-Target Search: A Real-Time Search for Changing Goals, IEEE Transactions in Pattern Analysis and Machine Intelligence, 6 (1995) 609-619

9. Cavazza, M.: An Integated TFG Parser with Explicit Tree Typing, Proceedings of the Fourth TAG+ Workshop, University of Pennsylvania (1998)

10. De Smedt, K., Kempen, G.: Segment Grammars: a Formalism for Incremental Sentence Generation, In: Paris, C.: Natural Language Generation and Computational Linguistics, Kluwer, Dodrecht (1990)

11. Abeillé, A.: Une grammaire léxicalisée d'arbres adjoints : application a l'analyse automatique. PhD Thesis, University of Paris 7 (1991)

12. Palmer, I.J, Grimsdale, R.L.: REALISM: Reusable Elements for Animation using Local Integrated Simulation Models, Proceedings of Computer Animation'94, IEEE Comp. Soc. Press (1994) 132-140

13. Nasr, A.: A Formalism and a Parser for Lexicalized Dependency Grammars, Proceedings of the Fourth International Workshop on Parsing technologies, Prague (1995)

14. Schabes, Y., Waters, R.: Tree-Insertion Grammar: A Cubic-Time Parsable Formalism That Lexicalizes Context-Free Grammars Without Changing the Trees Produced, Technical Report TR-94-13, Mitsubishi Electric Research Laboratories, Cambridge (1994)

3D Modeling from Captured Images Using Bi-directional Ray Traversal Method

Hisayoshi Zaima and Tsuyoshi Yamamoto

Hokkaido University, North-11, West-5, Kita-ku, Sapporo, Japan
{zaima, yamamoto}@cc.hokudai.ac.jp

Abstract. In general, modeling techniques are classified into the creative approach and the reproductive approach. We discuss the latter approach to reconstruct existing objects. Lately, computers and networks are significantly improved, so that application algorithms are also expected to be improved as well. For instance, capturing and modeling existing objects without special equipment is really desirable. We propose a method to reconstruct whole appearances of existing objects with voxel space from 2D images that are captured using ordinary video cameras. Our approach does not involve extracting and tracking feature points of target objects unlike some conventional methods. Our method identifies the voxel properties so as to keep the appearance from frame to frame consistent. We call the way of expression *screened voxel* expressions. The voxel properties are represented by state variables that represent shape and color, and they are calculated by backward and forward ray shooting. During the calculation each voxel has several candidate colors and the correct one is only determined at the end. In this paper, we will discuss the feature value assessment using some experiments. We will also explain the basic methodology of our approach.

1 Introduction

So far many approaches that reconstruct existing objects as 3D models have been introduced [1]∼[4]. However, they tend to have some restrictions with respect to hardware or capturing the environment. Some approaches employ extracting and tracking feature points of target objects that may be characterized by boundaries of textures or shapes. However, the problems of how to extract feature points of target objects and how to track each point between neighboring frames have not yet been established. Today, there is no choice but to rely on range finders or other special equipment for capturing and modeling 3D geometry. We propose a novel method to reconstruct 3D shapes and colors that uses a hand-held video camera to capture the appearances of target objects. Via camera calibration routines, the algorithm reconstructs whole shapes and colors of objects in voxel space. At present we use graph paper in order to extract control points for camera calibration, however there is no need to extract and track feature points of the target objects. Instead, the algorithm uses backward rays and forward rays so as to identify the property of each voxel by assessing the consistency of appearances from different viewpoints. It follows that the algorithm determines each voxel property so as to express outer surfaces of target objects. The required data are only *on the surface* state voxels and we call those extracted voxels *screened voxels*. Although it may be also significant to propose the way to convert these *screened voxels* to polygons by applying the marching cube method, our present objective is to generate high quality voxel models [5]. We have presented the fundamental idea of this approach [6]. In this paper we describe the assessment of proper feature values in order to improve usability of this approach in natural environments. We also describe our experimental results.

2   Related Works

Many approaches to generate 3D objects have been introduced so far. Modeling approaches from existing objects have been also studied a lot in the field of computer vision. Some promising ways have been developed by means of improving conventional methods such as the stereo algorithm or the SFM (Structure From Motion) [7]. In general, those methods require a number of feature points that are extracted as the boundaries of shapes or textures. However, extracting and tracking feature points have been difficult questions so that general and robust ways have not yet established. It also follows that the reconstructed results are strongly affected by the number and the accuracy of feature points. Some approaches that are improved in terms of this question have been introduced. Since it is not required to track feature points, the voting method seems promising. However, it is still required to extract a number of feature points [8][9]. We think it is significant to propose a new modeling method that does not require any feature points of the objects and represent whole appearances of the objects.

3   Bi-directional Ray Traversal Modeling

3.1   Outline

We call such feature values as texture colors and other factors that characterize objects' surfaces *appearance*. First, as can be seen in figure 1(a), we define voxel space, the space which surrounds target objects, as 128^3. Then, we extract outer surfaces by identifying each voxel property. Under ideal conditions, as can be seen from figure 1(b), voxel V_1 which is located on a certain surface, should basically appear identical even from different viewpoints. On the other hand, in the case of voxel V_2 which is located off the surfaces of objects, as can be seen from figure 1(c), will appear different from different viewpoints. When using a number of frames captured from different viewpoints, V_2 should not have a consistent appearance, nor should other off the surface voxels. Thus what the algorithm needs to do is to classify each voxel based on its consistency of *appearance*. In other words, each voxel is expected to be classified into two states depending on whether it has a consistent *appearance* among different frames or not. The reconstruction process consists of three sub-processes as shown in table 1 and each process is performed sequentially.

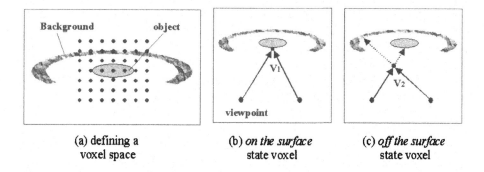

(a) defining a	(b) *on the surface*	(c) *off the surface*
voxel space	state voxel	state voxel

Fig. 1. Basic methodology.(a)Initially, we define a conventional voxel space.(b)On the surface state voxel, V1, should have a consistent appearance even from different viewpoints.(c)Off the surface state voxel, V2, should not.

Table 1. Reconstruction processes

No.	process	objective
1	Backward process	Set initial state for each voxel
2	Forward process (1)	Make inconsistent voxels invalid
3	Forward process (2)	Fix outer surfaces and colors

3.2 Advantages of Our Approach

We explain three advantages of our approach.

(1) No necessity of feature points
Some methods dealing with the feature points tend to have problems regarding the method and the accuracy when extracting and tracking them. Furthermore, it is sometimes the case that it is difficult to obtain a sufficient number of points on the surface, for instance with objects of a single color range (i.e. grayscale) or a curved surface with a single color. If the number of feature points is small, interpolation tends to be difficult. On the other hand, if there are a large number of points, incorrect correspondences often occur or human intervention is required, so it follows that the method becomes difficult to conduct. Although our method needs a number of control points on the background in order to perform camera calibration, it does not require any feature points on the objects. From this, even objects that are considered to be difficult to reconstruct, can be reconstructed.

(2) Outer surfaces of whole objects
If we use feature points, the reconstructed results depend on the distributions of those points. This means that the state of the results is affected by the num-

ber and density of the feature points. Furthermore, in regions where the feature points are dense, incorrect correspondences may be easily formed as described above. Interpolation errors are easily formed in sparse regions. In our method, the amount of final information depends only on the resolution of the voxel space, and it is suitable for calculating outer surfaces with uniform density. In addition, in our approach, it is possible to reconstruct whole appearance of objects regardless of the complexity of the shape and texture.

(3) Small core data
Screened voxel expressions keep the *core data* size for 3D geometry small. In our method, our programs extract and visualize the *core data* that are originally generated from conventional lattice located voxels. Voxels that are extracted as the *screened voxels* are located either on the surfaces or close to the surfaces of the objects. Polygon-based models have a tendency to keep the data size large because of their vertex data that are expressed with the floating decimal points. On the other hand, the *screened voxel* expressions do not involve vertex data so that *core data* can be kept smaller than other conventional expressions. *Core data* are constructed with voxel ids and voxel colors. We need only 6 bytes to define *on the surface* state voxel : 3 bytes for each voxel id and 3 bytes for each voxel color as long as we handle 256^3 voxel spaces or under.

3.3   Feature Values

When we try to compare the values of two or more voxels, certain special values are required. We call these special values *feature values* and use threshold values to compare them. Threshold values are given by maximum allowance ranges so we can regard two values as having the same appearance. In our experiments, we made input frames by translating NTSC video signals to RGB signals and performing a median filter process. We have generated several feature values from pixel values that are expressed as RGB signals. We have also evaluated the feature values through some experiments.

Table 2. Voxel properties

state	candidate colors
on the surface	$\{R_j, G_j, B_j \| j > 0\}$
off the surface	$\{-, -, -\}$

3.4   Voxel Properties

As can be seen from table 2, voxel properties are classified with two state variables, *on the surface* state and *off the surface* state. In the process of reconstruction, voxels that may possibly express outer surfaces of objects are given *on the surface* state and have more than one candidate color, meanwhile other voxels that have no possibility to express outer surfaces of objects are given *off the surface* state and have no candidate colors. Thus in the middle of reconstruction, as long as a voxel has at least one candidate color, the variable is set to *on the surface* state. Each voxel is in one or the other state at all times. If it is no longer possible for *on the surface* state voxels to express outer surfaces, in other words inconsistent *appearances* are found, the state variable is changed to *off the surface* state and all candidate colors are removed. This state changing is irreversible. Once a voxel is identified with *off the surface* state, it can never be reversed. After all processes are completed, voxels that maintain *on the surface* state should express the outer surfaces of target objects.

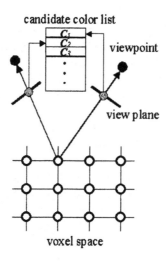

Fig. 2. The backward process. Backward rays are shot from each voxel to all viewpoints.

4   The Backward Process

We show the outline of the backward process in figure 2. Backward rays are shot from each voxel to all viewpoints. If the ray intersects the view plane, the algorithm obtains a feature value at the intersected pixel. So it can obtain a list of feature values. The number of feature values depends on how many view planes the backward rays from the voxel intersect. We mean it is not always true that the backward rays that are connected between a voxel and each viewpoint intersect the view plane. For example, even when we captured 20 frames as input images, the number of intersections could be 15. So the number of values on the list could be set to 15. We call this list *the candidate color list.* The backward process is expressed as follows schematically.

```
for ( each voxel )
{
    for ( each viewpoint )
    {
        shoot backward ray
        if ( intersected ) obtain the pixel value
    }
    obtain a candidate color list for current voxel
}
```

As long as a voxel is located on the surfaces of the object, the original color of the surface should be on *the candidate color list.* However, even in the case that the voxel is located on the surfaces of the object, the most frequently occurring color in the list does not always express the original color of the surface because there are a number of occlusions, or rear projections, shown in figure 3(a). This means that the candidate color lists necessarily contain various colors. Thus even if the number of times a color appears on *the candidate color list* is very small, we can never deny the possibility of expressing the original and final color. Meanwhile, it is possible even for voxels that are located off the surfaces of objects to have *a candidate color list* as described in figure 3(b). However in that case all feature values in the list are expected to be removed by the end of the reconstruction process. Unless these colors are removed, they will appear as artifacts.

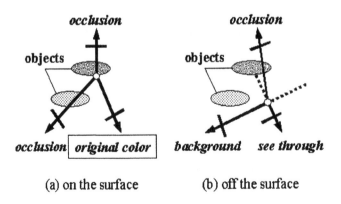

(a) on the surface   (b) off the surface

Fig. 3. Candidate colors on the list. (a)We need to identify the original color on the surface state voxel. (b)All candidate colors should be removed.

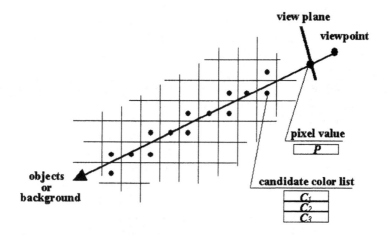

Fig. 4. The forward process. Forward rays are shot from each viewpoint to the voxel space through each pixel.

5   The Forward Process

In the forward process, rays are shot from each viewpoint to voxel space through each pixel as indicated in figure 4. These rays are expressed as traversal voxel lists using the 3DDDA (3 Dimensional Digital Differential Analyzer) [10]. Each forward ray has a feature value obtained from the pixel, and each traversal voxel also has *a candidate color list* obtained from the previous process. At this point, these values are compared using threshold values. When a difference between the values of forward ray (P) and the candidate colors (C_n) is found, the values on *the candidate color list* are removed. If a voxel loses all candidate colors, the state variable is changed to *off the surface* state. When the values of the forward ray (P) and the candidate colors (C_n) are identified as the same, the traversal of the current ray is discontinued and the traversal routine steps to the next ray. The forward process can be expressed as follows schematically.

```
for ( each viewpoint )
{
    for( each pixel )
    {
        shoot forward ray and obtain 'the candidate color list'
        compare feature values
    }
}
```

In our algorithm, the forward process is performed twice sequentially as shown in table 1. Strictly speaking, the voxel location can be classified as one of three states : inside, on the surface and off the surface of objects. The algorithm removes voxels that are located off the surfaces of objects by the first forward process. At this point inside voxels of objects remain and the final color of each voxel has not yet been narrowed down to one. In the second forward process, the algorithm identifies the outer surfaces of remaining voxels that are considered to be located inside or on the surfaces of objects at this point. At the beginning of the second forward process, the score of each feature value on the list is initialized to zero. When a forward ray intersects *on the surface* state voxel, it increases the score of the feature value which has the same value of the forward ray. Finally, the feature value that has the largest score on the list is selected as final value of the voxel. It also follows that a number of *on the surface* state voxels which have scores of zero can be identified with inside voxels. Therefore the algorithm removes those inside voxels in a lump. In the end, voxels that are located on the surfaces of objects remain with selected color.

6   Algorithm Assessment

6.1   Feature Value

Determining feature values in our algorithm required two aspects of assessments concerning the time-oriented properties and the plane-oriented properties. As for the time-oriented properties, it is required to express stable values for identical points on the surface of objects even from different viewpoints. This aspect plays a key role in keeping necessary voxels in *on the surface* state that are actually located on the surfaces of objects. As for the plane-oriented properties, whether the values can maintain sufficient differences based on their original RGB or not will be the target of assessment. This aspect is important to remove unnecessary outside voxels. We assessed the following values based on those requirements. As a preliminary investigation, we captured an existing object from arbitrary viewpoints using a hand-held video camera in a natural environment and extracted 10 frames as key frames. There is no special temporal or spatial relationship among the frames. We investigated the appearances and transitions of captured points. Figure 5 shows the intensities of respective values at an identical point for each frame. Table 3 summarizes standard deviation, maximum differential and band width for each candidate feature value. We also describe respective consideration as follows.

(1) RGB
Employing RGB values directly for feature values is reasonable because how objects appear to humans can be directly reflected with these values. That is the ideal concerning plane-oriented properties. However, the time-oriented properties are anything but stable so that RGB is not suitable for feature value in our algorithm. As can be seen from table 3, the maximum difference is 50, thus if we employ RGB as a feature value, we need to set the threshold value at more than 50 in order to be consistent. Using 50 as a threshold value against the band width that is 256 seems really impractical. The process of capturing images using

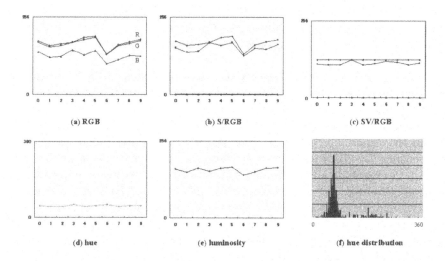

Fig. 5. Transmissions of feature values. (a)RGB (b)S/RGB (c)SV/RGB (d)Hue (e)Luminosity (f)Hue distribution

Table 3. Comparison of feature values

	Standard Division	Maximum Differential	Band Width
RGB	15.6	50	256
S/RGB	3.1	44	256
SV/RGB	23.2	17	256
Hue	7.3	8	360
Luminosity	6.6	26	256

NTSC and translating to RGB is sensitive to signal noise and the properties of objects. We have used RGB values for dull models in an indoor setting experimentally. The appearance of objects was mostly affected by ambient light, so that it sometimes worked well. However it might not work as well in other conditions.

(2) S/RGB

One important question to answer in our experiments was how to deal with NTSC signals. They are very sensitive to signal noise and do not reproduce the colors of scenes accurately. S/RGB stands for Saturated RGB which is produced by translating from RGB to HSV then reversing again to RGB after saturating the value of S. This value S indicates how whitish the recorded signals appear. Therefore saturating S is expected to absorb the dispersion of RGB signals caused by noises and other factors. We employed the Smith's method for inter-translation between RGB and HSV [11]. As can be seen from table 3, compared to RGB, it seems better with respect to time-oriented properties, however it is still not stable enough to be selected as a feature value.

(3) SV/RGB

This value is produced by saturating the value of V along with S. As can be seen from figure 5(c), while stable transitions on time-oriented properties can be found, another question is raised. Saturating a certain value in HSV involves setting the minimum value of RGB at zero or a middle value such as 128. In the region where two or three values in RGB are similar, people can not recognize the differences of these colors and may regard them as the same appearance. However, the translated values using HSV express completely different appearances. In other words, subtle differences in RGB are excessively extended and the translated values can hardly maintain stable appearances of plane-oriented properties. For instance, two pixels, $P_1\{R, G, B|100, 92, 90\}$ and $P_2\{R, G, B|100, 90, 92\}$, look about the same to humans. Even though the difference of G and B is small, these two values are translated to completely different RGB values in the end. This problem commonly occurs in capturing images by video camera because of signal noises and other factors. Reconstruction results are easily and significantly affected by the results of signal translation and camera calibration errors. This issue is found in S/RGB translation and is an even bigger problem in SV/RGB translation.

(4) Hue

RGB may be easily affected by the intensity of input signals but the original hue of objects seems not to be much affected by the input signals. As we expected hue is found to be stable in regard to time-oriented properties unlike RGB. The maximum difference of 8 against the band width of 360 seems to be stable. Having a large band width with a small threshold value is desirable for our algorithm. However, this value does not show sufficient differences in regard to plane-oriented properties. We also confirm the tendency from figure 5(f) that most values converge around particular values. It follows that we can not choose this value as a feature value for the algorithm. Naturally this phenomenon strongly depends on the environment captured. The environment captured may accidentally have had a preponderance of similar hues caused by trees or grasses. At any rate, employing hue seems not to be proper for this purpose.

(5) Luminosity

Since the NTSC signal was originally meant for monochrome images, it is not surprising that it is weak for color. So producing luminosity from NTSC is expected to be much more reliable than that of chromaticity. The value is calculated as YIQ signals translating from RGB. Compared to RGB, it is found to be relatively stable concerning time-oriented properties as well. As for plane-oriented properties, it is certainly true that the amount of information needed to recognize objects is smaller than that of RGB color images, however, it is still possible to recognize the target objects even with monochrome images. Therefore it is thought to be the optimum value among present candidate feature values for our algorithm.

It follows that it seems best for our algorithm to employ luminosity for the backward process and the first forward process and RGB for the second forward process as feature values.

6.2 EV Correction

In many cases, video users leave control of exposure to the camera. So when we capture images outdoors, the exposure values are controlled automatically by the state of light sources, backgrounds and the properties of objects at all times. Especially in our method, since arbitrary viewpoint locations are also allowed, the exposure values are easily changed from frame to frame. Changing exposure values necessarily affects the above-mentioned feature values. In particular, luminosity is easily affected by the exposure value. We could fix the exposure value while capturing images on purpose. However, we decided to give priority to freedom when capturing images and correct the exposure values by computer processing instead of fixing the exposure values. We used a Sony DCR-VX1000 for image capturing equipment because it records exposure values for each captured frame. This makes it possible for the algorithm to correct exposure values after capturing images. Figure 6(a) shows the relation between exposure values (EV) and luminosity (Z) obtained from captured frames. As a preliminary experiment, we observed the relation between EV and Z. In this experiment, we fixed the camera location and captured some frames of a color pallet while changing the exposure values artificially. Figure 6(b) shows the transitions of intensity. Though luminosity is easily affected by the exposure values, it is generally possible to correct the values linearly except for in the saturated region. Making use of the exposure correction based on this calibration, we performed some experiments.

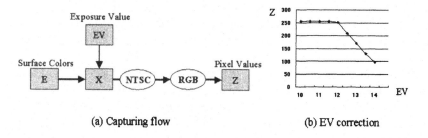

(a) Capturing flow   (b) EV correction

Fig. 6. Influence of exposure values. (a)Pixel values are affected by surface colors and current exposure value. (b)EV correction is available except the saturated region.

6.3 How To Decide Threshold Values

Not only feature value decisions, but also threshold value decisions should significantly affect results. At first, we set the values statically as a parameter and searched for the optimum value by feel. It was difficult to find a suitable value because there is a tradeoff in quality concerning threshold values. On the boundaries of textures or shapes, the accuracy of results is easily affected by camera calibration error. It follows that setting a small value easily causes unsuitable state changing from *on the surface* state to *off the surface* state in this area. Even with a one pixel gap, it could lead to a critical error in results. On the other hand, in the regions where similar appearance is continued in a frame, setting a small value causes effective state changing. This causes a reduction of artifacts. So when camera calibration can be done quite accurately and the feature values are also stable concerning the time-oriented properties, it is better to set small threshold values. In reality, it is difficult to meet all these conditions. Therefore, we may have to set the feature values manually depending on the situation. In the above-mentioned forward process, the algorithm changes the threshold values ray by ray. As can be seen from the following formula, each forward ray is dynamically given the threshold value TV by adding a factor of safety to the maximum differential between current pixel P_c and its surrounding eight pixels P_i.

$$TV = max|P_c - P_i| + \alpha$$

While these values become large on such regions as boundaries of textures and shapes, they become small where similar appearance is continuous.

7   Experimental Results

We show examples of captured frames and individual reconstructed figures in figure 7 and 8. Each model is reconstructed from 20 frames with 640 by 480 pixels and defined in 128^3 voxel space. We employed the Tsai's algorithm and used graph paper to obtain control points for camera calibration [12][13]. We performed all routines on an SGI Indigo^2(R10000-192MB). In the case of figure 8(b), the calculation time was 270 seconds for modeling and 4 seconds for rendering.

The number of input images is one of the most important factors that affect the accuracy of reconstructed models. In these experiments, we employed 20 frames as input images. It is the fact that the accuracy of results and calculation time vary depending on the number of input frames. We have not yet evaluated quantitatively the relationship between the number of frames and the results. It seems fairly affected by the complexity of objects. However, strictly speaking, the selection of camera angles is more important than the number of input images.

Fig. 7. How reconstruction is performed. (a)An example of input images. (b)Just after the backward process. (c)Just after the first forward process. (d)Just after the second forward process.

Figure 7 shows each process of reconstruction step by step. The algorithm identifies a tremendous number of *on the surface* state voxels just after the backward process. The 3D shape of the target object stands out in relief after performing the first forward process. After all processes are completed, the final result is obtained with surface colors along with the outer surfaces. Furthermore, the number of *on the surface* state voxels is reduced to around one tenth between the first forward process and the second one. This is because the voxels that are located inside objects are removed by the second forward process and only the voxels that are located on the surfaces of objects remained as *on the surface* state.

Figure 8(a) shows an example that deals with two objects and obvious occlusion. While we can confirm a good result for occluded objects, some artifacts caused by the graph paper are not negligible. The graph paper is located under the objects for camera calibration so that it is captured on all frames as a common background. Therefore the fact that the algorithm was not able to remove the common background produced artifacts as a result. We expect that this kind of artifact can be reduced by improving the accuracy of camera calibration.
Figure 8(b) shows an example that an object has several colors and occlusions. We confirm from this result that there are two types of artifacts. One type is floating voxels that are located outside the object where objects do not exist in reality. These artifacts are expected to be reduced by improving the camera calibration method as described above. The other one is identified as incorrectly colored voxels that appear different from the original despite being located on the surfaces of objects. We need to improve the color identification process so as to avoid this kind of problem.
In this case, by the end of the process, 3.8% of the voxels remain in *on voxel* state compared to the initial number of 128^3. The final *core data* size is approximately 360KB.

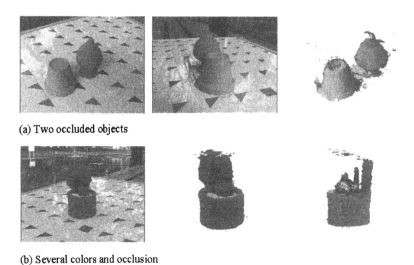

(a) Two occluded objects

(b) Several colors and occlusion

Fig. 8. Experimental results. (a)Two examples of input images and a rendering result of reconstructed model. (b)An example of input images and two rendering results of reconstructed models.

8   Conclusions

We have proposed a reconstruction approach for natural environments. We still have some restrictions such as using graph paper to locate objects, however, we have confirmed the possibility for improving our approach.

Reconstruction of 3D models from captured images has a wide range of applications. For example, reconstruction of the site of soil avalanches is difficult to perform by measuring or using range finders. Similarly, reconstruction of wild plants is difficult without touching them. In cases like the above, our approach will be considered preferable if the available resolution is improved more.

Our approach by no means produces more accurate models than using range finders or other methods. It is rather rough because of using voxel space. However it is portable and has a wide range of applications. Conventional methods that extract and track feature points of objects do not always produce satisfying results. Both approaches, conventional methods and our approach, have respective advantages. It may be desirable for users to apply one or the other method depending on the objects and objectives.

As for our approach in this paper, in order to cope with fully natural scenes, we need to reexamine how to deal with such optical phenomenon as specularly reflected light or highlights. Moreover, we would like to improve camera calibration and calculation time in order to improve effectiveness.

References

1. D.H.Ballard and C.M.Brown, "Computer Vision", Prentice-Hall, 1982
2. H.Murase and S.Nayar, "Visual Learning and Reconstruction of 3-D Objects from Appearance", International journal of Computer Vision, Vol.14, pp.5-24, 1995
3. P.Seutens and A.J.Hanson, "Computational Strategies for Object Recognition", ACM Computing Surveys, Vol.24, No.1, pp.5-61, 1992
4. P.E.Debevec, C.J.Taylor, and J.Malik, "Modeling and Rendering Architecture from Photographs : A hybrid geometry and image-based approach" In SIGGRAPH'96, 1996
5. Lorenson W.E., and Cline H.E., "Marching cubes : a high resolution 3D surface construction algorithm" Computer Graphics, 21(4), 163-9, 1987
6. H.Zaima and T.Yamamoto, "Reconstruction of Outer Surfaces by Bi- directional Rays", Proceedings of WSCG'98, pp141-148,1998
7. C.Tomasi and T.Kanade,"Shape and Motion from Image Streams under Orthography : Factorization Method", International Journal of Computer Vision, Vol 9.2, pp137-154, 1992
8. T.Hamano, K.Ishii and T.Yasuno,"Structure from motion by voting algorithm", Systems and Computers in Japan, Vol.24, No.4, pp23-33, 1993
9. S.Kawato, "Extraction of 3D Structure from Images of Multiple Viewpoints by Two-Step Voting", Journal of IEICE, D-II, Vol J77-D-II, No.12, pp.2334-2341, 1994

10. A.Fujimoto, T.Tanaka and K.Iwata, "ARTS : Accelerated Ray-Tracing System", IEEE Computer Graphics and Applications 6(4), pp.16-26, 1986
11. Smith, Alvey Ray, "Color Gamut Transformation Pairs", Computer Graphics, Vol 12, pp.12-19, 1978
12. R.Y.Tsai, "A Versatile Camera Calibration Technique for High- Accuracy 3D Machine Vision Metrology Using Off-the Shelf TV Cameras and Lenses", IEEE Journal of Robotics and Automation, VOL.RA-3, No.4, August, 1987
13. R.Y.Tsai, "An Efficient and Accurate Camera Calibration Technique for 3D Machine Vision", Proceedings of CVPR'86, pp.323-344, 1986

Face Models from Uncalibrated Video Sequences

P. Fua

Computer Graphics Lab (LIG)
EPFL
CH-1015 Lausanne
Switzerland
fua@lig.di.epfl.ch

Abstract. We show that we can effectively fit a very complex facial animation models to uncalibrated video sequences, without benefit of targets, structured light or any other active device.

Our approach is based on regularized bundle-adjustment followed by least-squares adjustment using a set of progressively finer control triangulations. It takes advantage of three complementary sources of information: stereo data, silhouette edges and 2-D feature points.

In this way, complete head models can be acquired with a cheap and entirely passive sensor, such as an ordinary video camera. They can then be fed to existing animation software to produce synthetic sequences.

1 Introduction

In this paper, we show that we can effectively and automatically fit a complex facial animation model to uncalibrated video sequences, without benefit of targets, structured light or any other active device.

To do so, we have developed a three-step process. First, our algorithm automatically recovers the head's relative motion with respect to the camera. Second, it computes disparity maps for each pair of consecutive images, derives clouds of 3-D points and fits local surface patches to these raw 3-D points. Finally, it uses a least-square adjustment technique to fit a generic animation mask to the 3-D data.

In recent years much work has been devoted to the modeling of faces from image and range data. There are many effective approaches to recovering face geometry. They rely on stereo [1], shading [2], structured light [3], silhouettes [4] or low-intensity lasers. Some of these systems such as the $C3D^{tm1}$, $Cyberware^{tm}$ or $Minolta^{tm}$ scanners are commercially available. However, recovering a head as a simple triangulated mesh does not suffice: To animate the face, one must further fit an actual animation model to the data.

Automated approaches to this task can be roughly classified into the following two categories:

---

[1] Turing Institute, Glasgow

Nadia Magnenat-Thalmann, Daniel Thalmann (Eds.): CAPTECH'98, LNAI 1537, pp. 214–228, 1998.

- Some concentrate on tracking the head motion and some features. They typically use a fairly coarse face model that is too simple for realistic face animation (e.g. [5]).
- Others use sophisticated face models with large numbers of degrees of freedom that are suitable for animation purposes but require very clean data to instantiate them. Such data can be produced by a laser scanner or structured light [6,3] or come from semi-automatically entered feature points and silhouettes [7].

The approach proposed here bridges the gap between these two classes by fitting to actual image data a detailed face model that has successfully been used to animate virtual actors. We can generate with very limited manual intervention a complete head model that can then be fed to existing animation software to create synthetic sequences.

Our contribution is twofold:

- We have introduced model-based regularization constraints in our bundle adjustment procedure that allows the effective recovery of the motion parameters, even though the quality of the points matches cannot be expected to very good.
- We have developed a robust fitting technique that allows the fitting of an animation mask with a great many degrees of freedom to noisy stereo data. The least-squares framework we propose allows us to pool several kinds of heterogeneous information sources—stereo or range, silhouettes and 2-D feature locations—without deterioration in the convergence properties of the algorithm. This is in contrast to typical optimization approaches whose convergence properties tend to degrade when using an objective function that is the sum of many incommensurate terms [8,9].

This has proved essential in dealing with ordinary video sequences of faces that typically exhibit relatively little texture. Our approach thus allows the automated instantiation of sophisticated animation models using a cheap, entirely passive and readily available sensor. As more and more people have video cameras attached to their computers, our approach could be used to quickly produce clones for video-conferencing purposes. It will also allow us to exploit ordinary movies to reconstruct the faces of actors or famous people that cannot be easily be scanned using active techniques, for example because they are unavailable or long dead.

2 Face Model

In this work, we use the facial animation model that has been developed at University of Geneva and EPFL [10]. It can produce the different facial expressions arising from speech and emotions. Its multilevel configuration reduces complexity and provides independent control for each level. At the lowest level, a deformation controller simulates muscle actions using rational free form deformations.

At a higher level, the controller produces animations corresponding to abstract entities such as speech and emotions.

The corresponding skin surface is shown in its rest position in Figure 1(a,b). We will refer to it as the *surface triangulation*. Our goal is to deform the surface without changing its topology. This is important because the facial animation software depends on the model's topology and its configuration files must be recomputed everytime it is changed, which is hard to do on an automated basis.

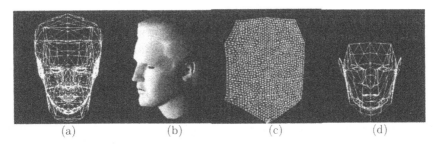

(a)   (b)   (c)   (d)

Fig. 1. Animation model. (a) Wireframe model used to animate complete heads. (b) Shaded view of the model (c) Regular sampling of the face used to perform bundle adjustment. (d) Control triangulation used to deform the face.

3   Relative Motion Recovery

To perform our computation, we first need to estimate the relative motion of the face with respect to the camera. In this work, we choose sequences in which the subjects keep a fairly neutral facial expression and we treat the head as a rigid object.

There are well established photogrammetric techniques to achieve this goal given reliable correspondences between images [11]. In recent years, there also has been much work in the area of autocalibration [12,13,14] and effective methods to compute the epipolar geometry [15] and the trifocal tensor [16] from point correspondences have been devised. However, most of these methods assume that it is possible to run an interest operator such as a corner detector [14,16] to extract from one of the images a sufficiently large number of points that can then be reliably matched in the other images.

In our case, however, because of the lack of texture on faces, we cannot depend on such interest points and must expect that whatever points we extract can only be matched with relatively little precision and a high probability of error. To overcome this problem, we take advantage of our rough knowledge of the face's shape and regularize the standard bundle-adjustment technique as described below.

We assume that the intrinsic camera parameters remain constant throughout the video sequence. In theory, given high precision matches, bundle-adjustment can recover both intrinsic parameters and camera motion. In practice however, we cannot expect out points matches to be very precise. We have therefore chosen to roughly estimate these intrinsic parameters and to concentrate on the computation of the extrinsic ones: We use an approximate value for the focal length and assume that the principal point remains in the center of the image. By so doing we generate 3-D models that are affine transforms of the real heads. Furthermore, we have verified experimentally that, when the estimate of the camera's focal length is not too different from the true value, this affine transform is relatively close to being a rotation and a scaling.

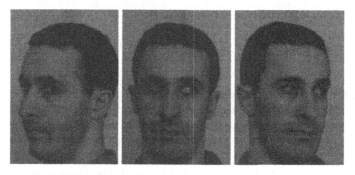

Fig. 2. Input video sequence: 6 of a sequence of 9 consecutive images of a video sequence used as input.

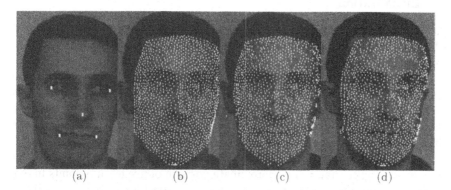

Fig. 3. Tie points: (a) The five manually supplied keypoints used to compute the orientation of the first camera. (b) The projections of the vertices of the bundle-adjustment triangulation of Figure 1(c) into the image of Figure 2(d). (c,d) The points in the images of Figure 2(c,e) that match those of (b). These matching points have been computed using a simple correlation algorithm.

3.1   Generic Bundle Adjustment

Let us assume that we are given n 3–D points that project into m images. We will refer to these points as *tie* points. For each point x_i, y_i, z_i that can be seen in image j, we write two observation equations:

$$Pr_u^j(x_i, y_i, z_i) = u_i^j + \epsilon_{u_i^j} \qquad (1)$$
$$Pr_v^j(x_i, y_i, z_i) = v_i^j + \epsilon_{v_i^j}$$

where $Pr_u^j(x, y, z)$ and $Pr_v^j(x, y, z)$ denote the two image coordinates of the projection of point (x, y, z) in image j and $\epsilon_{u_i^j}, \epsilon_{v_i^j}$ the projection errors to be minimized. For each j, Pr_u^j and Pr_v^j depend on the six external parameters that define the camera position and orientation.

These external parameters can be recovered by minimizing the observation errors in the least square sense, that is by minimizing the objective function $\mathcal{E}$:

$$\mathcal{E} = \sum_{1 \le i \le n} w_i \sum_{1 \le j \le m} \delta_i^j ((Pr_u^j(x_i, y_i, z_i) - u_i^j)^2 + (Pr_v^j(x_i, y_i, z_i) - v_i^j)^2)), \qquad (2)$$

with respect to the value of these parameters and of the x, y and z coordinates. δ_i^j is either zero or one depending on whether the tie point i is visible in image j or not. w_i is a weight associated to point i. It is initially taken to be 1 for all points and can then be adjusted as discussed below. The solution can only be found up to a global rotation, translation and scaling. To remove this ambiguity, we fix the position of the first camera and one additional parameter such as the distance between the first and the second camera.

3.2   Initialization

One well known limitation of bundle adjustment algorithms is the fact that, in order to ensure convergence, one must provide initial values for both camera positions and x, y and z coordinates that are not too far from their true values.

To fulfill this requirement, we begin by retriangulating the surface of the generic face model introduced in Section 2 to produce the regular mesh shown in Figure 1(c). We will refer to it as the *bundle-adjustment triangulation*. We take its vertices to be our tie points and use their x, y and z coordinates as the initial values of the $(x_i, y_i, z_i)_{1 \le i \le n}$ of Equation 2.

To initialize the process for a video sequence such as the one shown in Figure 2, we manually supply the approximate position of five feature points in one reference image: nose tip, outer corners of the eyes and outer mouth corners as shown in Figure 3(a). We usually choose as our reference image one in which the subject faces the camera and we take this image to be image number one.

We represent the camera models for all the cameras as 3x4 projection matrices. To compute them, the algorithm then goes through the following steps:

1. Generate an initial 3x4 projection matrix for the first camera with the principal point in the center of the image.

$$Prj = \begin{vmatrix} f & 0 & xdim/2 & 0 \\ 0 & f & ydim/2 & 0 \\ 0 & 0 & 1 & 0 \end{vmatrix}, \qquad (3)$$

where $xdim, ydim$ are the image dimensions and f is an estimate of the focal length.

2. Compute a 4x4 rotation-translation matrix M such that the five keypoints of Figure 3(a) once multiplied by this matrix project as close as possible to the hand-picked locations in the central image. The 3x4 matrix that represents the camera model for the first image is then be taken to be $Tr = Prj * M$, ensuring that the five keypoints project in the vicinity of the five hand-picked locations. As a consequence, all the other vertices of the bundle-adjustment triangulation also project on the face, as shown in Figure 3(b). These projections are taken to be the u_i^1, v_i^1 of Equation 2. We then match these points in the two images that immediately precede and succeed the central image in the video sequence. We use a simple correlation-based algorithm [17] to obtain the $(u_i^j, v_i^j)_{2 \leq j \leq 3}$ of Equation 2. Figure 3(c,d) depicts the results. Note that not all the points are matched and that there is a number of erroneous matches.

3. Take the initial positions of the other cameras to be equal to that of the first.

4. Given these initial values, use the Levenberg-Marquardt algorithm [18] to minimize the objective function $\mathcal{E}$ of Equation 2 with respect to the camera positions and the tie points' 3-D coordinates.

This yields the camera models for the two images on either side of the central image and an estimate of the bundle-adjustment triangulation's shape. To compute the following camera position, the image immediately succeeding the central image becomes the new central image. We project the bundle-adjustment triangulation's vertices into it, compute the matching points in the image that follows in the sequence and rerun the bundle-adjustment algorithm to compute the position of the corresponding camera. We then iterate until the end of the sequence. We proceed similarly for the images that precede the central image in the sequence.

3.3   Robust Bundle Adjustment

The last step of the procedure outlined above is regular bundle adjustment [11]. If the correspondences were perfect, this would be sufficient to retrieve the motion parameters. However the point correspondences can be expected to be noisy and to include mismatches. To increase the robustness of our algorithm, we augment the standard procedure in two ways:

1. **Iterative reweighted least squares** Because some of the point matches may be spurious, we use a variant of the Iterative Reweighted Least Squares [19] technique. We first run the bundle adjustment algorithm with all the weights w_i^j of Equation 2 being equal to 1. We then recompute these weights so that they are inversely proportional to the final residual errors. More specifically, for each tie point, we compute the average residual error ϵ_i:

$$\epsilon_i = \frac{\sum_j \delta_i^j (Pr_u^j(x_i, y_i, z_i) - u_i^j)^2 + (Pr_v^j(x_i, y_i, z_i) - v_i^j)^2}{\sum_j \delta_i^j} .$$

We take w_i to be

$$w_i = exp(\frac{-\epsilon_i}{\overline{\epsilon_i}}) \ ,$$

where $\overline{\epsilon_i}$ is the median value of the ϵ_i for $1 \le i \le n$. In effect, we use $\overline{\epsilon_i}$ as an estimate of the noise variance and we discount the influence of points that are more than a few standard deviations away.

2. **Regularization** The tie points are the vertices of our bundle-adjustment triangulation and represent a surface that is known to be smooth. We want to prevent excessive deformation by adding a regularization term $\mathcal{E}_D$ to the objective function $\mathcal{E}$ of Equation 2.

To compute this term, we first rewrite our observation equations as:

$$Pr_u^j(x_i + dx_i, y_i + dy_i, z_i + dz_i) = u_i^j \qquad (4)$$
$$Pr_v^j(x_i + dx_i, y_i + dy_i, z_i + dz_i) = v_i^j$$

where x_i, y_i, z_i are the vertex coordinates that are now fixed and dx_i, dy_i, dz_i are displacements that become the actual optimization variables.

If the surface was continuous, we could take $\mathcal{E}_D$ to be the sum of the square of derivatives of the dx_i, dy_i and dz_i across the surface. Because out bundle-adjustment triangulation is a triangulated surface, we can treat its facets as C^0 finite elements and evaluate $\mathcal{E}_D$ as follows: We introduce a stiffness matrix K such that

$$\mathcal{E}_D = 1/2(dX^t K dX + dY^t K dY + dZ^t K dZ) \ , \qquad (5)$$

approximates the sum of the square of the derivatives of displacements across the triangulated surface when dX, dY and dZ are the vectors of the dx_i, dy_i and dz_i.

We can now enforce smoothness by minimizing the regularized objective function $\mathcal{E}_T$:

$$\mathcal{E}_T = \mathcal{E} + \lambda \mathcal{E}_D \qquad (6)$$
$$\mathcal{E} = \sum_i w_i \sum_j \delta_i^j ((Pr_u^j(x_i + dx_i, y_i + dy_i, z_i + dz_i) - u_i^j)^2$$
$$+ (Pr_v^j(x_i + dx_i, y_i + dy_i, z_i + dz_i) - v_i^j)^2) \ ,$$

where λ is a smoothing coefficient.

To illustrate the algorithm's behavior and to quantify the influence of the λ regularization parameter of Equation 6, we have used the three synthetic images shown in Figure 4. They were generated by texture mapping the image of a face on a half sphere seen from several known viewpoints. The underlying half-sphere is shown in Figure 4(d) along with the pyramid shaped bundle-adjustment triangulation we have used in this example. We fixed the position of the first camera, used a regular sampling of the bundle-adjustment triangulation as our

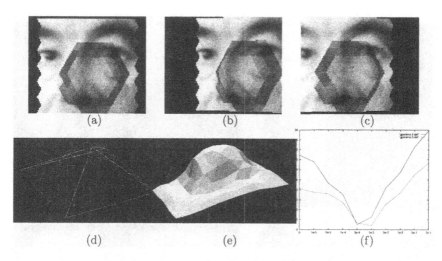

Fig. 4. Synthetic sphere images: (a,b,c) Three synthetic images of a textured half-sphere. (d) The "real" shape of the half sphere and the pyramid-shaped bundle-adjustment triangulation used in this experiment. (e) Recovered shape of the bundle-adjustment triangulation after recovery of the camera parameters for a give value of the regularization parameter λ. (f) Distance of the recovered position the camera centers to their true positions as a function of λ.

tie points and ran our algorithm for the following range of values of λ: 0.0, 1e-5, 5e-5, 1e-4, 5e-4, 1e-4, 1e-3, 5e-3, 5e-2, 1e-2, 5e-1 and 1e-1. In Figure 4(e) we show the shape of the bundle-adjustment surface at the end of the optimization for λ =5e-4. In Figure 4(f) we plot, for each camera, the distance of the recovered position of the optical center to the real one as a function of λ. For λ too small, there is not enough regularization and the algorithm tends to overfit the noisy data resulting in large errors. For λ too large, the regularization term prevents the bundle-adjustment surface to deform adequately, also resulting in a poor result. There is however a wide range of values of λ— approximately between 1e-4 and 5e-4— that yield minimal error.

These results were produced using the correct internal parameters—focal-length and principal points—to instantiate the projection matrix of Equation 3. Using the same data, we have also verified that when we perform the computation using internal parameters that differ from the real ones, the recovered shape is related to the original one by an affine transformation. The position of the principal points has little influence and, for values of the focal length that are within 20% of the real value, the affine transform is close to being a rotation-translation.

We now turn to the video sequence of Figure 2, we recover the camera positions shown in Figure 5(a). Figure 5(b,c) depicts the corresponding bundle-adjustment triangulation's shape. To check the quality of the result, we have used a Minolta^{tm} laser scanner to acquire the model of the same head shown in Figure 5(d,e). In theory, the bundle-adjustment triangulation and the output of the laser scanner—that we assume to be a fairly precise model of the real

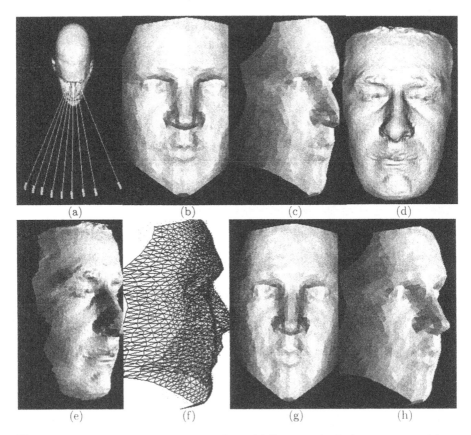

Fig. 5. Comparison with laser scanner data: (a) Recovered relative camera positions. (b,c) A shaded representation of the bundle-adjustment triangulation. (d,e) The laser scanner data. (f) The control triangulation, shown as wireframe, after an affine transform that projects it to the laser data, shown as red points. Note that they are well superposed (g,h) A shaded representation of the affine transformed bundle-adjustment triangulation.

face—should have the same shape up to an affine transform. We have therefore computed the affine transform that brings the bundle-adjustment triangulation closest to the laser-scanner model. As shown in Figure 5(f,g,h), the superposition is good and the deformation introduced by the affine transform is not very severe. We have performed the same experiment on the images of Figure 7 with similar results.

4   Model Fitting

Given the camera models computed above, we can now recover additional information about the surface by using a simple correlation-based algorithm [17] to compute a disparity map for each pair of consecutive images in the video sequences and by turning each valid disparity value into a 3–D point. Because,

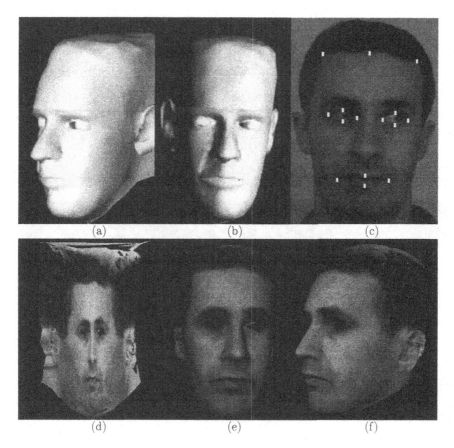

Fig. 6. Recovered head: (a,b) Shaded model of the head of Figure 2. (c) 2–D feature points used to constrain the reconstruction. (d) Computed texture map. (e,f) Texture mapped representations of the head.

these 3–D points typically form an extremely noisy and irregular sampling of the underlying global 3–D surface, we begin by robustly fitting surface patches to the raw 3–D points. This first step eliminates some of the outliers and generates meaningful local surface information for arbitrary surface orientation and topology. For additional details, we refer the interested reader to an earlier publication [20].

Our goal then is to deform the generic mask so that it conforms to the cloud of points, that is to treat each patch as an attractor and to minimize its distance to the final mask. In our implementation, this is achieved by computing the orthogonal distance d_i^a of each attractor to the closest facet as a function of the x,y, and z coordinates of its vertices and minimizing the sum of the squares of these distances

$$E_A = \sum_i w_i (d_i^a)^2 \tag{7}$$

where w_i is a weight associated to each attractor.

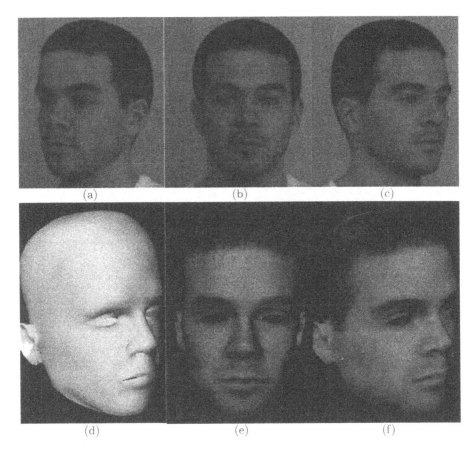

Fig. 7. Another video sequence: (a,b,c) Three images of a sequence of 9. (d) Shaded
model of the head (e,f) Texture mapped representation.

Finding this "closest facet" is computationally expensive if we exhaustively
search the list of facets. However, the search can be made efficient and fast if we
assume that the 3–D points can be identified by their projection in an image, as
is the case with stereo data. For each image, we use the Z-buffering capability
of our machines to compute what we call a "Facet-ID image:" We encode the
index i of each facet f_i as a unique color, and project the surface into the image
plane, using a standard hidden-surface algorithm. We can then trivially look up
the facet that projects at the same place as a given point.

4.1   Control Triangulation

In theory we could optimize with respect to the state vector P of all x, y, and
z coordinates of the surface triangulation. However, because the image data is
very noisy, we would have to impose a very strong regularization constraint. For
example, we have tried to treat the surface triangulation as finite element mesh.
Due to its great irregularity and its large number of vertices, we have found

the fitting process to be very brittle and the smoothing coefficients difficult to adjust. Therefore, we have developed the following scheme to achieve robustness.

Instead of directly modifying the vertex positions during the minimization, we introduce *control triangulations* such as the ones shown in Figure 1(d). The vertices of the surface triangulation are "attached" to the control triangulation and the range of allowable deformations of the surface triangulation is defined in terms of weighted averages of displacements of the vertices of the control triangulation.

More specifically, we project each vertex of the surface triangulation onto the control triangulation. If this projection falls in the middle of a control facet, we "attach" the vertex to the three vertices of the control facets and compute the corresponding barycentric coordinates. If this projection falls between two facets, we "attach" the vertex to the vertices of the corresponding edge. In effect, we take one of the barycentric coordinates to be zero.

Given these attachments, the surface triangulation's shape is defined by deformation vectors associated to the vertices of the control triangulation. The 3–D position P_i of vertex i of the surface triangulation is taken to be

$$P_i = P_i^0 + l_1^i \delta_{j1} + l_2^i \delta_{j2} + l_3^i \delta_{j3} \quad , \tag{8}$$

where P_i^0 is its initial position, $\delta_{j1}, \delta_{j2}, \delta_{j3}$ are the deformation vectors associated to the control triangulation vertices to which vertex i is attached, and l_1^i, l_2^i, l_3^i are the precomputed barycentric coordinates.

In this fashion, the shape of the surface triangulation becomes a function of the δ_j and the state vector to be optimized is taken to be the vector of the x, y and z components of these δ_j. Because the control triangulations have fewer vertices that are more regularly spaced than the surface triangulation, the least-squares optimization has better convergence properties. Of course the finer the control triangulation, the less smoothing it provides. By using a precomputed set of increasingly refined control triangulations, we implement a hierarchical fitting scheme that has proved very useful when dealing with noisy data.

4.2   Stiffness Matrix

Because there may be gaps in the image data, it is necessary to add a small stiffness term into the optimization to ensure that the δ_j of the control vertices located where there is little or no data are consistent with their neighbors. As discussed in Section 3.3, because our control triangulation is discrete, we can again treat its facets as C^0 finite elements and write our stiffness term as

$$E_S = \Delta_x^t K \Delta_x + \Delta_y^t K \Delta_y + \Delta_z^t K \Delta_z \tag{9}$$

where K is a stiffness matrix and Δ_x, Δ_y and Δ_z are the vectors of the x, y and z coordinates of the displacements δ. The objective function we actually optimize becomes

$$E = E_A + \lambda_S E_S \quad , \tag{10}$$

where λ_S is a small positive constant and E_A is the sum of the square distances to the attractors of Equation 7.

4.3   Weighing the Observations

We recompute the facet closest to each attractor at each stage of the hierarchical fitting scheme of Section 4.1, that is each time we introduce a new control triangulation.

Because the stereo data is noisy and may contain errors, we use again the Iterative Reweighted Least Squares technique introduced in section 3.3. Each time we recompute the attachments, we also recompute the weight w_i associated with attractor i and take it to be inversely proportional to the initial distance d_i of the data point to the surface triangulation.

4.4   Shape and Texture

This fitting procedure has been used to model the faces of the heads shown in Figures 6 and 7. Using the control triangulation of Figure 1(d). In both cases, to ensure that some of the key elements of the face—corners of the eyes, mouth and hairline—project at the right places we have manually supplied the location of the projection in one image of a few feature points such as the ones shown in Figure 6(c). We have then added a term to the objective function of Equation 10 that forces the projection of the corresponding vertices of the generic mask model to be close to those locations [21]. Note that the five manually supplied points used to initialize the bundle-adjustment procedure of Section 3.2 form a subset of these features points. To produce these face models, the manual intervention required therefore reduces to supplying these few points by clicking on their approximate locations in one single image, which can be done quickly.

The shape of the top of the head has been recovered by semi-automatically delineating in each image of the video sequence the boundary between the hair and the background and treating it as a silhouette that constrains the shape [21].

Given the final model of the head, we can compute a texture map by:

1. Generating a cylindrical projection of the head model.
2. For each projected point, finding the images in which it is visible and averaging the corresponding gray-levels.

This yields texture maps such as the one shown in Figure 6(d) and allows textured reconstruction such as the ones of Figures 6(e,f) and 7(e,f).

5   Conclusion

We have presented a technique that allows us to fit a complex animation model to uncalibrated video sequences with very limited manual intervention. As a result, these models can be produced cheaply and fast using an entirely passive sensor.

This has direct applications in the field of video communication and entertainment and will allow the the fast generation of realistic avatars from widely available data. Furthermore, the face model we use has been one of the starting points for the facial animation parameters defined in the MPEG-4 FBA work. When standardization is complete, it will therefore be easy to make the parameters of our model conformant with the MPEG-4 norm for facial animation and the work presented here will become directly relevant to video transmission.

Acknowledgements

We wish to thank Prof. Christian Heipke for the many illuminating discussions about bundle-adjustment we have had when we began the work reported here. We also wish to thank Prof. Nadia Magnenat Thalmann and Prof. Daniel Thalmann for having made their facial animation model available to us. We are also indebted to Mirco Sartor who spent many hours implementing the algorithm that generates the texture maps shown in this article.

References

1. F. Devernay and O. D. Faugeras, "Computing Differential Properties of 3–D Shapes from Stereoscopic Images without 3–D Models," in *Conference on Computer Vision and Pattern Recognition*, Seattle, WA, June 1994, pp. 208–213.
2. Y. G. Leclerc and A. F. Bobick, "The Direct Computation of Height from Shading," in *Conference on Computer Vision and Pattern Recognition*, Lahaina, Maui, Hawaii, June 1991.
3. M. Proesmans, L. Van Gool, and A. Oosterlinck, "Active acquisition of 3D shape for Moving Objects," in *International Conference on Image Processing*, Lausanne, Switzerland, September 1996.
4. L. Tang and T.S. Huang, "Analysis-based facial expression synthesis," *ICIP-III*, vol. 94, pp. 98–102.
5. D. DeCarlo and D. Metaxas, "The Integration of Optical Flow and Deformable Models with Applications to Human Face Shape and Motion Estimation," in *Conference on Computer Vision and Pattern Recognition*, 1996, pp. 231–238.
6. Y. Lee, D. Terzopoulos, and K. Waters, "Realistic Modeling for Facial Animation," in *Computer Graphics, SIGGRAPH Proceedings*, Los Angeles, CA, August 1995, pp. 191–198.
7. W.S. Lee and N. Magnenat Thalmann, "From Real Faces To Virtual Faces: Problems and Solutions," in *3IA*, Limoges, France, 1998.
8. P.E. Gill, W. Murray, and M.H. Wright, *Practical Optimization*, Academic Press, London a.o., 1981.
9. P. Fua and C. Brechbühler, "Imposing Hard Constraints on Deformable Models Through Optimization in Orthogonal Subspaces," *Computer Vision and Image Understanding*, vol. 24, no. 1, pp. 19–35, Feb. 1997.
10. P. Kalra, A. Mangili, N. Magnenat Thalmann, and D. Thalmann, "Simulation of Facial Muscle Actions Based on Rational Free Form Deformations," in *Eurographics*, 1992.
11. A.Gruen and H. Beyer, "System Calibration through Self-Calibration," in *Calibration and Orientation of Cameras in Computer Vision*, Washington D.C., August 1992.

12. O.D. Faugeras, Q.-T. Luong, and S.J. Maybank, "Camera self-calibration: theory and experiments," in *European Conference on Computer Vision*, Santa-Margerita, Italy, 1992, pp. 321–334.

13. B. Triggs, "Autocalibration and the Absolute Quadric," in *Conference on Computer Vision and Pattern Recognition*, 1997, pp. 609–614.

14. M. Pollefeys, R. Koch, and L. VanGool, "Self-Calibration and Metric Reconstruction In Spite of Varying and Unknown Internal Camera Parameters," in *International Conference on Computer Vision*, 1998.

15. Z. Zhang, R. Deriche, O. Faugeras, and Q. Luong, "A Robust Technique for Matching two Uncalibrated Images through the Recovery of the Unknown Epipolar Geometry," *Artificial Intelligence*, vol. 78, pp. 87–119, 1995.

16. A.W. Fitzgibbon and A. Zisserman, "Automatic Camera Recovery for Closed or Open Image Sequences," in *European Conference on Computer Vision*, Freiburg, Germany, June 1998, pp. 311–326.

17. P. Fua, "A Parallel Stereo Algorithm that Produces Dense Depth Maps and Preserves Image Features," *Machine Vision and Applications*, vol. 6, no. 1, pp. 35–49, Winter 1993.

18. W.H. Press, B.P. Flannery, S.A. Teukolsky, and W.T. Vetterling, *Numerical Recipes, the Art of Scientific Computing*, Cambridge U. Press, Cambridge, MA, 1986.

19. A. E. Beaton and J.W. Turkey, "The Fitting of Power Series, Meaning Polynomials, Illustrated on Band-Spectroscopic Data," *Technometrics*, vol. 16, pp. 147–185, 1974.

20. P. Fua, "From Multiple Stereo Views to Multiple 3–D Surfaces," *International Journal of Computer Vision*, vol. 24, no. 1, pp. 19–35, 1997.

21. P. Fua and C. Miccio, "From Regular Images to Animated Heads: A Least Squares Approach," in *European Conference on Computer Vision*, Freiburg, Germany, June 1998.

A 3D Reconstruction System for Human Body Modeling

Jin Gu[1], Terry Chang[2], Ivan Mak[1], S. Gopalsamy[1,3], H. C. Shen[1], and
M. M. F. Yuen[2]

[1] Department of Computer Science
Hong Kong University of Science and Technology
Clear Water Bay, Kowloon, Hong Kong.
{csgjx, ivanmak, gopal, helens}@cs.ust.hk
[2] Department of Mechanical Engineering
Hong Kong University of Science and Technology
Clear Water Bay, Kowloon, Hong Kong.
{meterry, meymf}@usthk.ust.hk
[3] Visiting Research Scientist from NCST, Bombay, India.

Abstract. A camera based image capturing and 3D reconstruction system for human body modeling is presented. The system is essentially based on shape from contour and uses deformable superquadrics as modeling primitive. From the superquadrics model, in the case of human body, a parametric surface model is derived which is used in mannequin modeling. The performance of the system is evaluated in terms of user interaction, time taken, and accuracy.

Keywords:

occluding contour, deformable superquadrics, human body modeling, parametric surface model, mannequin modeling.

1 Introduction

Three dimensional human body modeling has been an interesting topic for human factor engineers and researchers in ergonomics. Nowadays, it is finding its place in more and more applications, such as mannequin modeling for garment design in textile industry, computer games, and movie animation in entertainment field. In terms of requirements, human body modeling can be classified in to the following two categories:

1. Modeling of a specific human subject required in applications such as mannequin modeling for garment design [6], [3] where spatial accuracy is of prime concern. This is a particular case of 3D reconstruction traditionally addressed by computer vision people.

Nadia Magnenat-Thalmann, Daniel Thalmann (Eds.): CAPTECH'98, LNAI 1537, pp. 229–241, 1998.
© Springer-Verlag Berlin Heidelberg 1998

2. Modeling of a general human body required in animation and virtual reality applications dealing with virtual humans [2], [14], or modeling of a specific human for applications where visual realism dominates over spatial accuracy [11]. This is traditionally addressed by computer graphics and animation researchers.

In this paper, we are concerned with the first category. Here, in order to build human body model, three dimensional data needs to be captured from real human body or mannequin. There are mainly two categories of techniques for 3D data acquisition: active sensing and passive sensing. The active sensing techniques are commonly used for 3D data capturing due to the straight forward readiness in obtaining 3D data of object and/or its high precision and resolution. However, they project external energy on the object. Passive sensing is preferred in case the object is a life object such as human body. Camera is the commonly used sensor in this category. Stereo, shape-from-X (X can be occluding contours, shading, motion, focus/defocus, texture, surface contours), and volumetric intersections are techniques for passive sensing. Compared with laser scanner, such as the Cyberware whole body scanner[1], cameras are generally cheaper. On the other hand, camera can also capture visual information such as special markers on the body which may be important for later analysis of the human body.

In our laboratory, a camera-based data capturing and 3D reconstruction system has been designed and developed for the purpose of human body modeling [9], [5], [4], [10]. A system reported in the literature with similar scope and application is the Virtuosi system [3]. The Virtuosi system takes two views of a person to capture the data and uses a huge database of already computed 3D human models to select a close fit and then modify. Whereas our human body modeling system uses images from six views to reconstruct the 3D model and does not use any database of human models.

System overview: The human body modeling system consists of two major components – hardware and software. The hardware components include the following: the equipment supporting framework, cameras and lens, lighting arrangement, and sensor synchronization. The hardware design aims at a system which can provide a capturing environment which is friendly for users and the human being if it is to be imaged. In other words, we need to make the installation of the system simple and easy to use, at the same time, we need to make the time period during which the subject is required to stay stationary as short as possible.

The software consists of five modules:

- *Camera calibration module*: this module calibrates all the cameras, finding their positions and orientation in the global coordinate system, and their intrinsic parameters as well;
- *Image capturing module*: this module enables the system to obtain images from all the cameras in a certain amount of time;
- *Image processing module*: this module processes the intensity images and extracts occluding contours, fiducial marker positions, and grid-line intersections for stereo.

- *Model reconstruction module*: this module is the core of the whole system, it reconstructs the model of the imaged object by computer vision techniques [12, 9, 8, 7, 5];
- *Virtual measurement module*: this module extracts domain-dependent measurements from the reconstructed object model and finds application-oriented features. For our application of human body modeling for mannequin manufacturing and garment design, this module provides an interactive user interface for customized measurement and feature extraction.

The software aims at offering a friendly, easy-to-use environment where the user can easily calibrate the system, obtain the reconstructed object model and obtain the application-dependent information from the reconstructed model. In the following sections we give brief descriptions of above mentioned components and then present a performance evaluation of the system.

2   Hardware Components

2.1   The Equipment Supporting Framework

A hexagonal supporting framework is manufactured to form a closed space for imaging. The dimension of this space is $3m$ in radius and $2.5m$ high. The hexagonal supporting framework is made of six vertical ferro-chrome poles, six horizontal ones on the top and six horizontal ones on the floor for supporting and connection. In Figure 1, we show the top view and side view of the framework. Black cloth is hung around the framework as background of the imaging. Cameras will be installed along the vertical poles.

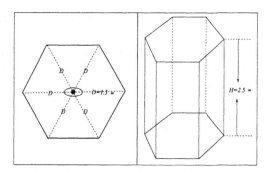

Fig. 1. Top view and side view of the supporting framework for imaging

The target object supposed to be imaged is up to $2.0m$ tall. Six views are used to cover the $360°$ circular reconstruction space. We add one more view for frontal image to be taken so that we can obtain better information of the chest, the armpit and the crotch in case of a human subject being imaged. Therefore seven views around the circular space are selected as viewing points for installing cameras. The first six views are approximately 60° apart from each other, the seventh view is between the first and the second view. In order to generate more feature points for the stereo to work, we use a slide projector which projects a grid pattern on the body surface. The slide projector is put at the position of the seventh view. In Figure 2, we show the viewpoints distribution in our system.

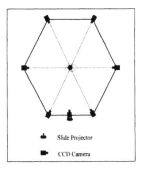

Fig. 2. View distribution of the system

2.2   Cameras and Lens

Currently, we have chosen ordinary B/W CCD cameras to acquire images of the objects. Considering the space available for imaging, and the required height of target objects, we select to use CCD cameras with $1/2''$ sense area and $8mm$ lens as our sensing equipments. The viewing angle α for our current system is 43.5^o. For each viewpoint, in order for the full length of the object to be sensed, two cameras are needed for each view based on such a selection of sense area-lens combination and the space constraints. The cameras are installed on the vertical poles in such a way that the whole body can be imaged and the shortening effect caused by perspective projection is minimized [4].

2.3   Sensor Synchronization

As we have mentioned, totally 12-13 cameras are used in our system. In order to capture the images in a time period during which a normal human being is able to stay relatively stationary, we need to synchronize all the cameras in the capturing process. It is impractical to use the same number of computers and grabber cards as cameras to achieve short capturing time. Instead, we use one computer only for image acquisition. We designed a 16-1 multiplex switch which can connect/disconnect the communication between cameras and the computer according to the signal sent by the computer software. With this switch box, the cameras send their images through network cables to the computer via the switch sequentially. The image capturing task can be accomplished within 15

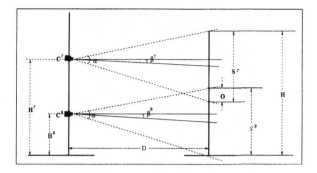

Fig. 3. Camera Positioning of the system

seconds. Through all of our experiments, with adult, this time period is shorter than acceptable. In Figure 4 we show the diagram of equipment connection.

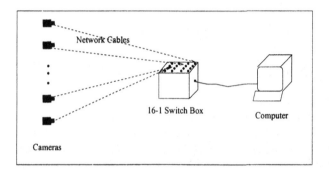

Fig. 4. Equipment Connection Diagram

3   Software Components

3.1   Camera Calibration

Calibration is a crucial step in any 3D measuring systems. To calibrate the cameras, we need a calibration target so that the calibration points can be easily identified in calibration images and their actual 3D coordinates can be easily and precisely determined. We have used a cylindrical object so that the patterns on its surface are visible to all cameras. Squares of known dimension are arranged on the surface of this object. The corners of the squares are used as the calibration points. Both 3D and 2D coordinates of these points are easily found. Tsai's camera model [13] is adopted and parameters are computed. Once the calibration is done, the cameras are not allowed to move, in other words, we fix the focus, the position and orientation of the cameras. Since they are stably installed on the framework, this can be guaranteed.

Fig. 5. Camera Calibration Object

3.2 Image Capturing

Intensity images are taken from multiple viewpoints. The human subject is required to wear tight clothing and stand in the center of the imaging space so that the body can be visible to all the cameras. To obtain clear contours of the body, the subject is asked to put the arms in a position so that they do not touch the torso part and also keep the two legs slightly apart. Special markers are put at crucial locations such as belly button and neck which will be used as reference points in the parametric representation of the human model. For surfaces such as frontal chest of female subjects, a grid pattern is projected onto the body surface to supply features for stereo cue to refine the details on the surface. The image acquisition procedure takes around 12-15 seconds in total. Within this period, the human body is asked to stand still. As a result 12 or 13 grey level images will be captured.

3.3 Image Processing

The captured images are processed in order to extract (i) occluding contours, (ii) the intersections of grid points for the images illuminated with grid patterns, and (iii) 3D coordinates of special markers. Occluding contour and grid intersections will be used in the subsequent steps of the reconstruction. Locations of special markers will be used in the parametric representation of the human model as explained later.

Contour extraction: In the first place, Canny edge detector is used to find the edges in the image. Edges with magnitude larger than a certain threshold value are considered major edge pixels. An edge linking algorithm is designed to link the major edge pixels to obtain the contours as connected components. The contours are then segmented into various parts corresponding to natural human body parts. The segmentation is done according to the curvature information of the contours and a prior knowledge of the imaged object structure.

Structural Lighting Feature Points Extraction: Grid lighting provides feature points for stereo cue. The intersections of grids are considered as the points used for stereo correspondence. In order to locate these feature points, two line detectors, that is horizontal and vertical line detectors are applied to the images with grid lighting. Pixels with high response to both detectors are taken as candidates for feature points.

Extraction of special markers: Their locations in the images are first extracted and the corresponding 3D coordinates are reconstructed by stereo.

In Figures 6, 7, we show the occluding contours and fiducial points extracted from intensity images.

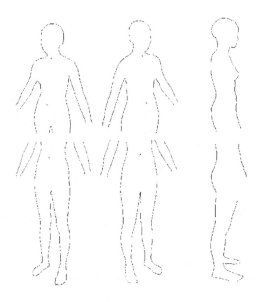

Fig. 6. Occluding Contours and Fiducial Points of Female Model – views 1, 2, 3

3.4   3D Model Reconstruction

Human Body Representation: In our system, a human body is represented by a set of deformable superquadrics(DFSQ). Briefly, deformable superquadric is a generalized ellipsoid with global parameters controlling the global shape of the superquadric and local parameters to capture the fine information of the object surface. The expressive range of such superquadric is rather wide. Allowed by local deformation, it can represent more detail information on the surface. These

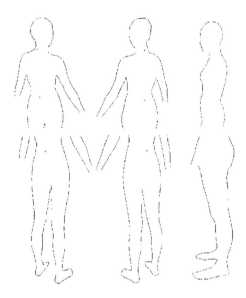

Fig. 7. Occluding Contours and Fiducial Points of Female Model – views 4, 5, 6

characteristics are suitable for representing human body surface. Except for the face, most of the human body surface is smooth. Most of the parts are in a shape of ellipsoid or cylinder. Therefore, deformable superquadrics are chosen to be the geometric primitive for our human body representation. Naturally we split the human body into 15 parts: head, neck, shoulder, arms(upper, forearm), torso, pelvis part, legs(thigh and calf), feet. Each part is represented by a deformable superquadric. For female adult human body, we add two more for the bosoms.

Superquadric Fitting: This is done in two steps – initialization and local deformation. The initialization of each DFSQ is done by computing an approximate bounding polyhedron by intersection of the viewing cones derived from occluding contours [5]. They are initialized into positions and orientations such that their projections by various cameras are roughly close to the image contours from the same cameras.

The process of local deformation is treated as the motion procedure of the points on the DFSQ under the external forces derived from the image contours and stereo-reconstructed points. This dynamic process is modeled by Lagrange's motion equation where the unknowns are simply the parameters of the superquadric including both global and local deformation. FEM method is used to solve the partial differential equation.

Experimental results: Figure 8 shows the reconstructed superquadrics of the female model. In Figure 9, we show the comparisons of measurements made on the real human body. It is agreed that the accuracy of the reconstruction is valid and reasonable for mannequin generation.

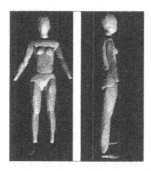

Fig. 8. Reconstruction of a female Model

	Estimated Measurements	Tailor Measurements	Difference
Height(cm)	170.53	171	0.47
Head Height(cm)	25.93	26	0.07
Neck(cm)	31.35	31	0.35
Chest(cm)	80.1	81	0.90
Waist(cm)	65.1	66	0.90
Waist Thickness (cm)	17.87	17	0.87
Hip(cm)	87.73	91	3.27
Thigh(cm)	46.86	46	0.86
Calf(cm)	34.26	33	1.26
Ankle(cm)	20.86	20	0.86

Fig. 9. Measurements of Female Model

3.5   Parametric Surface Representation

In our applications of mannequin manufacturing, we need a parametric surface representation of the reconstructed human model. The parametric representation is defined with respect to the following human-body-centered coordinate system (see Figure 10): the origin O is the mid point of the belly button (BB) and back belly button (BBB) points; the y-axis is the line through BBB; the plane through O, BB, and the front neck point (FN) is the yz plane. Secondly, the parametric representation is defined over individual parts of the human body. The parts of the human body are identified by a set of key feature points, Figure 11. For each part, section curves are defined at specific heights relative to key feature points and the part is obtained as a parametric surface passing through these section curves (Figure 12).

In order to obtain section curves from the superquadrics model, we first align the superquadrics with the human-body-centered coordinate system and then intersect with the planes defining the sections. Figure 13 shows the final parametric surface (shown in slices) of a female model computed using our system. Much effort was needed to fine tune the section curves extracted from the superquadrics model.

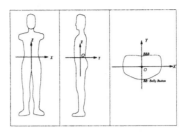

Fig. 10. Human-Body-Centered Coordinate System Definition

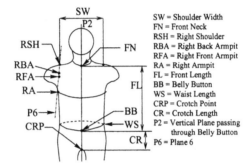

SW = Shoulder Width
FN = Front Neck
RSH = Right Shoulder
RBA = Right Back Armpit
RFA = Right Front Armpit
RA = Right Armpit
FL = Front Length
BB = Belly Button
WS = Waist Length
CRP = Crotch Point
CR = Crotch Length
P2 = Vertical Plane passing
     through Belly Button
P6 = Plane 6

Fig. 11. Key/Basic Features In Front View Of Human Body

Fig. 12. Section curves and surfaces

Fig. 13. Final parametric surface (shown in slices) of a female model

4   Practical Considerations of the System

Here we summarize and present the system from the practical point of view. We outline in a sequence, the various operations of the system which are to be performed in order to obtain a 3D human body model. For each operation, we point out the user interaction needed, interaction time, and computation time, wherever applicable.

1. *Camera calibration*: Since this involves image capturing and processing which takes time, this is done beforehand and the cameras are kept ready. This is to be redone whenever the cameras are disturbed or their parameters are changed. Camera calibration requires user interaction for (a) previewing the target image and adjusting the cameras if necessary, and (b) interactive cleaning of noises in the image after the captured images have been processed by the system. User interaction usually takes a few minutes for each camera and computation time is not significant.
2. *Human model clothing and posture*: As mentioned in the previous section on image capturing, the human subject should wear tight clothes, put up some markers on belly button, and front and back neck points, and stand still in an upright posture facing the front camera for about 15 seconds. User interaction is needed to preview the images to see if they are proper.
3. *Image capturing*: The 13 images are automatically captured in sequence and stored within 15 seconds.
4. *Image processing*: Image processing is done to obtain the image contours as collection of connected segments. It requires user interaction for interactive cleaning of noises in the image after the computation of the contours. User

interaction usually takes a few minutes for each image and computation time is not significant.

5. *Segmentation*: The image contours are associated with the corresponding body parts – head, torso, arms, etc. It is done interactively and over all the images it takes only a few minutes.

6. *Superquadrics model fitting*: This involves (i) computation of initial super-quadrics corresponding to various parts and (ii) computation of local deformations. Initialization takes a few minutes and computation for local deformations takes a few hours.

7. *Computing parametric representation*: This involves two steps: (i) aligning the superquadrics with the human-body-centered coordinate system, and (ii) computation of section curves and surface patches. Some of the section curves extracted from the superquadrics may not be smooth and it requires manual editing of such section curves in order to obtain a satisfactory parametric surface model. This takes a considerable amount of time.

5   Conclusion

In this paper, we have presented a camera based image capturing and 3D reconstruction system for human body modeling. As demonstrated by the experiments, realistic human body models can be generated in parametric form without the need of any databases of human models. The most time consuming task in this system is the superquadrics model fitting. Currently, we are exploring ways to improve the computation time but preserve the accuracy. One possibility is to use representation other than superquadrics. Another area that can be further improved is the user interface. Even though, most of the interactive "noise cleaning" features are easy to use, we are still trying to automate as much as possible in tasks such as camera calibration; image processing; and parametric surface model.

Acknowledgments

This research project is supported by grants from the Industry and Technology Development Council (grant no. AF/122/96), Research Grants Council of the Hong Kong Special Administrative Region, China (competitive earmarked research grant no. HKUST/754/96E), and UGC-UST Research Infrastructure (grant no. RI 95/96, EG18). Domain knowledge and expertise of the Garment Industry has been provided by Mr. Alexandre Kung of TPC (HK) Limited. The multiplex switch was built by the CAD/CAM facility of HKUST.

References

[1] Stephen Addleman. Whole-body 3d scanner and scan data report. In Richard N. Ellson and J. H. Hurre, editors, *Three-Dimensional Image Capture*, volume 3023, pages 2–5, 1997.

[2] J. E. Chadwick, D. R. Haumann, and R. E. Parent. Layered construction for deformable animated characters. In *Proceedings of SIGGRAPH '89*, pages 243–252, 1989.

[3] S. Gray. Virtual fashion. *IEEE Spectrum*, pages 19–25, February 1998.

[4] J. GU, N. Jojic, H. C. Shen, S. Gopalsamy, and T. S. Huang. Design of a camera-based 3d acquisition system. In *Proceedings of 5th International Conference on Mechatronics and Machine Vision in Practice, Nanjing, China*, pages 93–98, 1998.

[5] Jin Gu. *3D Reconstruction of Sculptured Objects*. PhD thesis, Department of Computer Science, Hong Kong University of Science and Technology, 1998.

[6] B. K. Hinds and J. McCartney. Interactive garment design. *The Visual Computer*, 6:53–61, 1990.

[7] N. Jojic, J. Gu, T. S. Huang, and H. C. Shen. Computer modeling, analysis and synthesis of dressed humans. *IEEE Transactions on Circuits and System for Video Technology - Special Issue on Synthetic-Natural Hybrid Coding(to appear)*.

[8] N. Jojic, J. Gu, I. Mak, H. C. Shen, and T. S. Huang. Computer modeling, anlysis and synthesis of dressed humans. In *Computer Vision and Pattern Recognition, June'98, Santa Barbara, CA, USA*, pages 528–534, 1998.

[9] N. Jojic, J. Gu, H. C. Shen, and T. S. Huang. 3d reconstruction of multipart, self-occluding objects. In *Computer Vision-ACCV'98, Proceedings of the Third Asian Conference on Computer Vision, Hong Kong, China, 1998.*, pages 455–462, 1998.

[10] I. Mak, Q. F. Wang, T. Chang, J. Gu, S. Gopalsamy, H. Shen, and M. Y. Yuen. Feature points based parametric modeling of a human body. In *Proceedings of 5th International Conference on Mechatronics and Machine Vision in Practice, Nanjing, China*, pages 99–104, 1998.

[11] K. Singh, J. Ohya, and R. Parent. Human figure synthesis and animation for virtual space teleconferencing. In *Proceedings of Virtual Reality Annual International Symposium '95*, pages 118–126, 1995.

[12] D. Terzopoulos and D. Metaxas. Dynamic 3d models with local and global deformations: Deformable superquadrics. *IEEE Transactions on Pattern Analysis and Machine Intelligence*, 13(7):703–14, 1991.

[13] R.Y. Tsai. A versatile camera calibration technique for high-accuracy 3d machine vision metrology using off-the-shelf tv cameras and lenses. *IEEE Journal of Robotics and Automation*, 3(4):323–44, 1987.

[14] P. Volino, N. M. Thalmann, J. Shen, and D. Thalmann. The evolution of a 3d system for simulating deformable cloths on virtual actors. *IEEE Computer Graphics and Applications*, pages 42–50, September 1996.

Bézier Volume Deformation Model for Facial Animation and Video Tracking

Hai Tao and Thomas S. Huang

Beckman Institute, Department of Electrical and Computer Engineering
University of Illinois at Urbana-Champaign, Urbana, IL 61801, USA
{tao, huang}@ifp.uiuc.edu

Abstract. Capturing real motions from video sequences is a powerful approach to automatically build facial deformation model. In this paper, a 3D Bézier volume deformation model is proposed for both synthesis and analysis of facial movements. Since this model is independent of the mesh structure provided the feature points are given, it is capable of animating geometric facial models of different shapes and structures. Of the same importance, the linear property of this model implies a simple and robust analysis algorithm, from which a customized facial deformation model is derived. Experimental results on animation and video analysis are demonstrated in this paper.

1 Introduction

Many applications in human computer interface, 3D games, model-based video coding, talking agent, and distant learning demand realistic human facial animation. Two closely related important issues are geometric representation and deformation modeling. The geometric representation defines the shape and features of a face. The deformation model, on the other hand, deals with the deformation of static geometric models to generate various dynamic effects for intelligible reproduction of facial expressions.

Basic deformation parameters, which have to be constantly updated to drive a face model, play a key role in model-based talking head systems. The well-known facial action coding system (FACS) developed by Ekman and Friesen [1] describes the action of each group of muscles by a parameter called action unit. These perceptually meaningful deformation parameters need to be converted into 3-D displacements of facial mesh vertices by a deformation model. Since the conversion is generally non-linear and complicated, several approximation methods have been proposed and can be classified into four major categories: parameterized model [2][3], physical muscle model [4][5], free-form deformation model [6], and performance-driven animation model [7][8].

Built upon these parameters, higher levels of deformation models are usually derived to generate animation sequences. They are expression/visual speech layer and scene description layer (Figure 1). In this paper, a free-form deformation model and its corresponding tracking algorithm are proposed.

Nadia Magnenat-Thalmann, Daniel Thalmann (Eds.): CAPTECH'98, LNAI 1537, pp. 242–253, 1998.
© Springer-Verlag Berlin Heidelberg 1998

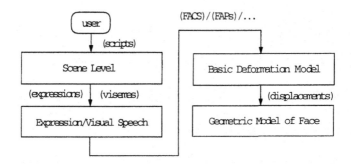

Fig. 1. Deformation layers in facial animation system.

The remaining sections are organized as follows. A brief description of our geometric facial model is given in Section 2. A linear free-form facial deformation model is described in Section 3. Section 4 focuses on the facial motion tracking problem using this deformation model. Implementation issue and experimental results are discussed and shown in Section 5, which is followed by concluding remarks in Section 6.

2   Geometric Facial Model

To build a generic face model, the first step is to obtain the positions of sample points on the surface of a real human face. Several techniques are available to accomplish this task. Using CyberWare 3D color scanner data is a handy method. However, the problem is that the internal structures of a human face, such as the bone surface, tongue, teeth, and the muscles, are not observable. An alternative method is to analyze magnetic resonance imaging (MRI) volume data, which reveal more information about the anatomic structures. Our process of modeling face surface using MRI data includes the following two steps:

- Contour fitting in each interested MRI data slice
  In this stage, fixed number (25 points in our model) of sample points on the surface contour in each interested MRI data slice are manually extracted. 41 data slices are sampled in our system for the face surface.
- Refining of interested regions
  This step is accomplished by repeating the previous step around facial features such as the nose and the ears. For example, in our model, the nose is refined to a 10×8 mesh and each ear is refined to a 12×15 mesh. Picture of the original MRI data and the derived generic face model is shown in Figure 2.

After a generic geometric facial model has been derived from a MRI data set, the next step is to fit the model to a particular person. This process is called model fitting. If 3D range data such as CyberWare scanner data is available, the

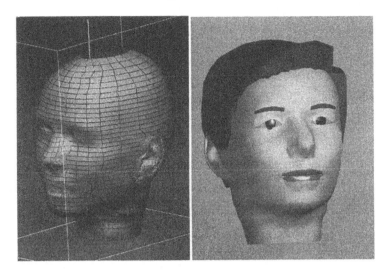

Fig. 2. Generic face model derived from MRI data: the mesh from the volume data (left) and the generic model (right).

model fitting process is equivalent to a 3D warping problem. Weighted Voronoi diagram method is applied in our system [9]. A fitted face model is shown in Figure 3.

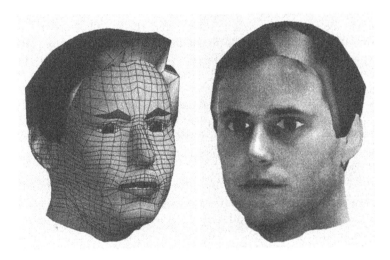

Fig. 3. Face model fitted from CyberWare range data: the mesh (left) and the texture mapped model (right).

3 Bézier Volume Deformation (BVD) Model

Animation of the polygonal face mesh is achieved using deformation at different descriptive levels. As shown in Figure 1, a basic deformation model is used to describe the local deformation behaviors of a geometric model. The inputs to this module could be deformation parameters such as facial action coding system (FACS) parameters suggested by Ekman [1] or MPEG-4 facial animation parameters (FAPs) [10]. The outputs are 3D displacement vectors of vertices in the mesh model. At a higher level, more meaningful facial expression and visual speech information is translated into these deformation parameters. Usually, users only manipulate the face model at expression or visual speech level, which is more efficient and reliable. Animating face at expression and visual speech level is still considerably tedious. Scene level description simplifies this process by depicting multiple threads of facial activities and the synchronization between these threads.

3.1 Facial Deformation Models - Properties

The common goal of deformation models is to regulate deformations of a geometric model by providing smoothness constraints. Some desired properties are:

- Generality
  An ideal deformation model needs a structure that works on geometric facial models of different shapes or even different mesh structures if facial fiducial points are provided. Since constructing a deformation model is a tedious procedure, this property is highly desirable.
- Adaptability
  Each individual person possesses certain characteristics in facial movements. These characteristics should be easily represented using the deformation model. A learning procedure should be facilitated for model customizing.
- Computational simplicity
  For many applications such as computer agents and teleconferencing, real-time performance is the key to a successful product. Computationally expensive model may fail to meet the real-time requirement.

3.2 Bézier Volume Deformation Model

The free-form deformation method was proposed in [6][11]. In our system, a mesh-independent free-form deformation model is proposed. First, connected piece-wise 3D Bézier volumes are generated automatically from a given face mesh according to facial feature points. These volumes cover most regions of a face that can be deformed. Then, by moving the control points of each volume, face mesh is deformed. The main difference between this approach and [6] is that by using non-parallel volumes, irregular 3D manifolds are formed. As a result, smaller number of deform volumes are necessary and the number of freedom in control points are reduced. This is a preferable property for motion tracking algorithm.

Moreover, based on facial feature points, this model is mesh independent, which means that it can be easily adopted to deform any face model.

A Bézier curve in 3D space is defined as

$$\mathbf{x}(u) = \sum_{i=0}^{n} \mathbf{b}_i \binom{n}{i} u^i (1-u)^{n-i} = \sum_{i=0}^{n} \mathbf{b}_i B_i^n(u) \ , \tag{1}$$

where u is the parameter in the range of $[0,1]$, $\mathbf{x}(u)$ is a point on the curve, $\mathbf{b}_i$ are the control points, and B_i^n are Bernstein polynomials. By moving control points $\mathbf{b}_i$, the curve is deformed in a smooth fashion, or

$$\mathbf{v}(u) = \sum_{i=0}^{n} \mathbf{d}_i B_i^n(u) \ , \tag{2}$$

where $\mathbf{v}(u)$ is the displacement of a point on the curve, $\mathbf{d}_i$ is the displacement vector of control point $\mathbf{b}_i$. For a Bézier volume, the displacement vector of a point inside the volume with parameter (u, v, w) is

$$\mathbf{v}(u, v, w) = \sum_{i=0}^{n} \sum_{j=0}^{m} \sum_{k=0}^{l} \mathbf{d}_{i,j,k} B_i^n(u) B_j^m(v) B_k^l(w) \ . \tag{3}$$

From above equation, it is trivial to observe that the evaluation of the deformation can be decomposed into three Bézier curve evaluations. Figure 4 shows a Bézier volume containing a part of the face mesh. By moving the control nodes, or applying $\mathbf{d}_{i,j,k}$, the embedded mesh is deformed. A good analogue is to deform a piece of elastic sheet embedded in a rubber block by bending the rubber.

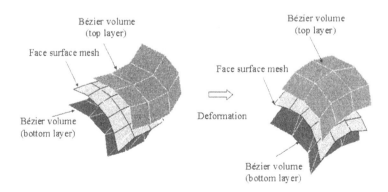

Fig. 4. Bézier volume deformation.

In order to do so, parametric coordinates for each mesh points must be derived. When the order of Bézier volume is high, there is no analytic solution to this problem. Numerical searching algorithm is applied in our implementation. Since this process only needs to be performed once during the formation of the deformation model, it does not slow the actual animation process.

3.3   Mesh Independent Face Deformation Model

Bézier volumes are formed based on facial feature points such as eye corners, mouth corners, etc. Each Bézier volume contains two layers, the outside layer and the inside layer. They form the volume that contains a part of the face mesh. Norm vectors of each facial feature points are used to form these volumes. To ensure that no gap appears during deformation process, neighboring Bézier volumes must have the same order along the dimension connected. In other words, on each side of a boundary, there must be the same number of control points. Additionally, the corresponding control points must always be at the same 3D locations. The Bézier volume structure used in our implementation is shown in Figure 5.

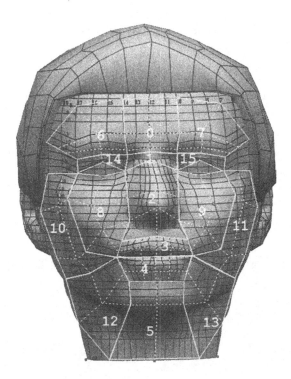

Fig. 5. The face model is deformed by 16 Bézier volumes.

After this mesh is constructed, for each vertex on the mesh, it needs to be determined which particular Bézier volume it belongs to and what values the parameters u, v, w are. Then, moving control points of Bézier volumes in 3D will cause smooth facial deformation. This deformation is written in matrices as

$$\mathbf{V} = BD \ , \tag{4}$$

where $\mathbf{V}$ is the nodal displacements of face mesh, D is the displacement vectors of Bézier volume control nodes. B is the mapping matrix composed of Bernstein polynomials. An interactive tool is programmed to manipulate control points D to achieve desired expressions and visual speech. Basic expression units are neutral, smile, surprise, sad, anger, disgust, and fear. In Figure 6, the real control mesh and the generated expression *smile* are illustrated. For each time instance, the non-rigid motion of a face is modeled as a linear combination of different expressions or visemes (visual phonemes), or

$$\mathbf{V} = B[D_0, D_1, \ldots, D_r] \begin{bmatrix} p_0 \\ p_1 \\ \vdots \\ p_r \end{bmatrix} = B\mathbf{D}P = LP \ , \tag{5}$$

where D_i are expressions or visemes, p_i are their corresponding intensities. The deformed head/face model is

$$R(\mathbf{V}_0 + LP) + T \ , \tag{6}$$

where $\mathbf{V}_0$ is the geometric facial model, R is the rotation decided by three rotation angles $W = (w_x, w_y, w_z)$, and T is the 3D translation.

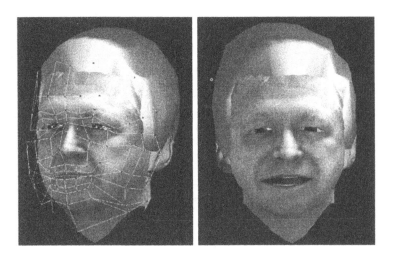

Fig. 6. The face model with the control mesh (left) and the expression *smile* (right).

4   Motion Capturing from Video Sequences

Motion information captured in video sequences can be applied to animate a geometric facial model. Two of the many algorithms for facial motion tracking were proposed by Essa [12] and by DeCarlo [13]. The first one is based on a physical muscle deformation model which detects muscle contraction parameters in video sequences. The latter one applies specific local geometric deformation model as constraints. In this paper, we propose a algorithm for Bézier volume deformation model. The block diagram is shown in Figure 7.

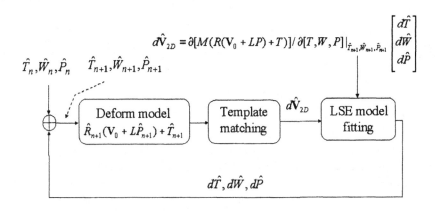

Fig. 7. Block diagram of the BVD tracking system.

At the initialization stage, or for the first video frame, the face needs to be approximately frontal view so that the generic 3D model is fitted. The inputs to the fitting algorithms are positions of facial feature points, which currently are manually picked. All motion parameters are set to be zeroes, which means a neutral face is required. The camera parameters are known in our implementation. Otherwise, a small segment of the video sequence is needed to estimate these parameter using SFM (structure from motion) techniques.

Then for each frame, the 2D movements of many mesh nodal points are estimated using template matching algorithm. From these displacement vectors, 3D global motion parameters (rotation and translation) and non-rigid motion parameters (intensities of expressions/visemes or action units) are computed using a least square estimator. Since the Bézier volume deformation model is linear, only the perspective projection and rotation introduce non-linearity. This property makes the algorithm simpler and more robust. The inter-frame 2D displacement vector for each node is written as

$$dV_{2D} \approx \left. \frac{\partial[M(R(\mathbf{V}_0 + LP))]}{\partial[T, W, P]} \right|_{\hat{T}_n, \hat{W}_n, \hat{P}_n} \begin{bmatrix} d\hat{T} \\ d\hat{W} \\ d\hat{P} \end{bmatrix}$$

$$= M \left[\begin{bmatrix} 1\ 0\ -x/z \\ 0\ 1\ -y/z \end{bmatrix}, \begin{bmatrix} G_0 - x/zG_2 \\ G_1 - y/zG_2 \end{bmatrix}, \begin{bmatrix} [RL]_0 - x/z[RL]_2 \\ [RL]_1 - y/z[RL]_2 \end{bmatrix} \right] \begin{bmatrix} d\hat{T} \\ d\hat{W} \\ d\hat{P} \end{bmatrix}, (7)$$

where G_i means the ith row of matrix G and $[RL]_i$ denotes the ith row of matrix RL. The projection matrix M is

$$M = \begin{bmatrix} fs/z & 0 \\ 0 & fs/z \end{bmatrix}. \tag{8}$$

f is the focal length of the camera and s is the scale factor. The vector (x, y, z) represents the 3D mesh nodal position after rigid and non-rigid motion T_n, W_n, and P_n.

$$G = \begin{bmatrix} 0 & z_1 & -y_1 \\ -z_1 & 0 & x_1 \\ y_1 & -x_1 & 0 \end{bmatrix}, \tag{9}$$

where the vector (x_1, y_1, z_1) represents the 3D mesh nodal position after only non-rigid deformation, or $\mathbf{V}_0 + LP$ (without translation and rotation). Since many 2D inter-frame displacement vectors are calculated, an over-constrained system is constructed. As a result, inter-frame motion parameter differences $d\hat{T}$, $d\hat{W}$, and $d\hat{P}$ are induced using least square estimator. By adding these derivatives to previously estimated motion parameters, new motion parameters T_{n+1}, W_{n+1}, and P_{n+1} are derived.

5   Implementation and Experimental Results

The Bézier volume deformation model has been implemented on an SGI ONYX machine with VTX graphics engine. Real-time animation has been achieved. Currently, the tracking algorithm is relatively slow (7 frames/sec) due to the simple template matching algorithm with large template size and searching area.

5.1   Facial Animation Using Bézier Volume

Based on our deformation model, facial action units are constructed using interactive tools in which the control nodes are manipulated. Then various expressions and visemes are created either from these action units or directly by moving control nodes.

In our implementation of talking head, text script is written down and is read by a speaker. The phoneme segmentation is obtained using a speech recognition tool from the acoustic signal. An alternative approach is to use text to speech system (TTS) to generate both acoustic data and phoneme segmentation.

Based on phoneme segmentation, mouth shapes and expressions are computed using a coarticulation model similar to [14]. Then audio and animation results are synchronized to generate realistic talking head sequences. Figure 8 shows frames from a speech sequence.

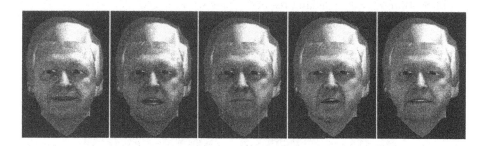

Fig. 8. An animation sequence with smile and speech "I am George McConkie".

5.2 Facial Motion Tracking

1. Input video sequences
   The proposed algorithm has been implemented to extract facial motion parameters from video sequences. Each video frame contains 720 × 486 pixels. The subjects are required to perform different expressions such as smile, surprise, sad, anger, disgust, fear, and various local facial motions like raising eyebrows. As previously mentioned, the first frame needs to be approximately frontal view and with no expression.
2. Facial model initialization
   From the first frame, facial feature points are extracted manually. The 3D fitting algorithm is then applied to warp the generic model for the person whose face appears in the video sequence. However, since we only have 2D information, the warping process is performed in 2D except the initial scaling. Then from facial feature points and their norms, Bézier volumes are automatically generated. In our model, 16 Bézier volumes are formed.
3. Motion field
   To relieve the drifting problem in template matching algorithm, templates from the previous frame and templates from the initial frame are applied randomly with equal probabilities. For example, the even nodes of the face mesh are tracked using templates of previous frame and the odd nodes are tracked using those of the initial frame. Our experiments show that this approach is very effective.
4. Motion model fitting
   The computed 2D facial motions are assumed being caused by dozens of parameters corresponding to global motions and various non-rigid facial motion

units. Depending upon the purpose of the tracker, these motion units may include expressions, visemes, or local facial motions such eyebrow raising. In our implementation, around 25 local facial motion units are applied. The inter-frame difference of these motion units, together with that of the six global motion parameters, are then computed using LSE method described in Section 4. Some tracking results are shown in Figure 9.

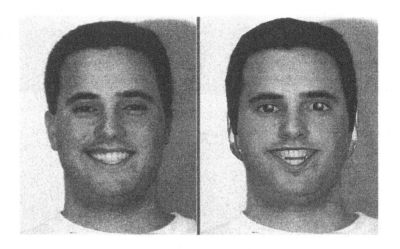

Fig. 9. The original video frame (left) and the synthesized tracking result (right).

6   Conclusions

A deformation model is proposed for successful facial animation and facial motion tracking. This deformation model is independent of the actual face mesh and is linear. These features make algorithms simple and robust. However, we also realize that to accomplish automatic, robust, and accurate facial motion tracking, other techniques such as face detection, facial feature detection, structure from motion, and 3D shape reconstruction also need to be integrated into the system.

Acknowledgments

This work was supported in part by Army Research Laboratory under Cooperative Agreement No. DAAL01-96-2-0003, and in part by Joint Services Electronics Program Grant ONR N00014-96-1-0129.

References

1. Ekman P., Friesen W. V.: *Facial Action Coding System.* Consulting Psychologists Press Inc (1977)
2. Parke F. I.: Computer generated animation of faces. in *Proc. ACM Annual Conf..* August (1972)
3. Thalmann N. M., Primeau N. E., Thalmann D.: Abstract muscle action procedures for human face animation. Vis. Comput. **3** (1988) 290–297
4. Platt S. M.: Animating facial expressions. in *Proc. SIGGRAPH 81*, (1981) 245–252
5. Lee Y., Terzopoulos D., Waters K.: Realistic modeling for facial animation. in *Proc. SIGGRAPH 95*, (1995) 55–62
6. Kalra P., Mangili A., Thalmann N. M., Thalmann D.: Smile: a multi-layered facial animation system. in *Proc. IFIP Conf. on Modeling in Comput. Graphics* (1991) 189–198
7. Williams L.: Performance-driven facial animation. in *Proc. SIGGRAPH 90* (1990) 235–242
8. Guenter B., Terzopoulos D., Waters K.: Realistic modeling for facial animation. in *Proc. SIGGRAPH 98* (1998)
9. Tao H., Huang T. S.: Multi-scale image warping using weighted Voronoi diagram. in *Proc. IEEE Int. Conf. on Image Processing (ICIP'96)* (1996) 241–244
10. MPEG-4 document: Text for CD 14496-2 video. ISO/IEC JTC1/SC29/WG11 N1902 (1997)
11. Sederberg T. W., Parry S. R.: Free-form deformation of solid geometric models. in *Proc. SIGGRAPH 86* (1986) 151–160
12. Essa I.: Analysis, interpretation, and synthesis of facial expressions. Ph.D. thesis, MIT (1994)
13. DeCarlo D., Metaxas D.: The integration of optical flow and deformable models with applications to human face shape and motion estimation. in *Proc. CVPR 96* (1996) 231–238
14. Massaro D. W., Cohen M. M.: Modeling coarticulation in synthetic visual speech. in *Models and Techniques in Computer Animation.* Springer-Verlag, Tokyo (1993)

Head Modeling from Pictures and Morphing in 3D with Image Metamorphosis Based on Triangulation

WON-SOOK LEE, NADIA MAGNENAT THALMANN

MIRALab, CUI, University of Geneva
24, rue General-Dufour, CH-1211, Geneva, Switzerland
Tel: +41-22-705-7763 Fax: +41-22-705-7780
E-mail: {wslee, lee, thalmann}@cui.unige.ch

Abstract. This paper describes a combined method of facial reconstruction and morphing between two heads, showing the extensive usage of feature points detected from pictures. We first present an efficient method to generate a 3D head for animation from picture data and then a simple method to do 3D-shape interpolation and 2D morphing based on triangulation. The basic idea is to generate an individualized head modified from a generic model using orthogonal picture input, then process automatic texture mapping with texture image generation by combining orthogonal pictures and coordinate generation by projection from a resulted head in front, right and left views, which results a nice triangulation on texture image. Then an intermediate shape can be obtained from interpolation between two different persons. The morphing between 2D images is processed by generating an intermediate image and new texture coordinate. Texture coordinates are interpolated linearly, and the texture image is created using Barycentric coordinates for each pixel in each triangle given from a 3D head. Various experiments, with different ratio between shape, images and various expressions, are illustrated.

Keywords: clone, a generic model, automatic texture mapping, interpolation, Barycentric coordinate, image morphing, and expression.

1. Introduction

Ask any animator what is the most difficult character to model and animate, and nine out of ten may respond "humans". There is a simple reason for that: we all know what humans are supposed to look like; we are all experts in recognizing realistic person.

In this paper, we describe a method for individualized face modeling and morphing them in 3D with texture metamorphosis. There are various approaches to reconstruct a realistic person using a Laser scanner [7], a stereoscopic camera [2], or an active light stripper [10]. There is also an approach to reconstruct a person from picture data [6][12]. However most of them have limitation when compared

Nadia Magnenat-Thalmann, Daniel Thalmann (Eds.): CAPTECH'98, LNAI 1537, pp. 254-267, 1998.

practically to a commercial product (such as a camera) for the input of data for reconstruction and finally animation.

Other techniques for metamorphosis, or "morphing", involve the transformation between 2D images [14][17] and one between 3D models [15][16] including facial expression interpolation. Most methods for image metamorphosis are complicated or computationally expensive, including energy minimization and free-form deformation.

We present a method not only for reconstruction of a person in 3D for animation but also for morphing them in 3D. Our reconstruction method makes morphing between two people possible through 3D-shape interpolation based on the same topology and 2D morphing for texture images to get an intermediate head in 3D.

We first introduce, in Section 2, a fast head modeling method to reconstruct an individualized head modified from a generic head. In Section 3, texture mapping is described in detail how to compose two images and obtain automatic coordinate mapping. Then Section 4 is devoted to image morphing based on triangulation. In following Section 5, several results are illustrated to show 3D realistic morphing among several people. It includes shape interpolation, image morphing and expression interpolation. Finally conclusion is given.

2. Face Modeling for Individualized Head

In this section, we present a way to reconstruct a head for animation from orthogonal pictures, which looks photo-realistic. First, we prepare a generic model with animation structure and two orthogonal pictures of the front and side views. The generic model has efficient triangulation, with finer triangles over the highly curved and/or highly articulated regions of the face and larger triangles elsewhere, that includes eyes and teeth.

The main idea to get an individualized head is to detect feature points on the two images and obtain 3D position of the feature points to modify a generic model using a geometrical deformation. The feature detection is processed in a semiautomatic way using the structured snake method with some anchor functionality as described in paper [12].

Figure 1 (a) shows an orthogonal pair of images. Detected features on a normalized image pair are also shown in **Figure 1** (b). Feature points are overlaid on image even though the space has different origin and different scaling.

Then two 2D position coordinates in front and side views, which are the (x, y) and the (z, y) planes, are combined to be a 3D point. First, we use a global transformation to move the 3D feature points to the space for a generic head. Then Dirichlet Free Form Deformations (DFFD) [8] are used to get new geometrical coordinates of a generic model adapting to the detected feature points. Then the shapes of the eyes and teeth are recovered to the original shape with translation and scaling adapted to a new head. The control points for the DFFD are feature points detected from the images. As shown in **Figure 2**, it is a rough matching method that does not get the exact points for every point except feature points. However, it is useful to reduce the data size of a head to accelerate animation speed. To get it to be realistic looking, we use automatic texture mapping, which is described in UNTER section.

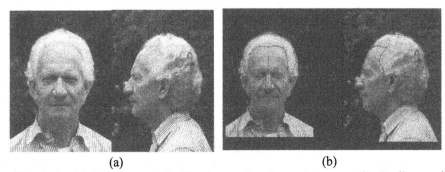

(a)   (b)

Figure 1: (a) The front and side views of a Caucasian man. (b) Scaling and translation of given images after normalization and detected features.

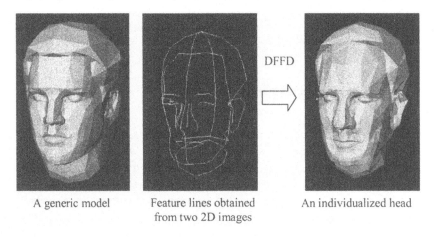

A generic model   Feature lines obtained   An individualized head
                        from two 2D images

Figure 2: Modification of a generic head with detected feature points

3. Texture Mapping

Texture mapping is useful not only to cover the rough matched shape, here the shape is obtained only by feature point matching, but also to get a more realistic colorful face.

The information of detected feature points is used for automatic texture generation combining two views. The main idea of texture mapping is to get an image by combining two orthogonal pictures in a proper way to get highest resolution for most detailed parts. We first connect two pictures on predefined feature lines using a geometrical deformation and a multiresolution technique for smoothness without boundary effect, and then give proper texture coordinates of every point on a head following same transformation with image transformation.

3.1.   Texture Generation

Image Deformation

A front view is kept as it is to keep high resolution and side view is deformed to be connected to front view in certain defined feature points lines. We deform the side view face to attach to the front view face in right and left direction. In the front image, we can draw feature lines as we can see two red lines on front face in **Figure 4**. There is a corresponding feature line on a side image. We deform the side image to transform the feature line, the same as the one on the front view. Image pixels in right side of feature lines are transformed with the same transform as the line transform as shown in **Figure 3**. To get the right image, we utilize side image as it is and deform it with the right the red feature line on the front image. For a left image, we flip a side image vertically and deform it with the left-hand red feature line on the front image. The resulted three images are shown in **Figure 4**.

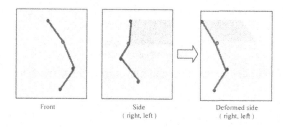

Front   Side   Deformed side
           (right, left)   (right, left)

Figure 3: The side views are deformed to transform certain lines in side view to ones in front view.

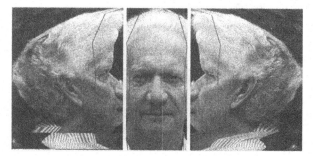

Figure 4: Three images after deformation ready for merging.

Multiresolution Image Mosaic

The two resulted images after deformation are merged using pyramid decomposition of image [4] using the Gaussian operator. We utilize REDUCE and EXPAND operators to obtain G_k (Gaussian image) and L_k (Laplacian image) and merge three L_k images on each level on any given curves, here they are feature lines for combination. Then the merged images P_k is augmented to get S_k, which is the resulted image for each level obtained from P_k and S_{k+1}. The final image is S_0.

Figure 5 shows the whole process of the multiresolution technique to merge three images and
Figure 6 shows an example from level 3 to level 2.

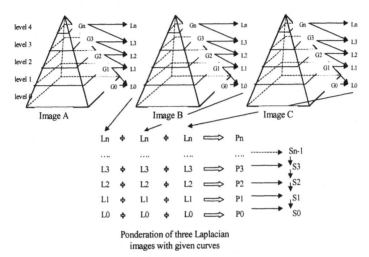

Ponderation of three Laplacian
images with given curves

Figure 5: Pyramid decomposition and merging of three images.

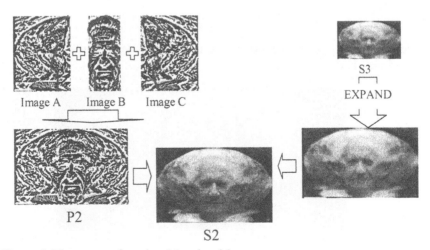

Figure 6: The process from level 3 to level 2.

This multiresolution technique is very useful to remove boundaries between the three images. Although we try as much as possible to take pictures in a perfect environment, boundaries are always visible in real life. As we can see in **Figure 7** (a) and (c), skin colors are quite different when we do not use the multiresolution technique. The images in (b) and (d) show the results after the multiresolution technique, which removes boundaries and makes a smooth connection between images.

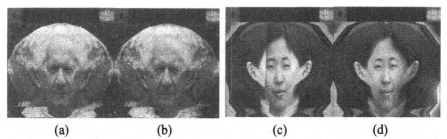

(a)   (b)   (c)   (d)

Figure 7: The generated texture images combined from the three (front, right, and left) images without multiresolution techniques in (a) and (c) and with the technique in (b) and (d).

Eyes and teeth images are added automatically on top of an image, which are necessary for animation of eyes and mouth region.

3.2. Texture Fitting

To give a proper coordinate on a combined image for every point on a head, we first project an individualized 3D head onto three planes. With the information of feature lines, which are used for image merging in ÜBER section, we decide which plane a point on a 3D head is projected. Then projected points on one of three planes are transferred to one of feature points spaces between the front and the side in 2D. Finally, one more transform on the image space is processed to obtain the texture coordinates. The origins of each space are shown in **Figure 8** (a) and the final mapping of points on a texture image is generated. 3D head space is the space for 3D head model, 2D feature points space is the one for feature points which are used for feature detection, 2D image space is the one for space for orthogonal images which are used for input, and 2D texture image space is for the generated image space. The 2D-feature point space is different from 2D-image space even though they are displayed together in **Figure 1**.

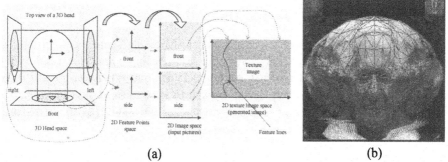

(a)   (b)

Figure 8: (a) Texture fitting process to give a texture coordinate on an image for each point on a head. (b) Texture coordinates overlaid on a texture image.

The final texture fitting on a texture image is shown in **Figure 8** (b). The eyes and teeth fitting process are done with predefined coordinates and transformation related to the resulted texture image size, which is fully automatic after one process for a generic model.

The brighter points in **Figure 8** (b) are feature points while the others are non-feature points and the triangles are a projection of triangular faces on a 3D head. Since we utilize a triangular mesh for our generic model, the texture mapping is resulted on efficient triangulation of texture image showing finer triangles over the highly curved and/or highly articulated regions of the face and larger triangles elsewhere as the generic model does. This resulting triangulation is used for 3D-image morphing in Section 4.2.

The final texture mapping results in smoothly connected images inside triangles of texture coordinate points, which are given accurately. **Figure 9** shows several views of the reconstructed head out of two pictures in **Figure 1** (a).

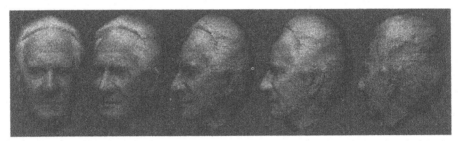

Figure 9: snapshots of a reconstructed head of a Caucasian male in several views

4. 3D Morphing between Two Persons

When we morph one person to another person in 3D, there are two things needed. One is the shape variation and the other is texture variation.

4.1. 3D Interpolation in Shape Based on Same Topology

Every head generated from a generic model shares the same topology with a generic model and has similar characteristic for texture coordinates. Then resulted 3D several shapes are easily interpolated. An interpolated point P between P_L and P_R is found using a simple linear interpolation. **Figure 10** shows a head after interpolation where $a = b = 0.5$. The left head is slightly rotated and the middle has an interpolated shape and an interpolated position with some rotation.

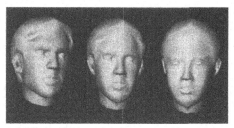

Figure 10: Shape interpolation

4.2.   Image Morphing

Beside shape interpolation, we need two items to obtain intermediate texture mapping. First texture coordinate interpolation is performed and image morphing follows.

2D Interpolation of Texture Coordinate

It is straightforward as 3D-shape interpolation. An interpolated texture coordinate C between C_L and C_R is found using a simple linear interpolation in 2D.

2D-Image Metamorphosis Based on Triangulation

We morph two images with a given ratio using texture coordinates and the triangular face information of the texture mapping; we first interpolate every 3D vertex on the two heads. Then to generate new intermediate texture image, we morph triangle by triangle for every face on a 3D head. Parts of image, which are used for the texture mapping, are triangulated by projection of triangular faces of 3D heads since the generic head is a triangular mesh. See **Figure 8** (b). With this information for triangles, Barycentric coordinate interpolation is employed for image morphing. **Figure 11** shows that each pixel of a triangle of an intermediate image has a color value decided by mixing color values of two corresponding pixels on two images. Three vertexes of each triangle are interpolated and pixel values inside triangles are obtained from interpolation between two pixels in two triangles with the same Barycentric coordinate. To obtain smooth image pixels, bilinear interpolation among four neighboring pixels is processed.

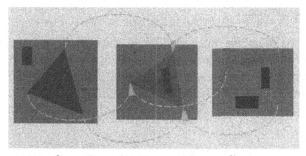

Figure 11: Image transformation using Barycentric coordinates.

We process the triangles on the image one by one. The new problem is how to fill the triangle in an efficient way. For the three vertexes *P1*, *P2*, and *P3* of a triangle, we rename them according to the x coordinate in descending order like $P1_x \le P2_x \le P3_x$. Then a line between *P1* and *P2* and one between *P1* and *P3* are compared to fill the triangle to find the range of y for a given x where $P1_x \le x \le P2_x$. After similar checking is performed to find (x, y) where $P2_x \le x \le P3_x$.

For each pixel (x, y) in an intermediate image, the Barycentric coordinate (u, v, w) is found inside a triangle with three points *P1*, *P2*, and *P3*. There are corresponding points in two input images, say *P1L*, *P2L*, and *P3L* for the first image and *P1R*, *P2R*, and *P3R* for the second one. Then $u*P1L + v*P2L + w*P3L$ is the corresponding pixel in the first image and vice versa for the second. The color value $M(x, y)$ of a given pixel (x, y) is found from linear interpolation between the color value $ML(x, y)$ of the first image and $MR(x, y)$ of the second as the formula below.

$$M(x,y) = aM_L(uP1_{Lx} + vP2_{Lx} + wP3_{Lx}, uP1_{Ly} + vP2_{Ly} + wP3_{Ly})$$
$$+$$
$$bM_R(uP1_{Rx} + vP2_{Rx} + wP3_{Rx}, uP1_{Ry} + vP2_{Ry} + wP3_{Ry})$$

To show 2D-image metamorphosis, we show another example of a face as seen in **Figure 12**. It shows very similar structure to the Caucasian male example.

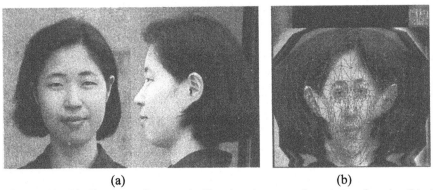

(a)   (b)

Figure 12: (a) The input front and side view images of an Asian female. (b) A generated texture image with visual texture coordinate for triangular faces of a corresponding 3D head.

We vary the morphing ratio a and b to show dynamic morphing. **Figure 13** illustrates intermediate texture images between one in **Figure 8** (b) and the one in **Figure 12** (b). Pixels like eyes, mouth and some part of hair regions which are not covered by triangles are not calculated to get intermediate values, but are not used for texture mapping anyway. If different eye colors are used, it interpolates eye colors too.

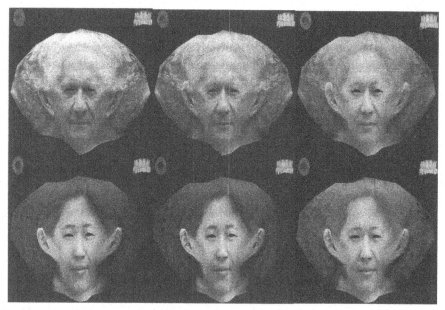

Figure 13: Intermediate images. Starting from top left going in a clockwise direction, it is mixed for (Caucasian male, Asian female).

5. Various Morphing Experiments

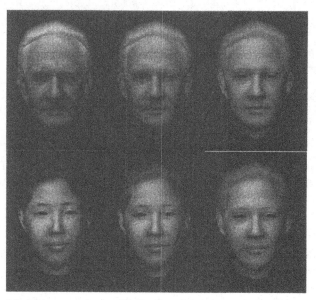

Figure 14: Morphing steps in clockwise direction starting from left-up for (Caucasian male, Asian female).

The resulting head shows very smooth images without any hole in the textured parts. **Figure 14** shows the final result of 3D morphing. It shows how to interpolates the shapes and skin and hair colors between old Caucasian male and young Asian female and **Figure 15** shows another variation of an Asian female mixing with a Caucasian female. The middle ones have mixed characteristics.

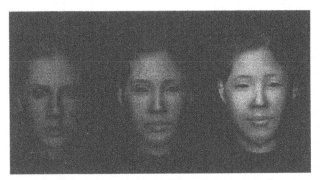

Figure 15: 50% morphing between Caucasian and Asian females.

Since it is a morphing in 3D, changing the view is an easy task to enable the visualization of various profiles. **Figure 16** shows two examples. Left-hand shows a Caucasian male with the Asian female and right-hand shows the Caucasian male with another male.

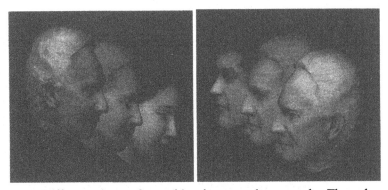

Figure 16: Different views of morphing between three people. They show the change of shape and image morphing. Each middle head is mixed with a ratio of 50%.

A Different Ratio for Shape and Image Variation

It is possible to set different ratios for the interpolation of the 3D shapes and for morphing images. **Figure 17** shows different ratios of morphing for shape and texture images. The Asian female looks older with a lot of wrinkles and white hair, which are borrowed from a Caucasian male on the left side.

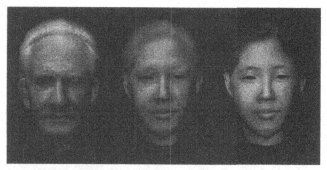

Figure 17: 90% of shape is from the Asian female and the image is mixed 50% for each of Caucasian male and Asian female.

Interpolation between Several Expressions

Since a reconstructed head can be animated in active way, which keeps the same topology and texture mapping, it shows an easy solution for the experimentation of mixing people with different expressions. **Figure 18** and **Figure 19** show other example for reconstruction. Input pictures in **Figure 19** are rotated interactively to get orthogonal pair.

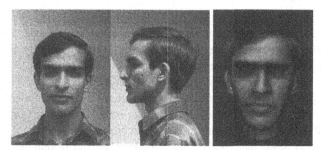

Figure 18: A reconstructed Indian man from orthogonal pictures

Figure 19: Input images in gray for J.F.K and reconstructed J.F.K.

The (generic) face model is an irregular structure defined as a polygonal mesh. The face is decomposed into regions where muscular activity is simulated using rational free form deformation [13]. As model fitting transforms the generic face without changing the underlying structure, the resulting new face can be animated.

Animation can be controlled on several levels. On the lowest level, we use a set of 65 minimal perceptible actions (MPAs) related to muscle movements.

The two heads in **Figure 20** have different expressions and head positions. The middle head with in-between shape and in-between texture shows in-between expression.

Figure 20: Morphing in 3D with various expressions.

6. Conclusion

We introduced methods from for realistic looking face reconstruction from two pictures and to for 3D morphing between given two faces, which is not only 3D-shape interpolation or 2D-image metamorphosis, but both of them.

We have first shown an efficient face modeling for animation with new texture techniques. It shows the processes modifying a generic model for shape acquirement and producing texture images combining orthogonal pair input deforming geometrically and then using multiresolution technique.

The resulting heads have wide range covering man and woman, and also different kinds of race from only one generic model. These models have the same topological structure for the 3D shape and similar characteristic for texture images, which enables 2D-image metamorphosis based on triangulation that results from our reconstruction method. The 2D-image morphing using Barycentric coordinate interpolation is possible with triangulation, which comes from an individualized head reconstruction from a generic head.

Various experiments show a potential area to develop a family and aging simulation from different ratios for 3D-shape interpolation and 2D-image morphing.

7. Acknowledgment

The authors would like to thank other members of MIRALab for their help, particularly Laurent Moccozet, Pierre Beylot and especially Chris Joslin for proof reading this document.

8. References

[1]   Exhibition On the 10th and 11th September 1996 at the Industrial Exhibition of the British Machine Vision Conference.

[2]   http://www.turing.gla.ac.uk/turing/copyrigh.htm

[3]   Takaaki Akimoto, Yasuhito Suenaga, and Richard S. Wallace, Automatic Creation of 3D Facial Models, IEEE Computer Graphics & Applications, Sep., 1993.

[4]   Peter J. Burt and Edward H. Andelson, A Multiresolution Spline With Application to Image Mosaics, ACM Transactions on Graphics, 2(4):217-236, Oct., 1983.

[5]   Horace H.S. Ip, Lijin Yin, Constructing a 3D individual head model from two orthogonal views. The Visual Computer, Springer-Verlag, 12:254-266, 1996.

[6]   Tsuneya Kurihara and Kiyoshi Arai, A Transformation Method for Modeling and Animation of the Human Face from Photographs, Computer Animation, Springer-Verlag Tokyo, pp. 45-58, 1991.

[7]   Yuencheng Lee, Demetri Terzopoulos, and Keith Waters, Realistic Modeling for Facial Animation, In Computer Graphics (Proc. SIGGRAPH), pp. 55-62, 1996.

[8]   L. Moccozet, N. Magnenat-Thalmann, Dirichlet Free-Form Deformations and their Application to Hand Simulation, Proc. Computer Animation, IEEE Computer Society, pp. 93-102, 1997.

[9]   Meet Geri: The New Face of Animation, Computer Graphics World, Volume 21, Number 2, February 1998.

[10]   Marc Proesmans, Luc Van Gool. Reading between the lines - a method for extracting dynamic 3D with texture. In Proceedings of VRST, pp. 95-102, 1997.

[11]   http://www.viewpoint/com/freestuff/cyberscan

[12]   Lee W. S., Kalra P., Magenat Thalmann N, Model Based Face Reconstruction for Animation, In Proc. Multimedia Modeling (MMM) '97, Singapore, pp. 323-338, 1997.

[13]   P. Kalra (1993) An Interactive Multimodal Facial Animation System, PH.D. Thesis, Ecole Polytechnique Federale de Lausanne.

[14]   T. Beier, S. Neely, Feature-based image metamorphosis, In Computer Graphics (Proc. SIGGRAPH) pp. 35-42, 1992.

[15]   J. Kent, W. Carlson , R. Parent, Shape Transformation for Polygon Objects, In Computer Graphics (Proc. SIGGRAPH) pp. 47-54, 1992.

[16]   Kiyoshi Arai, Tsuneya Kurihara, Ken-ichi Anjyo, Bilinear interpolation for facial expression and metamorphosis in real-time animation, Visual Computer, Volume 12, number 3, 1996.

[17]   S.-Y. Lee, K.-Y. Chwa, S.-Y. Shin, G. Wolberg, Image metamorphosis using Snakes and Free-Form deformations, In Computer Graphics (Proc. SIGGRAPH) pp. 439-448, 1995.

Facial Animation by Synthesis of Captured and Artificial Data

Zsófia Ruttkay, Paul ten Hagen, Han Noot, and Mark Savenije

CWI, Kruislaan 413, 1098 SJ Amsterdam, The Netherlands
{zsofi, paulh, han, markjoe}@cwi.nl

1 Introduction

Performer-driven animation has been used with success [1], first of all to reproduce human body motion. While there are different capturing hardware-software
systems to map the motion of a performer on the motion of a model of the body
or face, little has been done both on the technical and on the theoretical level
to support the inventive re-use of captured data.

The topic of this paper is an animation editing environment, which can be
used to visualize and analyze captured animation data as well as to process the
captured data and re-use it several times in different ways.

The Animation Editor has been designed in the framework of the FASE
project, aiming at performer-driven facial animation. The performer data is used
to drive both a physically-based 3D realistic model, as well as different, cartoon-
like 2D faces. We are also experimenting with driving non-human faces with
(processed) performer data. The editor is coupled to the models in such a way,
that snapshots of the animation or selected parts of it can be seen interwoven
with editing.

We will discuss animation editing in the context of facial animation. However,
most of the ideas could be applied to other animation domains.

When animating the human body, techniques used to animate or describe
joints the dynamics of motion of physical bodies can be applied. The situation
is different in the case of facial animation. The 'laws' of facial movements are
based on too complex and partly unknown physical structures (friction between
muscles, precise location and parameters of muscles and tissue, etc.). In addition,
there is still very little known about generic and individual characteristics of the
dynamics of the face [2]. Hence, both the physical as well as the behavioral laws
of facial motion could be, and should be learnt from a large body of empirical
captured data. Once generic and individual characteristics of certain facial motions, e.g. expressions, are known, these can be used to process captured data
or make facial animations from scratch.

2 Capturing Facial Data

The motion of the performer's face is coded in terms of feature point based
MPEG action units (further on: AUs) [3]. In the present stage of the project

Nadia Magnenat-Thalmann, Daniel Thalmann (Eds.): CAPTECH'98, LNAI 1537, pp. 268–271, 1998.

we can recognize the feature points identified in the MPEG standard by applying marker points to the performer's face. Later, more AUs will be captured, and based only on video recordings of the face without markers. The recognition based capturing subsystem is being developed by our partners in the FASE project [4]. We assume for this paper that captured data are provided through the above interface. The paper will not discuss the recognition task further but concentrate on the synthesis aspects, in particular by means of interactive animation editing.

3   The Animation Editor

Animation Editor is an interactive tool for the graphical specification, presentation and modification of the values of animation parameters for computer (facial) models. The parameters can represent muscle contraction values, coordinates of feature points or any parameters used to control a facial model.

The animation editor is as much a research tool as it is an animators tool. In body animation performer input is still superior to model-input for driving animations. In facial animation the situation is more complicated because accurate performer data are hard to get. Moreover the correct interpretation of observed data needs better underlying models than currently available. The animation editor will in our approach play an important role in finding better models. It can be used to do a detailed analysis of performer input parameter values including time dependent behavior. The analysis can be about individual parameters or ensembles of them. Hypotheses can immediately be 'edited in' and tested (visually) on a variety of models. Particular attention can be given to the possibilities of analyzing the dynamics of facial behavior.

Underlying utilities allow for controlled superposition of animation (e.g. speed and expressions). The strategy is to let the analysis tools smoothly evolve towards animators tools. The current version has been evaluated by animation artists through hands on exercising. The results are encouraging. During this experimental phase it is vital to maintain access to the lowest level editing operations, as they are the building blocks for higher level actions targeted for.

The animation editor operates on a window which looks like a musical score. There is a 'staff' for every animation parameter; the lines on each staff reflects the values the parameter can take. The behavior in time of an animation parameter is specified by placing points on its staff. They are entered, moved and deleted by mouse-operations.

One can perform editing operations — cut and paste operations, time- and value scaling — on portions of curves and on sets of them. Performer data can be read in and presented in the scores. Parts of earlier made animations — also performer data — can be copied and pasted to a different set of parameters, allowing e.g. to animate different — realistic 3D as well as 2D cartoon-like — faces on the bases of performer data.

The editor can produce as output animation scripts (movies) in ASCII format by sampling the curves at a rate which is set by the user. Such a file can be used as

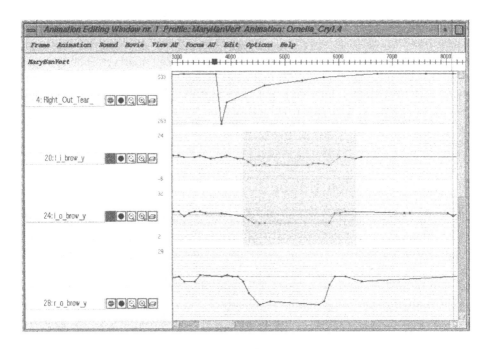

Fig. 1. Snapshot of an Animation Editor window, showing 4 animation parameter staves, the top with artificial data, the 3 below with captured data. Part of the left eyebrow movements are selected.

input for the corresponding model, or the corresponding model can communicate directly with the editor, allowing for feed back — snapshots, replay of selected parts — while editing the animation curves.

4   Processing Captured Data

The Animation Editor supports the (re-)usage of captured data in different ways:
Analysis The curves of the captured data give an overview of the 'content' of the facial movement. One can quickly identify certain events (jaw opening, eyebrow movements). Also, from the extreme values and shape of the curves one can evaluate the animation by large, at a glance.
Scaling Parts of the captured data can be scaled in magnitude and/or time. The selection can be restricted to certain parameters in a given time interval (e.g. to make an eyebrow movement more emphasized or shorter), or to one parameter (e.g. to achieve asymmetrical motion).
Editing and Extension of Captured Data The editing environment can be used to add non-captured motion (e.g. eye-gaze movement) and change the captured data locally (e.g. to eliminate recognition mistakes, to smoothen the animation, to refine synchronization).

Re-using Library Entries Pieces of captured (and possibly processed) animations can be saved and re-used later. When re-using an animation, different sets of motion parameter channels can be used than the ones of the saved animation. Automatic bi-linear re-scaling takes place when pasting a curve of one channel to another one.

Constraint-Based Editing Constraints can be used to express both the physical and behavioral 'laws' of the face to be animated (e.g. co-activation of action units, limits on ranges and derivate of parameters, symmetric motion of the face) to define compound animations as 'building blocks' to be used (e.g. a smile is an animation fulfilling certain constraints), to prescribe synchronization and other requirements according to the 'story' of the animation (eyes should be fixed somewhere, at the time of a noise effect the face should blink).

5   Implementation and Future Plans

The first version of the Animation Editor supporting the most essential constraints only has been implemented in Java, and is being tested by potential users. This version has been used with success in our environment. (Demos are available.)

For the next version, the constraint-related features will be added [5], allowing the user to define, switch on/off constraints, helping him to fulfill the current set of constraints during editing, adjusting an animation to a new set of constraints. The latter feature will allow to define transformations of captured data on a high conceptual level (e.g vigorous facial data can be transformed to an animation of the face of a tired/sleepy person).

Based on a large body of empirical captured data, we will support the inclusion and blending of animations as high-level building blocks (expressions). In the next version, for the mapping of channels a choice of possibilities will be available, allowing the definition of interesting, not one-to-one usage of performer data channels and animation parameters.

The work has been carried out in the framework of the ongoing FASE project, supported by STW grant CWI66.4088.

References

1. L. Williams, "Performance-driven facial animation," in *Computer Graphics (SIG-GRAPH '90 Proceedings)* (F. Baskett, ed.), vol. 24, pp. 235–242, aug 1990.
2. I. Essa, S. Basu, T. Darrel, and A. Pentlands, "Modeling, tracking and interactive animation of faces and heads using input from video," in *Proceedings of Computer Animation '96*, pp. 68–79, 1996.
3. ISO/IEC 14496-2, "Coding of audio-visual objects: Visual," tech. rep., International Organisation for Standardisation, Tokyo, March 1998.
4. FASE home page: http://www-it.et.tudelft.nl/FASE.
5. Z. Ruttkay, P. ten Hagen, and H. Noot, "Constrained-based keyframing," in *Proceedings of the ECAI '98 workshop on Constraint technologies for artistic applications*, ECAI, August 1998.

Author Index

Springer
and the
environment

At Springer we firmly believe that an
international science publisher has a
special obligation to the environment,
and our corporate policies consistently
reflect this conviction.

We also expect our business partners –
paper mills, printers, packaging
manufacturers, etc. – to commit
themselves to using materials and
production processes that do not harm
the environment. The paper in this
book is made from low- or no-chlorine
pulp and is acid free, in conformance
with international standards for paper
permanency.

Springer

Lecture Notes in Artificial Intelligence (LNAI)

Lecture Notes in Computer Science